VANCOUVER AND VICTORIA

COLOURGUIDE
Third Edition

Edited by Constance Brissenden
Photography by Hamid Attie

FORMAC PUBLISHING COMPANY LIMITED
HALIFAX

CONTENTS

For photo credits and acknowledgements, see page 216.

CONTENTS

Library and Archives Canada Cataloguing in Publication

Vancouver and Victoria : colourguide / edited by Constance
Brissenden ; photography by Hamid Attie. -- 3rd ed.

(Colourguide series)
Includes index.
ISBN 10: 0-88780-691-0 ISBN 13: 978-0-88780-691-9
    1. Vancouver (B.C.)--Guidebooks. 2. Victoria (B.C.)--Guidebooks.
I. Brissenden, Connie, 1947- I. Attie, Hamid III. Series.

FC3847.18.V34 2006   917.11'33045   C2005-907393-4

Formac Publishing Company   Distributed in the   Distributed in the
5502 Atlantic Street   United States by: United Kingdom by:
Halifax, Nova Scotia B3H 1G4 Casemate   Portfolio Books Limited
www.formac.ca   2114 Darby Road, 2nd Floor   Unit 5, Perivale Industrial Park
                              Havertown, PA 19083   Horsenden Lane South,
Printed and bound in China   Greenford, UK UB6 7RL

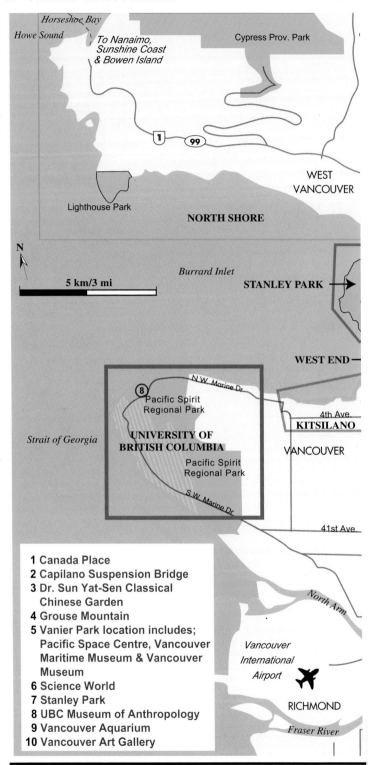

1 Canada Place
2 Capilano Suspension Bridge
3 Dr. Sun Yat-Sen Classical
   Chinese Garden
4 Grouse Mountain
5 Vanier Park location includes;
   Pacific Space Centre, Vancouver
   Maritime Museum & Vancouver
   Museum
6 Science World
7 Stanley Park
8 UBC Museum of Anthropology
9 Vancouver Aquarium
10 Vancouver Art Gallery

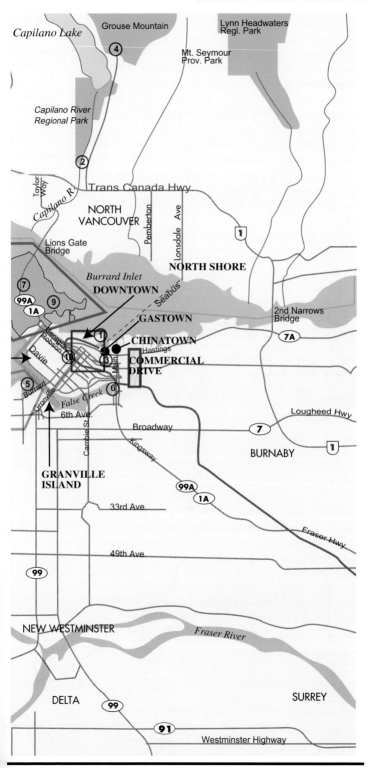

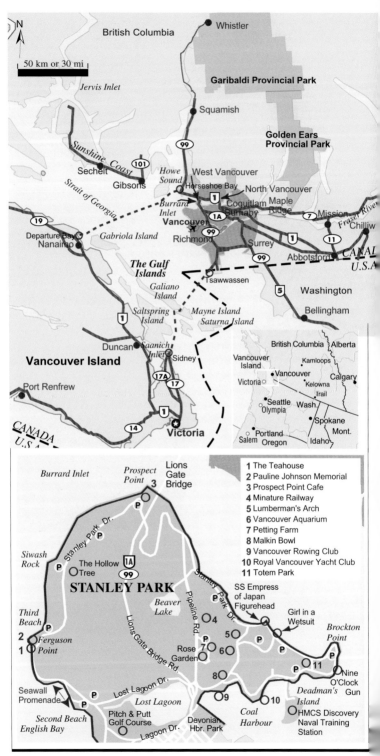

N

50 km or 30 mi

British Columbia

Whistler

Garibaldi Provincial Park

Jervis Inlet

Squamish

99

Golden Ears Provincial Park

Sunshine Coast

101

Howe Sound

West Vancouver

Sechelt

Gibsons

Horseshoe Bay

North Vancouver

Maple Ridge

Burrard Inlet

Coquitlam

Burnaby

7

Mission

Fraser River

Chilliw

Strait of Georgia

1A

Vancouver

19

Departure Bay

Nanaimo

Gabriola Island

Richmond

99

Surrey

1

11

Abbotsford

CANAL

U.S.A

The Gulf Islands

Tsawwassen

99

5

Washington

Galiano Island

Saltspring Island

Mayne Island

Saturna Island

Bellingham

1

Sidney

Duncan

Saanich Inlet

Vancouver Island

17A

17

Port Renfrew

1

14

Victoria

CANADA

U.S.A

British Columbia | Alberta

Vancouver Island

Kamloops

Vancouver

Calgary

Victoria

Kelowna

Trail

Seattle

Olympia

Wash.

Spokane

Mont.

Portland

Oregon

Idaho

Salem

Burrard Inlet

Prospect Point

Lions Gate Bridge

P

3

1	The Teahouse
2	Pauline Johnson Memorial
3	Prospect Point Cafe
4	Minature Railway
5	Lumberman's Arch
6	Vancouver Aquarium
7	Petting Farm
8	Malkin Bowl
9	Vancouver Rowing Club
10	Royal Vancouver Yacht Club
11	Totem Park

Stanley Park Dr.

P

Siwash Rock

The Hollow Tree

1A

99

STANLEY PARK

Beaver Lake

Stanley Park Dr.

SS Empress of Japan Figurehead

Girl in a Wetsuit

Third Beach

P

Pipeline Rd.

4

Brockton Point

2

Ferguson Point

1

Lions Gate Bridge Rd.

Rose Garden

7

5

6

P

11

Nine O'Clock Gun

Seawall Promenade

P

8

Deadman's Island

P

Lost Lagoon Dr.

9

10

HMCS Discovery Naval Training Station

Second Beach

English Bay

Pitch & Putt Golf Course

Lost Lagoon

Lagoon Dr.

Devonian Hbr. Park

Coal Harbour

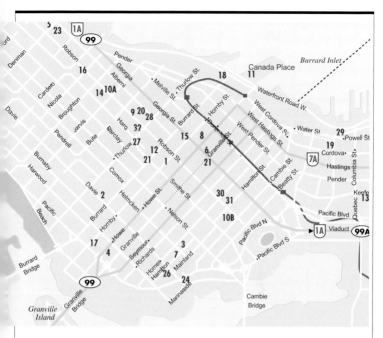

1. 900 West Sea & Steakfood Restaurant
2. Bacchus Ristorante
3. Bin 941 Tapas Parlour
4. C
5. Café de Paris
6. Chartwell
7. Cioppino's Mediterranean Grill
8. Diva at the Met
9. Earl's Restaurants
10. Ezogiku Noodle Café
11. Five Sails Restaurant
12. Fleuri Restaurant
13. Floata Seafood Restaurant
14. Hon's Wun Tun House
15. Imperial Chinese Seafood Restaurant
16. Il Giardino di Umberto
17. Kirin Mandarin Restaurant
18. Le Crocodile
19. Liliget Feast House
20. Musashi Japanese Restaurant
21. Notte's Bon Ton Bakery and Confectionary
22. Piccolo Mondo
23. Raincity Grill
24. Rodney's Oyster House
25. Shanghai Chinese Bistro
26. Steamworks Brewing Co.
27. Subeez
28. Villa Del Lupo
29. White Spot Triple O
30. Won More Szechuan Cuisine

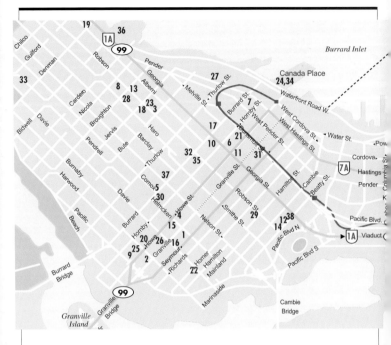

1. Best Western Chateau Granville Hotel
2. Best Western Downtown Vancouver
3. Blue Horizon Hotel
4. Bosman's Hotel
5. Century Plaza Hotel and Spa
6. Crowne Plaza Hotel Georgia
7. Days Inn Vancouver Downtown
8. Empire Landmark Hotel — Downtown Vancouver
9. Executive Hotel Downtown Vancouver
10. Fairmont Hotel Vancouver
11. Four Seasons Hotel Vancouver
12. Georgian Court Hotel
13. Greenbrier Hotel
14. Hampton Inn & Suites
15. Holiday Inn Hotel & Suites
16. Howard Johnson Hotel
17. Hyatt Regency Vancouver
18. Listel Vancouver
19. Lord Stanley Suites on the Park
20. Marriott Pinnacle Hotel
21. Metropolitan Hotel
22. Opus Hotel
23. Pacific Palisades Hotel
24. Pan Pacific Hotel Vancouver
25. Quality Hotel Downtown
26. Ramada Inn & Suites Downtown Vancouver
27. Renaissance Vancouver Hotel Harbourside
28. Robsonstrasse Hotel
29. Rosedale on Robson
30. Sheraton Vancouver Wall Centre Hotel
31. St. Regis Hotel
31. Sutton Place Hotel
33. Sylvia Hotel
34. Waterfront Centre Hotel
35. Wedgewood Hotel
36. Westin Bayshore Resort & Marina Vancouver
37. YMCA Hotel
38. YWCA Hotel

ABOUT THIS GUIDE

This guide has been written to help you get the most out of your stay in Canada's favourite West Coast destinations — Vancouver, Victoria and the surrounding areas including Whistler and the Gulf Islands. It will enrich your stay by directing you to the top attractions as well as to places off the beaten track. The contributors to this book are people who know and love these destinations and want to share their knowledge with you.

The guide is divided by city with the Vancouver section beginning on page 11 and the Victoria section on page 125. The Vancouver section offers nine chapters focusing on top attractions and activities. It also offers 10 chapters dedicated to some of Vancouver's most exciting neighbourhoods.

The Victoria section of the guide includes general information, a brief history of the city, the top things to see and do and chapters on shopping and dining.

Following the section on Victoria, the guide explores Whistler, the Gulf Islands and the Sunshine Coast. Listings are carried at the end of the book. City and neighbourhood maps, as well as maps showing the locations of restaurants, hotels and attractions, appear at key points throughout the guide.

Like the other books in the Colourguide series, this is an independent publication. No payments or contributions have been solicited or accepted by the creators or publishers of this guide.

While every effort was made to ensure that the information was up to date when it went to press, things do change over time. It is always wise to phone ahead to confirm that the information presented here is still current.

Brief biographies of the contributors follow.

KEVIN BARKER (Sunshine Coast) is a business writer and long-time resident of the Sunshine Coast.

MELANEY BLACK (Victoria Shopping) is a contributing writer for Victoria's *Monday Magazine*.

SHAWN BORDOFF (Entertainment) is an actor, scriptwriter and a TV producer who teaches for the Vancouver School Board.

CONSTANCE BRISSENDEN (editor; Exploring Vancouver; Whistler) is a Vancouver writer and editor with seven books and hundreds of magazine articles about Vancouver to her credit.

VIEW FROM PROSPECT POINT

GAIL BUENTE (Vancouver's Top Attractions; Annual Events) has written for many magazines and publications, with a special emphasis on the arts and music.

BRIAN BUSBY (Yaletown) editor of seven literary anthologies, lives in Yaletown.

CHUCK DAVIS (A Brief History of Vancouver) has shared his in-depth knowledge Vancouver history in many books and articles, including *Chuck Davis' Guide to Vancouver* and *Vancouver, An Illustrated Chronology*.

PATRICIA FRASER (Vancouver Shopping) is the coordinator for international programming, Fairchild Radio, and covers shopping for *Vancouver* magazine.

MARIAN GILMOUR (Kids' Stuff) is the manager of one of Vancouver's most beautiful historic buildings, Heritage Hall.

GARY HYNES (Victoria Dining) is a veteran food critic and publisher of *EAT* (Epicure and Travel).

LESLEY KENNY (Victoria's Top Attractions) is a researcher and writer who has organized tours for conference delegates and visiting business people.

TRUDE LABOSSIERE Huebner has been writing lifestyle pieces about British Columbia and its people for print, radio and television since 1964.

ALMA LEE (Granville Island and False Creek) is the producer of the Vancouver International Writers Festival.

BOB MACKIN (Activities & Spectator Sports) is a sports reporter for the *North Shore News* and the author of *Baseball Trivia*.

GARY MCFARLANE (Commercial Drive) is a writer who lives and works in the Commercial Drive neighbourhood.

MARG MEIKLE (Parks and Gardens) is the author of *Garden City: Vancouver*, as well as numerous other fact-based books and children's books.

JAMES OAKES (West End) is a veteran journalist and the former editor of a West End business newsletter.

CHRIS PETTY (UBC), a UBC graduate and historian, edits the *UBC Chronicle* alumni magazine.

JOANNE POON (Chinatown) has a degree in Chinese social history from UBC and works in Chinatown.

D. C. (DENNIS) REID (Exploring Victoria; A Brief History of Victoria) is a Victoria resident, published poet and historical novelist.

ANN ROSENBERG (Galleries), a retired art teacher, is now an independent curator and art critic.

LEANORE SALI (Gastown) is the director of the Gastown Business Improvement Society.

ANNE SMART (Gulf Islands) is the author of *All About Salt Spring Island*.

BARBARA TOWELL (Downtown Vancouver) has a BA in Art History and an MA in Archival Studies from the UBC.

ROCHELLE VAN HALM (North Shore) was born, raised and still lives on the North Shore; she is a veteran freelance writer.

KASEY WILSON (Vancouver Dining) is Vancouver's leading food writer and broadcaster; she is the author of the highly successful *Best of Vancouver*.

VANCOUVER

EXPLORING VANCOUVER

CONSTANCE BRISSENDEN

Since the mid-1980s, Vancouver has grown up before the astonished eyes of its populace. Expo '86 (the 1986 World Exposition on Transportation and Communication), was the launching pad for the revitalization of areas such as Yaletown, which overlooks the former Expo site on False Creek. Just two decades ago, Yaletown was a neglected, rundown enclave of warehouses and railway yards. It is now a gleaming community of high-rises and converted heritage buildings, with chic restaurants deemed the best in the West.

Vancouver's newest honour, being named host to the 2010 Olympic and Paralympic Winter Games (sharing the glory with Whistler, B.C.), is furthering the transformation of the city. New buildings are springing up, new attractions are appearing, and established ones are expanding. A bubbling energy is evident in the streets.

Visitors will benefit from improvements that are reshaping an urban centre already known as one of the best in the world both to live in and to visit. For the Greater Vancouver area, road and transit improvements will include a faster link from downtown to the Vancouver International Airport. Many millions will be spent renovating Vancouver venues and building new facilities. Vancouver's tourism infrastructure is already benefitting from international promotion as a world-class destination worthy of the Winter Olympics. That's good news for visitors who already enjoy a high

degree of service, mobility and safety in the Pacific Rim city.

AN IDEAL CITY

Vancouver is a superbly livable place. The weather is moderate, as befits a coastal rain forest, the grass is always green and flowers bloom year-round. The Coast Mountains make the perfect backdrop to the Pacific Ocean, especially in winter when they are brushed with a fresh coat of snow. All in all, it's an ideal environment, which explains why Canadians flock here to live. The city centre is home to more than 572,000 people, while the fast-growing Greater Vancouver area counts 2 million residents.

LIONS GATE BRIDGE

Growth is good news for Vancouver's tourist attractions, services and infrastructure. What was once a small provincial town is now a cosmopolitan Pacific Rim player, with excellent hotels, impressive restaurants and plenty to see and do year-round. The mix of people here is unique, a blend of West meets East, with 30 per cent of the population of Asian descent. Vancouver also has many First Nations people. Their influence is evident in the city's galleries, museums, at special events like powwows and in the stores, which often feature clothing and jewellery by native designers.

**BELOW: STANLEY PARK CYCLIST
BOTTOM: SNOWBOARDING AT CYPRESS MOUNTAIN**

While some residents complain about traffic, getting around the city is easy for visitors. Public transit is provided by the SkyTrain, a light rapid-transit system, the SeaBus, which crosses Vancouver harbour, and bus. With a TransLink day pass, you can visit the North Shore cities of West Vancouver and North Vancouver, or head south to explore the historic Steveston fishing village where the Gulf of Georgia Cannery National Historic Site is housed. For real efficiency, call TransLink's Customer Information number for routes and schedules at (604) 953-3333. You don't even need a car to travel the 120 kilometres (75 miles) to Whistler: transportation is available by Greyhound Canada, tour companies and by air. If you prefer driving, however, the roads in and around Vancouver are good, although rush hours can be slow.

FAVOURITE SPOTS TO EXPLORE

Ask any Vancouverite where the best places are to visit, and they'll enthuse about their favourite things to see and do in the city. For some, it's a walk along English Bay to Stanley Park. Depending on how ambitious you are, you may want to walk around the park's 10-kilometre (6-mile) seawall perimeter, passing under the Lions Gate Bridge and past Brockton Point with its array of totem poles. Or you may simply

HARBOUR CENTRE

want to stop at a park bench and watch the world stroll, skate or bike by. Granville Island, with its busy market, multitude of small arts and crafts shops and hustle and bustle, is completely different from Stanley Park. Yet here, too, you can find quiet spots and quiet moments. On a clear day, you may even see towering Mount Baker to the south in Washington State from your Granville Island viewpoint.

Across the water, on the North Shore, the pace of life slows, with strolls along Ambleside beach in West Vancouver and picnics in Mt. Seymour Provincial Park in North Vancouver. Grouse Mountain offers expansive views of Vancouver from the top of the peak. Rivers have carved deep canyons through the lush forests. These canyons can be viewed at several spots, the best known of which is North Vancouver's Capilano Suspension Bridge.

To get to know the Vancouver area quickly, contact a local tour company. If you'd like to tour and explore at the same time, the Vancouver Trolley Company's "jump on, jump off" bus is ideal. Many other types of tours are available, from horse-drawn wagons through Stanley Park to boats up Howe Sound.

Unique and informative walking tours are available in several of the city's neighbourhoods. If you're interested in history, Walkabout Historic Vancouver offers walking tours of downtown, Gastown and Granville Island from mid-March to mid-November. Gastown and Chinatown also have walking tours. Note that some excursions are not available year-round. For a 360-degree view of the city and the North Shore, visit The Lookout! atop Harbour Centre Tower. The revolving observation deck is 167 metres (547 feet) up via glass elevators.

SEAWALL AT STANLEY PARK

This guide takes you through a variety of Vancouver's fascinating neighbourhoods. For more information, the Vancouver Tourist InfoCentre is extremely helpful. Its website, www.tourismvancouver.com, provides lots of great information. If you visit the centre in person, the staff can make reservations for you at hotels throughout B.C. You can also book your hotels online. For current information on entertainment, attractions and dining in Vancouver, check the Thursday editions of the *Province*, *Vancouver Sun* and the free weekly, the *Georgia Strait*.

This book also explores the highlights of Victoria. For more on Victoria, see the Exploring Victoria section. Under the Top Attractions sections, you will find in-depth descriptions of the main attractions in both cities.

For detailed information on climate, travel arrangements, currency, customs, shopping, dining, accommodation, emergency care, telephone numbers and other key information, refer to the Listings section at the end of this guide.

A Brief History

Chuck Davis

There are several accounts relating to Vancouver's origins, but a favourite involves the 1792 meeting between a Spanish exploration party and some of the local Salish people. (An earlier expedition, a 1791 visit by Don José Marie Narvaez, marked the first contact between Europeans and native people in this area.) It happens that 1792 was the same year Captain George Vancouver was exploring these waters. In fact, Vancouver met Dionisio Galiano, the leader of the Spanish expedition, here and the two men hit it off and became friends. Vancouver gave the name Spanish Banks to the area where that meeting occurred, and it bears that name more than 200 years later. Aside from Indian Arm, an arm of the Burrard Inlet (today the city's harbour), Vancouver bestowed no native-inspired names, even though he had the Musqueam, the Squamish, the Kwantlen, the Tsawwassen and many other groups to choose from. Some of these groups were seasonal, coming down from the interior to the mouth of the Fraser River when the salmon were running.

ABOVE: INUIT SCULPTURE IN STANLEY PARK

TOP LEFT: CAPTAIN GEORGE VANCOUVER

Simon Fraser made a very brief visit in 1808 before being chased back up the river by angry Musqueam men. Nearly 60 years were to pass before the white people returned ... this time to stay. What attracted them first were the area's magnificent trees. The forest industry then attracted other kinds of enterprise.

ORIGINS

September 30, 1867, marks the arrival in what is now Vancouver of John "Gassy Jack" Deighton. The

Yorkshire-born Deighton, with a complexion, according to a chum, of "muddy purple," rowed into the Burrard Inlet with his native wife, her mother, her cousin, a yellow dog, two chairs and a barrel of whiskey. A busy sawmill stood where Gassy landed on the south shore of the inlet. A busier, bigger one existed on the North Shore. A kilometre or so to the west through the trees three fellows derisively nicknamed the "Three Greenhorns" (for paying the exorbitant price of $1 an acre for their land) were trying to make bricks from a vein of clay.

Gassy, retired from his career as a riverboat captain, jovially greeted the men who worked at the mill. He knew that the nearest drink for these thirsty fellows was a five-kilometre row east along the inlet to the North Road, then a long walk along a rude trail built by the Royal Engineers to New Westminster through the forest, the elk and the bears. A saloon near the mill on the South Shore was an ideal business opportunity. Gassy avowed that if the mill workers helped him build a bar, they could have all they could drink. The Globe Saloon was up within 24 hours.

The Globe is gone now, but it stood in the heart of what is now Vancouver's Gastown. The voluble Mr. Deighton, who well deserved his nickname because he never shut up, chose his location more wisely than he knew. The new country of Canada had been formed just two months earlier. British Columbia would soon join this Confederation, lured by the Canadian Pacific Railway's promise that it would link B.C. to Eastern markets. If they had known it would take 15 years to arrive, they might not have agreed so readily. But in 1871, B.C. signed on, and now British Columbians were also Canadians. The population grew and Gassy Jack thrived. So did the Greenhorns. Their landholdings are today's apartment-crammed West End.

By the spring of 1886 there were enough people in Vancouver to form a city. The little ramshackle collection of tents and wooden shacks was incorporated on April 6. A little more than two months later, on June 13, the whole thing was destroyed by fire. A freak wind sprang up while some CPR workmen were burning brush, and in less than 45 minutes the town disappeared. "Vancouver didn't burn," one of the survivors said, "it exploded." The heat was so intense that the bell at St. James Anglican Church melted into a puddle. You can see it today at the Vancouver Museum. The survivors began to build, more solidly this time, while the ashes were still smoking.

THE RAILWAY

The CPR's first train arrived on July 4, 1886, at Port Moody. Contrary to expectations, it didn't stop there: the railway extended the line to Coal Harbour, what is now part of the Vancouver waterfront. That enraged the speculators who had bought land at Port Moody based on the CPR's promise to put a terminal there. It turns out that the water at the end of the inlet wasn't deep enough for the oceangoing ships that were part of the CPR's plans to establish links to China and other Far Eastern points.

Complaints were useless; the CPR was a hard-nosed firm, led by a single-minded, stocky, bearded bull of a man named William Van Horne, who ran his railway his way. Van Horne named Vancouver. It was originally named Granville, for the colonial secretary of the time, but Van Horne declared no one would ever know where "Granville" was. But "Vancouver," now that was a different matter. Everyone knew of Captain George Vancouver's famous Pacific Coast explorations. Van Horne had his way. He nearly always did.

William Van Horne was an American. Americans have played an important part in Vancouver's past: William Shaughnessy, a later CPR president and the man for whom the city's old-money neighbourhood is named, was an American. So was Benjamin Tingley Rogers, who built the huge B.C. Sugar Refinery company. L.D. Taylor, the man elected mayor of Vancouver eight times, more often than anyone, was from Michigan.

The first thing Vancouver's first city council did in 1886 was petition the federal government to lease it a 405-hectare military reserve at the entrance to the harbour. The heavily forested reserve had been established as a potential defense point just in case the bumptious Americans tried to take over the area. That's how Vancouver got Stanley Park, one of the world's great city parks.

INSET: WILLIAM VAN HORNE

BOTTOM: FIRST CPR TRAIN ARRIVES IN VANCOUVER

The railway, which had received thousands of acres of free land in return for coming into Vancouver, established a hotel named Hotel Vancouver some distance south of Gastown that, in effect, pulled the city's downtown around it. When Van Horne arrived in the city and saw the hotel, he confronted the architect: "So you're the damned fool who made it look like a hospital!" You see today the third Hotel Vancouver. This imposing, green-turreted landmark (now Fairmont Hotel Vancouver) has hosted royal guests since 1939, beginning with King George VI and Queen Elizabeth, later the Queen Mother.

One very tangible result of the Great Depression of the 1930s is still visible in Vancouver: the Lions Gate Bridge. This big, splendid and beautiful bridge opened in 1938, paid for and built by the Guinness Brewing Company of Ireland. The brewers had bought, at distress Depression prices of less than $19 an acre, a vast tract of land on the wooded slopes of the North Shore and began to sell the property. They built the bridge to encourage traffic, and buyers, to come on over. It worked British Pacific Properties is still the most affluent neighborhood in Greater Vancouver.

TOP: THE SECOND HOTEL VANCOUVER
ABOVE: FAIRMONT HOTEL VANCOUVER TODAY

The residents in one of its postal zones have the highest per capita income in the country.

NEW GROWTH

After some years of relative quiet, Vancouver began to show signs of growth in the 1950s. A handsome office building erected on Burrard Street in 1955 by B.C. Electric was the first skyscraper built south of downtown. Much of what has been built since is distinctive, too. The city has given Canada some important architects, including Ron Thom, Bing Thom, Bruno Freschi, C. B. K. Van Norman and, pre-eminently, Arthur Erickson. Erickson's unique buildings dot the metropolitan area, and his provincial courthouse complex still draws admiring crowds in the city's downtown heart. His MacMillan Bloedel Building at 1075 W. Georgia (no longer occupied by the giant forest company) is a striking and lofty landmark, noted for its immensely deep windows. Simon Fraser University, also his creation, in the suburb of Burnaby to the east, provided an apt setting for the hotbed of student revolt in the 1960s. Erickson's magnificent Museum of Anthropology on the University of British Columbia campus to the west is further evidence of the work of this globally famous architect.

Vancouver inherited a reputation as "Lotus Land" in the swinging 1960s and 1970s. More global attention

MUSEUM OF ANTHROPOLOGY

was heaped on it in 1986 with the terrifically successful Expo 86, a world exposition that attracted more than 20 million paying visitors. The Expo lands were sold to Hong Kong financier Li Ka-Shing at a bargain-basement price and spawned a high-rise boom. In the past decade, Lotus Land has been superseded by the same frenetic energy that has infected cities worldwide. Today, the up-and-coming live in lofty "smart" high-rises, bristling with high-tech features. What remains are the breathtaking views of the city, the harbour and the looming Coast Mountains.

INFLUX OF NEWCOMERS

Suburban growth continues to this day, and so does the number of newcomers: over the last couple of decades, there has been a huge influx of Asian immigrants: Hong Kong Chinese (many of whom decided to leave Hong Kong in advance of the 1997 takeover by China), Vietnamese, Korean, Thai, Filipino and other South Asians. They've established neighbourhoods: suburban Richmond is one-third Chinese; suburban Surrey has attracted thousands of East Indian residents. By opening shops and restaurants and participating in the business, social and community lives of the region, these newcomers have added verve to the Lower Mainland.

Besides the jolt to the economy the newcomers provide, Vancouver and its suburbs are thriving because of their fervent embrace of high technology. The slow decline of resource-based industries like forestry, mining and fishing is being counterbalanced by the growth in biotechnology and computer-related companies, new media, film, television and related trades. Tourism is now one of the pillars of B.C.'s economy, and Vancouver is consistently ranked as one of the world's most liveable cities. Its centre is alive with people who live and work downtown, notably in the West End where examples of late nineteenth-century houses still nestle among the high-rise towers overlooking English Bay. The population continues to grow, expanding by more than 20 per cent since 1996. "Our city," says Larry Beasley, a Vancouver city planner, "is emerging as an unbelievably unique place. We have tens of thousands of citizens who have elected to move into the city. Most of North America has an anti-urban philosophy. But here, people want to move into the downtown."

BOTTOM: ENGLISH BAY

TOP ATTRACTIONS

GAIL BUENTE

TOTEMS IN STANLEY PARK	**STANLEY PARK** Ask any Vancouverite to recommend one must-see attraction, and the answer will be Stanley Park. At 20 times the size of New York's Central Park, it is North America's third-largest urban park. Its location, almost entirely surrounded by the Pacific Ocean and adjacent to Vancouver's West End, makes it unique and beloved. In 1889, Governor General Lord Stanley dedicated Stanley Park "to the use and enjoyment of people of all colours, creeds and customs for all time." With an estimated 8 million visitors a year, this 405-hectare (1,000-acre) urban wilderness is treasured by all. Any
STANLEY PARK'S MINIATURE TRAIN	time of year, the trails and footpaths buzz with the sound of dozens of languages, spoken by people of all

ages, races and beliefs.

Back in Lord Stanley's day, a day in the park was a dignified affair, culminating in a posed family snapshot inside the Hollow Tree. But Vancouver has grown and changed, and so has the park. It has come to symbolize all the traits of this vibrant city: informality, naturalness, energy and diversity. But the century-plus since it became a park is only a brief moment in the life of this ageless patch of earth.

Stanley Park is full of geological hints of a past far older than the high-rise buildings around it. Fossils indicate that semi-tropical palms and sequoia trees thrived here millions of years ago. Cougars prowled in the not-so-distant past. Remnants of Indian middens (garbage dumps) tell of thousands of years of native habitation when villagers hunted, fished and held potlatches on the peninsula. Lumberman's Arch was once the site of the Squamish village of Whoi Whoi. Deadman's Island, now a military base, was once a funeral ground for early peoples.

THE HOLLOW TREE

Stanley Park is really two distinct parks: a tame, well-used outer rim, and a wilder, more natural inner heart. A 10-kilometre (6-mile) seawall surrounds the outer portion's recreational attractions: rowing and yacht clubs, the Vancouver Aquarium Marine Science Centre, cricket and rugby fields, a petting farm and miniature railway, picnic areas, swimming beaches, a pitch-and-putt course, lawn bowling and tennis courts. Walkers can stop at a variety of restaurants: Sequoia Grill (the Teahouse), Prospect Point Café, the Fish House or the Stanley Park Pavilion. On weekends, artists display their works at an impromptu gallery on the grass.

STANLEY PARK TOTEM

A walk along the seawall takes you past the *Girl in a Wetsuit* sculpture, the Brockton Point Lighthouse, the huge wooden Lumberman's Arch monument and Vancouver's unique acoustic landmark, the Nine-O'Clock Gun. Originally, the gunshot helped mariners set their chronometers, but continues simply out of affection for tradition. Nearby, sightseers snap pictures of nineteenth-century totem poles by Haida, Kwakwaka'wakw and Nuu-chah-nulth carvers. Farther along is another favourite with photographers, the lookout at Prospect Point, the highest point in the park.

At Second Beach, a city beach par excellence, you'll find

21

LOST LAGOON

a saltwater swimming pool, playground, baseball diamonds and picnic areas. The aroma of fish and chips, a Stanley Park tradition, wafts by. Lost Lagoon is perhaps the most representative feature of the "outer park." Once a favourite canoeing spot for Mohawk poet Pauline Johnson, it now provides an urban spot to feed swans in the shade of willow trees.

The interior park, in contrast, is densely forested, with a network of bike and footpaths crisscrossing beneath fir and cedar boughs. Beaver Lake, the inner park's counterpart to Lost Lagoon, is a natural-state pond, edged with cattails and teeming with frogs croaking from water lilies. When venturing into the park's wilder interior, don't be misled by the apparently easy-to-follow trailways. It's quite possible to get lost. Explore with a friend and a map.

VANCOUVER AQUARIUM MARINE SCIENCE CENTRE

Since 1956, when it opened in Stanley Park, more than 30 million visitors have been entertained and amazed by the Vancouver Aquarium Marine Science Centre. The aquarium's 167 aquatic displays provide an up-close look at the 60,000 creatures living here.

In the steamy jungle environment of the Amazon Rainforest gallery, two caimans, second cousins to the crocodile, set the tone. Every hour, "rainstorms" are created inside this space. Adding to the atmosphere are giant freshwater Amazon fish that play a vital role in the survival of the rainforest, scarlet ibises and a pair of sloths.

Once a day in the Tropical Gallery, a research naturalist dives with the sharks. Twice a week the diver feeds the sharks with dramatic results. The waters literally thrash as the sharks gulp down their food. Overall, the gallery mimics a tropical reef at Indonesia's Bunaken National Marine Park, including black-tipped reef sharks, stone fish and rainbow-coloured tropical species.

Five beluga whales in the Arctic Canada Habitat can be viewed through an underwater gallery on the lower level. The Beluga Whale Encounter is a unique

chance to touch the whales and feed them a fishy snack, while discovering more about their curious behaviours.

Outside, in the Wild Coast exhibit, three sea otters, Milo, Nyac and newcomer Tanu, keep company. The sea otters, like the belugas, are under constant study. Nyac is the oldest living female sea otter survivor of the Valdez, Alaska, oil spill of 1989. Outdoor shows featuring belugas and sea otters are a summertime favourite. Spinnaker, a Pacific white-sided dolphin, and the Steller sea lions are members of a shrinking population. Their presence is significant for public education and scientific observation.

Local waters are the focus of Treasures of the British Columbia Coast. Elusive wolf eels and giant Pacific octopi dwell here. In Clownfish Cove, children eight years of age and younger will delight in an interactive play zone. Featured are live animals such as seahorses, horseshoe crabs, toads, and, of course, clownfish. In a make-believe marine mammal rescue hospital, little ones take care of a sick or injured seal pup.

After viewing the galleries, visitors can drop by the UpStream Café, and colourful ClamShell Gift Shop, where souvenirs from soapstone carvings to local postcards come in many price ranges.

Acclaimed for its innovative programming, the aquarium was the first in Canada to add professional naturalists on-site. Its Marine Mammal Rescue and Rehabilitation Program program is respected world-wide.

SEA OTTER

BELOW: DISCOVERING MARINE LIFE AT THE AQUARIUM BOTTOM: MEETING A BELUGA

SCIENCE WORLD ACTIVITY

SCIENCE WORLD/ALCAN OMNIMAX THEATRE AT SCIENCE WORLD

Science World is housed in a geodesic dome built for Expo '86, Vancouver's successful 1986 world exposition. Originally called the Expo Centre, it was affectionately dubbed "the golf ball" at the time. Three years later, in 1989, the silver ball reopened as Science World, with Queen Elizabeth II on hand for the ceremonies. By day, the exterior reflects the waters of False Creek. At night, the dome sparkles with 391 exterior lights.

Science World is now a hugely popular, hands-on family attraction. More than 500,000 people visit each year, 62,000 of which are students on school trips.

Adults and children come to Science World to be dazzled by science as entertainment. It certainly works. Hundreds of creative exhibits ensure that even science dropouts can find something intriguing and new. One exhibit makes your hair stand on end; another lets you blow square bubbles.

Science World houses six permanent galleries, including Kidspace, an evolving environment for children three to six years of age, and Eureka! where children of all ages learn about everything from heat sensitivity to making music with their feet. Visitors can also check out the Feature Gallery to see the bright and unusual variety of exhibitions that Science World hosts throughout the year.

The Alcan OMNIMAX Theatre is found inside the multi-million-dollar geodesic dome. The steeply raked, 400-seat viewing room boasts one of the world's largest screens, capable of projecting an image nine times larger than a conventional movie. Sound pumps out of 28 digital sound speakers backed by 10 tons of equipment. The most comfortable viewing experience

SCIENCE WORLD

is near the top of the amphitheatre. Fifty-minute documentaries vary in subject from dolphins to the mysteries of Egypt. The theatre presents six shows each weekday, with an added show at 5 p.m. on weekends and holidays. An additional fee is charged for Alcan OMNIMAX shows.

For lunch or a coffee, the White Spot Triple O's café overlooks False Creek. The Science World Gift Shop displays some of the most amusing souvenirs in the city, including kid-pleasing choices like a science book featuring "really gross experiments."

THE MUSEUM OF ANTHROPOLOGY

In the Great Hall of the museum of Anthropology (MOA), sunlight streams in through 15-metre (50-foot) glass walls. Immense totem poles, graceful cedar canoes and many other First Nations artifacts appear as they might have in remote coastal villages. Displays include sturdy boxes, made by steaming red cedar planks, which were also used for everything from cooking to cradles to coffins. Bowls and feast dishes take the form of mythical beings like Tsonoqua, the wild woman of the woods. All these artifacts conjure images of huge potlatches, traditional ceremonies where social status was publicly affirmed, lavish feasts were served and gifts exchanged.

Movingly displayed, the University of British Columbia Museum of Anthropology's research collection of approximately 230,000 artifacts includes ethnographic and archeological materials from Europe, Africa, the Americas, Asia and the South Pacific. Undeniably, the focal point of the museum is its collection of Kwakwaka'wakw, Nisga'a, Gitksan, Haida and Coast Salish art. Experts agree it is one of the finest collections of Northwest Coast First Nations art in the world.

While the museum gives careful treatment to these historic objects, they are also appreciated as works of art. Only the most fragile items are kept in darkness,

MUSEUM OF ANTHROPOLOGY GREAT HALL

HOUSE POSTS CIRCA 1906 AT THE MOA

and even those are accessible through innovative "visible storage" in glass-topped drawers and glass cabinets. While most museums display only 2 to 5 per cent of their collections, more than 90 per cent of the Museum of Anthropology's permanent collection is viewable. Row upon row of Kwakwaka'wakw dance masks stare out in an eerie display of variations on a theme. Forty-three black raven heads with wild cedar-bark manes raise their red beaks defiantly, and look out through steely, white-rimmed eyes.

The museum pioneered both the visible storage system and the use of natural light, a concept that has since been incorporated into the National Gallery in Ottawa. Both these innovations, now widely copied, were considered controversial back in 1976 when the museum opened its doors, leading to citations for both best design and worst design.

The architecture, evoking the plank houses of the Northwest Coast First Nations, is by Vancouver's Arthur Erickson. His unique challenge was to create a building to house an already well-established

HAIDA DANCERS AT THE MOA

collection. From its beginning in 1949, with a humble collection of oceanic materials housed in the basement of the university's main library, the holdings had grown over many years. Erickson's design is magnificent, worthy of its subject matter and its majestic location overlooking Howe Sound.

In the Masterpiece Gallery, exquisitely carved jewellery and small sculptures of argillite, silver, gold and bone are evidence of an age of painstaking craftsmanship.

In the museum's central rotunda, a skylight illuminates master artist Bill Reid's sculpture *Raven and the First Men*. The massive yellow cedar carving portrays Raven, the magical trickster, as, according to Haida legend, he discovers the first humans in a clamshell and coaxes them out. The Museum of Anthropology's collection of Bill Reid's art is the largest assemblage anywhere of his influential works, which fuse modern design with traditional Northwest Coastal native forms.

VANCOUVER ART GALLERY

The Vancouver Art Gallery houses British Columbia's largest collection of artworks, from classical to avant-garde. Established in 1931, it moved into its present location in 1983. Formerly a provincial courthouse, the neo-classical-style heritage building was redesigned by renowned local architect Arthur Erickson to accommodate an additional 3,716 square metres (40,000 square feet) of exhibition space. The internationally recognized gallery touches all the bases, with exciting touring exhibits alongside an outstanding permanent collection of close to 7,000 works.

The Vancouver Art Gallery mission statement calls it a place "to inspire and please through visual art," and that describes it well. Visit the four floors of exhibition space and you'll find numerous delightful surprises: one-person and group shows by established and emerging artists, thematic shows and travelling exhibitions from other museums. You may see an exhibit of familiar paintings by Impressionist masters, or a show of vibrant new works by up-and-coming local artists.

Yet for many guests, the highlight of the gallery is the permanent collection of works by B.C. artist and writer Emily Carr. Now well known in Canada and internationally, for most of her life Carr's art was ignored. Though respected by other painters, including Canada's influential Group of Seven, many saw her as simply an eccentric Victoria boardinghouse keeper with a penchant for pet monkeys. This dowdy, down-to-earth, observant woman carted her paint box and canvases to isolated

ABOVE: EXHIBITS AT THE MOA
BELOW: PAINTINGS BY EMILY CARR AT THE VAG

GEORGE NORRIS'S STAINLESS STEEL SCULPTURE *THE CRAB* OUTSIDE THE H.R. MACMILLAN PACIFIC SPACE CENTRE

First Nations settlements. Her treks in a dilapidated caravan took her deep into the ancient forests to capture the essence of coastal British Columbia.

When success finally did arrive, the modest artist was unprepared for it. In 1937, when the Vancouver Art Gallery purchased its first Carr painting, *Totem Poles, Kitseulka*, she wrote in her diary that "this sudden desire to obtain 'Emily Carrs'" made her afraid that the attention might "knock me into conceit." The Vancouver Art Gallery's Carr holdings, including 150 paintings and 100 works in other media, constitute the most important single Carr collection. Among them are some of Carr's most famous works, including *Big Raven, Tree Trunk* and *Scorned as Timber, Beloved of the Sky*.

Tours and gallery talks add to the enjoyment of the Carr exhibit as well as many of the touring exhibitions. Finish your visit by browsing for quality posters, books and artist-made gifts in the Gallery Shop before making a relaxed stop at the licensed Gallery Café and patio.

H.R. MACMILLAN PACIFIC SPACE CENTRE

VANCOUVER MUSEUM, H.R. MACMILLAN PACIFIC SPACE CENTRE, H.R. MACMILLAN PLANETARIUM, VANCOUVER MARITIME MUSEUM

Four Vancouver gems are clustered in Vanier Park, on the south shore of English Bay.

Some say the Vancouver Museum resembles a First Nations woven hat. Outside its front door is the equally distinctive stainless steel sculpture, *The Crab*. The museum got its start just a few years after the birth of Vancouver, when a far-sighted group of citizens gathered a few artifacts in a rented space on Granville Street. By 1905, the museum had moved into the Carnegie Library at Main and Hastings streets, now a community centre. The collection moved to its present site in 1968, becoming the largest administered and interpreted permanent collection of any Canadian civic museum. Only 2 per cent of the museum's holdings are on display. The rest is stored in a football field-sized storage vault.

All museums are time machines, and this one is no exception. The curators bring Vancouver's past to life with delightful permanent hands-on displays such as the recreation of a genteel Victorian home as well as a 1950s soda shop, supplemented by ever-changing short-term exhibits. Planned renovations will only enhance the local and international quality of the museum's exhibits.

VANCOUVER MUSEUM EXHIBIT

You can access the H. R. MacMillan Pacific Space Centre from the same foyer as the Vancouver Museum. Launched in October 1997, 29 years after the venerable H.R. MacMillan Planetarium opened, the space centre features many styles of programming. Here's the place where the wonders of space come down to earth with innovative programs like the Cosmic Courtyard hands-on gallery. Visitors discover the ups and downs of travelling the solar system, including the chance to touch a real moon rock or play state-of-the-art computer games. Daily multimedia shows and live demonstrations are fun for all ages.

Evening laser shows, the staple of the H.R. MacMillan Planetarium, have long been a major draw. Donated by one of the province's lumber barons in 1967 as a Canadian centennial gift to the City of Vancouver, the planetarium is a city icon. These days, the famed multimedia shows are presented in the renovated Star Theatre. Its dome, Zeiss star projector and theatre interior have been fully upgraded and a large-format video, new laser projection and other technological enhancements have been added. Sit back — well, lie back really — in the comfortable lounge chairs and view the night sky unfolding overhead.

VANCOUVER MARITIME MUSEUM

ZEISS STAR PROJECTOR, H.R. MACMILLAN PLANETARIUM

A short five-minute walk from the museum and planetarium, you'll find the Vancouver Maritime Museum on the waterfront at the foot of Cypress Street. Permanent exhibits as well as temporary feature exhibits bolster the Maritime Museum's most famous display, the RCMP schooner *St. Roch*, the first ship to cross the treacherous Northwest Passage in both directions, as well as the first ship to circumnavigate North America. Kids will also enjoy the Children's Maritime Discovery Centre, with its full-scale replica tugboat wheelhouse and remote-controlled underwater robot, as well as the area known as Pirates!, complete with a treasure chest, pirate weapons and costumes and the pirate ship *Shark*. Outside the museum, Heritage Harbour provides a closer look at heritage vessels of all types, including a small boat-building and repair workshop.

CANADA PLACE

CANADA PLACE/CN IMAX THEATRE AT CANADA PLACE

Built for Expo '86, Canada's 1986 world exposition, Canada Place was designed to give the stylish Sydney Opera House in Australia a run for its money. With five white, Teflon-coated "sails" echoing a nautical theme, the Canada Place complex stands out against the high-rise hotels of Vancouver's waterfront. Canada Place continues to be a popular tourist destination, home to a harbour-view promenade, cruise ship terminal, the CN IMAX Theatre, Vancouver Trade and Convention Centre, and Vancouver's World Trade Centre. The domed Pan Pacific Hotel is one of several major hotels in the area.

The complex resembles an immense ocean-going vessel, stretching three city blocks into Burrard Inlet. The open-air promenade around the building affords one of the best views of busy Port Vancouver. The parade of pleasure craft, working vessels, SeaBuses to the North Shore, and seaplanes make this a great place to sit and have lunch.

Luxury cruise ships, en route to Alaska, dock at Canada Place, as well as the nearby Ballantyne Pier. Between May and October, passengers depart Vancouver to enjoy the famed Vancouver-Alaska cruise, one of the world's most popular cruises.

Whether trekking to the top of Everest or walking in the footsteps of dinosaurs, CN IMAX Theatre film presentations dazzle viewers with sound and images. IMAX technology is the largest film format in motion picture history, 10 times the size of conventional 35-mm film. The 440-seat, steeply pitched amphitheatre features a towering five-storey screen and six-channel Digital wraparound sound. Open daily, for afternoon and evening features, films are approximately 40 minutes long.

CAPILANO SUSPENSION BRIDGE

What an adventure it must have been in the late nineteenth century when George Mackay's buddies, calling themselves the Capilano tramps, trudged to the pioneering Scotsman's secluded cabin on the north shore of Burrard Inlet. Seventy metres (230 feet) above the Capilano River canyon, George suspended a

CRUISE SHIP PASSING UNDER LION'S GATE BRIDGE

CAPILANO SUSPENSION BRIDGE

rickety rope-and-cedar bridge for what certainly must have been a petrifying crossing. Today's bridge, built of sturdy steel cables, petrifies and captivates 800,000 visitors each year. The 140-metre (450-foot) bridge is certainly safer and more accessible now, but the lush forest property is no less breathtaking than in Mackay's time.

Capilano Suspension Bridge's swaying span is the world's longest and highest suspension footbridge. Since 1899, when the original bridge was built, the attraction has been improved and enhanced by each of its six successive owners. The Story Centre traces the history of the bridge and the development of the city around it. Exhibits include an English country garden planted with rhododendrons and azaleas, the Living Forest interactive ecology display, a tranquil nature park and a gift shop. Totem Park features a display of locally carved Coast Salish poles collected since the 1930s. In nearby Big House, visitors can watch First Nations carvers at work and ask them about their techniques.

The newest enhancement, Treetops Adventure, is the most dramatic ever. After its completion in 2005, the park won a National Tourism Excellence Award as Innovator of the Year for its series of elevated boardwalks crossing from one tall Douglas fir to another. Viewers climb ever higher for a bird's eye view of a coastal rainforest, without endangering the environment. An ingenious compression system allows the walkways and observation platforms to be supported without harming the tree trunks in any way.

Tours, displays and special activities are designed to give guests a glimpse into the historic and botanical roots of the area. The full-service Bridge House restaurant and two casual eateries serve hungry visitors with fresh West Coast-style cuisine as well as snacks. The suspension bridge is a 20-minute drive from downtown Vancouver.

GROUSE MOUNTAIN

It takes only eight minutes for the Grouse Mountain Skyride to climb to 1,128 metres (3,700 feet) above sea level. That's the only disappointing part of the Grouse Mountain experience because on a clear day, the panoramic view of Vancouver, the Strait of Georgia and far-off Vancouver Island is unsurpassed. From here, the Peak Chair continues the ascent to 1,250 metres (4,100 feet), providing a 360-degree view that includes Vancouver Island across the Strait of Georgia.

Grouse Mountain was named in 1894 after a hunting party caught some blue grouse there. The mountain was one of the earliest ski areas developed near Vancouver. In 1911, a Swede named Rudolph Verne became the first to ski the slope. Today, hardy types make their way to the top with a strenuous 2.9-kilometre (1.8-mile) hike known as the Grouse Grind. The Grind is a badge of honour for many, with the fittest of the fit running up the steep rise. But the majority of visitors prefer the more sedate Skyride.

Grouse attracts year-round visitors. In winter, downhill skiing, snowboarding, snowshoeing, sleigh rides and a mountaintop ice-skating pond are always fun. Ski lessons and equipment rentals are available. For summer visitors, there's the Refuge for Endangered Wildlife, an enclosed natural habitat of

DR. SUN YAT-SEN GARDEN

just under a hectare (two acres). Two orphaned grizzly bears, Grinder and Coola, live here year-round. The larger bear, Coola, is a Coastal grizzly, with salmon as part of its natural diet. Grinder, the smaller one, is an Interior grizzly, eating a diet that is up to 85 per cent wild vegetation. In the summertime, rescued peregrine falcons, red-tailed hawks, a golden eagle and a barred owl join the grizzly pair on display. Naturalists are on hand to share insights into these magnificent birds. Loggers' shows, forest hikes and rides to the top on the Peak Chair add up to hours of activity.

If you're not the outdoorsy type, enjoy the free Theatre in the Sky show. The theatre features a high-definition video presentation, *Born to Fly,* as part of the Skyride pass. Fine dining at the Observatory (advance reservations allow you to ride the Skyride free) makes the most of the views. Open daily are the Bar 98 Bistro, a casual dining area with a large outdoor rooftop patio, and Lupin's Café for fresh, self-serve food.

DR. SUN YAT-SEN CLASSICAL CHINESE GARDEN

In Vancouver's Chinatown, local families in search of the freshest vegetables mingle with out-of-town visitors exploring exotic herb shops. Traffic inches alongside throngs of pedestrians crowding the sidewalks. In the midst of all this kinetic energy, it would be easy to miss the tranquil Dr. Sun Yat-Sen Classical Chinese Garden tucked away just a few steps off Pender Street. But you won't want to miss this peaceful "Refreshment for the Heart."

Enter the garden near the intersection of Pender and Carrall streets, through a whitewashed wall behind the Chinese Cultural Centre. As soon as you pass through the doorway marked Yi Yuan, or Garden of Ease, you'll find yourself slowing your steps to the pace of another time and place.

Classical Chinese gardens are an art form 20

centuries old. The most famous are in the city of Suzhou in China's Chiangsu province. These contemplative "scholar's gardens" have influenced garden design worldwide. In 1986, the Dr. Sun Yat-Sen Garden became the first full-scale classical Chinese garden outside China, and the first to be built anywhere in nearly 500 years. Built in Ming Dynasty style, the garden reflects nature through the four elements of rock, water, plants and architecture. Inside, a microcosmic world of less than half an acre is cleverly laid out to maximize its intricacy and complexity. Framed by round moon gates and lacy latticework, glimpses of exquisite vistas emerge, disappear and reappear to create infinite visual space.

More than 50 skilled Chinese artisans came to Vancouver to build the garden using centuries-old techniques, ancient tools and authentic building materials. The Yun Wei Ting gazebo, for example, perches atop a miniature mountain built of a unique rock found only on the bottom of Lake Tai in Suzhou. But the garden is also an original, incorporating local plants and materials.

Admission to the Dr. Sun Yat-Sen Classical Chinese Garden includes tea and a tour. The gift shop features a large selection of English-language books about Chinese culture.

DR. SUN YAT-SEN GARDEN

STORYEUM

Vancouver's latest attraction is one that will take you back to its earliest times. The journey begins in a lobby decorated with historic photos of Western Canada's significant events and famous figures. A tour group is assembled and guided onto Storyeum's enormous elevator, a reincarnated antique water tank large enough to carry 200 passengers. Once on board this time machine, the descent into Vancouver's past begins.

Far beneath the streets of Gastown, lively scenes of old B.C. are brought to life by a troupe of actors and singers. Storyeum is one of the biggest and most exciting attractions in Vancouver, with the goal of making history entertaining as well as informative.

A series of stages are arranged in an underground space bigger than six hockey rinks. As the audience moves through the stages — and ages — of history, a 65-minute presentation takes them from a scene depicting ancient native myths, right up through Canada's participation in the Second World War. Along the way, viewers witness the ups and downs of the province's history, the dashed hopes and the fulfilled dreams of the pioneers who built B.C.

Beginning with a scene set in a primordial forest, the arrival of Europeans is still far in the future. Hear how the world began according to West Coast aboriginal myths and witness the traditions of the earliest people to live here.

The arrival of Europeans with the resultant trade, and smallpox, is portrayed on a stunning stage resembling a Pacific coast bay. A Hudson's Bay schooner lies at anchor. It's a landscape full of courageous, and sometimes oddball, characters. Even Queen Victoria and U.S. President James Polk make cameo appearances in a hilarious Punch-and-Judy style scenario.

The next stop is Barkerville, featuring larger-than-life personalities of British Columbia's gold rush era. Among them, Judge Matthew Begbie, known as "the Hanging Judge," makes an appearance. Stroll into the next panorama to learn how the transcontinental railway changed life in Canada's westernmost province. Logging, fishing and mining industries flourished as British Columbia entered an era of prosperity. This period is also remembered for its injustices toward Chinese immigrant workers. A view of Vancouver at the close of the Second World War ends the show. The city's residents gaze confidently into the future, believing it will bring unlimited peace and prosperity for all.

The tour returns to the modern world accompanied by a colourful 360-degree, 14-metre (46-foot) high film finale celebrating British Columbia's diverse landscapes and its multicultural heritage.

PRESENTATION AT STORYEUM

DINING

KASEY WILSON

Vancouver's culinary reputation is built on fresh food and fresh flavours. The variety of dining experiences continues to grow each year, with some of the country's finest chefs bringing distinction to food that is innovative and, in many cases, unique to the West Coast.

If there is a quintessential West Coast food, it is wild salmon. It comes in five varieties: sockeye, pink, coho, spring and chum, and can be cooked in a multitude of ways. The original inhabitants, First Nations people both on the Pacific as well as the inland rivers, barbecued or baked it. Today, specialty restaurants like Salmon House on the Hill, feature traditional delicacies such as alderwood-grilled wild British Columbia salmon.

With some 30 per cent of Vancouver's population of Asian origin, it's not surprising that Oriental cooking is plentiful throughout the city. No matter where you go within Vancouver or its neighbouring suburbs — Richmond, Burnaby, New Westminster, or the North Shore communities of North and West Vancouver — you'll find the diversity of Asia represented in

PACIFIC SALMON DINNER

SUN SUI WAH SEAFOOD RESTAURANT

B.C. SALMON DINNER

the kitchens. With a light touch, the chefs offer up a tasty mix of texture and colour, flavour and flair.

These days, dining in Vancouver encompasses a great many nationalities: French, Italian, Lebanese, Hungarian, Swiss, Persian, Portuguese and Spanish are but a few examples. No matter what the style, cooking on the coast is buoyed with top-quality ingredients, brought in from the individualistic farms and ranchers of the hinterlands.

The perfect complement to fine dining in Vancouver are the internationally recognized icewines grown in the Okanagan Valley. Canada is now recognized as the world's leading producer of icewine. Unlike any other dessert wine, frozen icewine grapes are harvested by hand in the Okanagan during the nights in December and January when the temperature reaches –8° C (18° F) or colder. Just as wonderful are the ales, beers and stouts from local micro-breweries. And don't forget the coffee. It's not just a pick-me-up but a way of life in the multitude of coffee bars that dot the city's streets.

HON'S WUN TON HOUSE

CHINESE

Chinatown is, of course, the first place to go in search of Chinese food.

Getting a table at the Floata Seafood Restaurant on Keefer Street shouldn't be hard, even at the notoriously busy dim sum hour. With 1,000 seats, it is immense. The ease and skill evident in the service and cooking, however, belie its size. A second Floata Seafood serves Richmond. A bit further along Keefer Street is Hon's Wun Tun House, an institution revered for fast, inexpensive servings of Cantonese-style rice and noodle dishes and vegetarian dim sum.

Just outside Chinatown, the Pink Pearl on Hastings Street is crowded with discriminating Chinese families, especially between 11 a.m. and 2 p.m. on weekends, when dim sum is a tradition. Lunch-time dining is easy here for visitors: servers urge you to make choices from the dishes displayed on their carts. Coming for dinner instead? You could catch a glimpse — and get an earful — of a Chinese wedding banquet, usually a boisterous affair.

The Chinese food experience doesn't end at

DIM SUM AT SUN SUI WAH

Chinatown's border. Across the Oak Street Bridge in Richmond are a number of Asian-style malls, complete with eateries. The Yaohan Centre's food courts offer a wide range of Asian street eats at bargain prices. Next to the Yaohan Centre, the Radisson President Hotel harbours the Richmond Mandarin Chinese Restaurant, distinguished by its creative dim sum menu and masterful repertoire of Cantonese dishes.

Between the new Asian centre of Richmond and the pioneering region of Vancouver's Chinatown are literally hundreds more Chinese restaurants. The popularity of humble Hon's, for instance, has translated into additional venues in downtown Vancouver, Richmond, New Westminster and Coquitlam. Hon's has also spawned a thriving trade in frozen potstickers, buns and dim sum, as well as won ton noodles and chili oil. Most visiting food writers dine at Sun Sui Wah, on Main Street in Vancouver, designed by noted B.C. architect Bing Thom; owner Simon Chan developed the Cantonese-style menu of dim sum specialties. The Won More Szechuan Restaurant serves reasonably-priced hot and sour soup, potstickers and other dishes, mainly spicy, in a crowded, upstairs space in West End Vancouver and bigger, slightly more expensive digs in Kitsilano. At the downtown Shanghai Chinese Bistro, a skein of noodles makes its first appearance as a rope of dough, undergoes a fascinating ritual of twisting and stretching, and ends up as your plate as Tan Tan

BEEF AND MIXED VEGGIES AT HON'S

noodles with peanut sauce. Szechuan cuisine reappears in a slightly costlier incarnation at the Szechuan Chongqing Seafood Restaurant with locations in both Vancouver and Burnaby. Both restaurants showcase

KIRIN MANDARIN

cooking from the Chongqing region and specialize in seafood.

The Imperial Chinese Seafood Restaurant brings Chinese fine dining with a view to the downtown business district. Its serene atmosphere frequently breaks down in the face of giggles from its younger patrons. It's equally likely to be shattered by the adults, whose unsuppressed admiration for a perfect, glistening rock cod, whole and steamed with ginger and scallions, is often hearty and spontaneous. Look to the elegant Kirin Mandarin, also downtown, for specialties such as Shanghai smoked eel, Beijing duck and Szechuan hot and spicy scallops.

JAPANESE

The popularity of teriyaki, teppan and especially sushi has taken Japanese food far from the small stretch of Powell Street known as Japantown. At Tojo's, on busy Broadway, the privileged and prudent few who reserved a place at the ten-seat sushi bar are treated to a show of Hidekazu Tojo's consummate skill with sushi. Tojo's edible masterpieces are the main draw for the knowing Japanese businesspeople, filmmakers and celebrities that crowd the establishment, but a wide range of non-sushi dishes round out the somewhat pricey menu. In contrast to tiny Tojo's, the large and lush Kamei Royale, in its second floor downtown

TOJO'S RESTAURANT

location overlooking Burrard Street, is home to a steady stream of barbecue grill dishes, free-style special rolls and, of course, a wide range of sushi.

The West End's Musashi Japanese Restaurant offers more sensibly priced sushi and sashimi. Its menu includes the usual soups, salads, tempura, teriyaki chicken and beef, as well as rice and noodles, many assembled nicely into combination dinners. Yuji's Japanese tapas offers a unique menu of Japanese appetizer dishes perfect for snacking and socializing at reasonable prices.

Gyoza King has a much narrower focus. While noodle dishes and inexpensive specials do appear on the menu, there's no sushi to be seen in this West End eatery. The place is crammed with locals and tourists alike, who consume one plateful of plump meat, seafood or vegetable gyozas after another. And for ramen in all its forms — regular (pork), miso and soy

— try Ezogiku Noodle Café, a short walk away, where little else, only a fried rice dish, a fried noodle dish, a curry and gyozas, are offered. There's a second Ezogiku near the Vancouver Public Library.

SOUTH ASIAN

In many parts of Greater Vancouver, South Asian restaurants are easy to find. Vij's Restaurant showcases B.C.-influenced Indian curries and other specials. The West Side's Maurya has an incredible wine list and the tandoori quail served over spinach and chickpea cakes is a must. There's a lunch buffet for $9.95 — a bargain you can't afford to pass up. Both places are modern, high-profile eateries.

VIJ'S RESTAURANT

THAI AND OTHER ASIAN

Thai restaurants represent yet another sector of the city's multi-faceted Asian community. Montri's Thai in Kitsilano is hot, in every sense of the word (but you can ask for milder). Often cited as the city's best Thai, Montri's presents authentically-spiced dishes that make the scaled heat ratings — from one chili (mildest) to five chilies (hottest) — required reading. The Phnom Penh is family-run, with a focus on Vietnamese and Cambodian food with some Chinese dishes. While the surroundings may be rather plain, the hot and sour soup, tender flash-fried squid tubes and fresh-oyster omelettes are anything but.

FRENCH AND ITALIAN/MEDITERRANEAN

For French dining, look to Le Crocodile. Located downtown, it offers roomy, luxurious surroundings with a patio, and French wines and Alsace regional dishes that are well worth the expense. Owner and chef Michel Jacob's Alsatian onion tart has been hailed as the best in Vancouver. For a bistro experience, try Café de Paris in the West End. The warm dark woods, wine racks and lace curtains instantly bring to mind a Paris bistro. The menu includes moderately priced classics: duck confit, steak tartare and cassoulet; all are served with the pommes frites that have become legendary in the city. A table d'hôte, as well as original contemporary French creations, is available. Saveur, on

LE CROCODILE

Thurlow, sources local organic produce to create fine French dining at a prix-fixe of under 40 dollars. Bistro Pastis also produces solid country fare. Look for an outstanding cheese plate and, in cooler weather, satisfying braises, cassoulets and roasts. The Smoking Dog Grill will sate a hunger for uncomplicated food such as coq au vin, steak au poivre, duck à l'orange, and

QUATTRO ON FOURTH

salade niçoise. On a sunny afternoon, watch the Kitsilano crowd from the patio.

In West Vancouver, the unpretentious La Régalade is winning awards for no-nonsense country cooking inspired by the neighbourhood bistros in France. Don't miss the escargots or the homemade pâtés. Italian, French and Spanish flavours meld at Cioppino's Mediterranean Grill, where chef and owner Pino Posteraro infuses his philosophy of "cucina naturale" into light, fresh dishes. In the same Yaletown area, Villa Del Lupo delivers a generous and contemporary menu of excellent pastas and favourites such as lamb shank osso buco.

IL GIARDINO DI UMBERTO

Another bit of Italy resides in Il Giardino di

Umberto, a seaside villa recreated on Hornby Street. The Tuscan menu emphasizes pasta and game. And at Quattro on Fourth and Gusto di Quattro, the rooms are mosaic-tiled and mahogany-trimmed. Quattro prepares some unusual Italian pastas; the combination plate provides a good overview. Across the Lions Gate Bridge, the Beach Side Café in West Vancouver has deck dining to capitalize on views of Stanley Park and Kitsilano across the water. A strong wine list and Italian food preparation characterize the restaurant.

PACIFIC NORTHWEST

The Pacific Northwest's original First Nations cuisine cannot be ignored. The Liliget Feast House occupies a stunning longhouse near the beach in the West End. There are wood walkways, pebbled floors, cedar plank tables and walls hung with contemporary native art. A feast, or potlatch, platter ensures a wide sampling; it includes bannock, baked sweet potato with hazelnuts, alder-grilled salmon, toasted seaweed with rice, steamed fern shoots and barbecued venison.

LILIGET FEAST HOUSE

Plentiful, readily available seafood is a characteristic of Pacific Northwest cuisine. The Yaletown area has been transformed since Expo '86 into an urbane playground of streetside cafes and stylish diners. At Rodney's Oyster House, oysters are the main attraction: a dozen or so varieties lie on ice, in long stainless steel beds, while customers line the oyster bar. Other fresh seafoods, chowders and slapjacks are also popular. Exceptional seafood is served at Blue Water Café and Raw Bar in a century-old heritage warehouse. Provence Marinaside's husband-and-wife team have matched a rustic décor with Mediterranean fare, in a perfect location overlooking False Creek. The trendy glowbal grill & satay bar is yet another Yaletown winner. Try the regional dishes such as grilled veal chops and tuna tartare.

STILTON CHEESECAKE AT DIVA

Search out The Cannery Seafood Restaurant, isolated among the Burrard Inlet wharves. The interior is lined with seafaring memorabilia and, fittingly, the Cannery always makes good on the seafood promises offered by the "daily fresh" sheet. The Beach House, on the other side of the Burrard Inlet, is also especially strong on seafood. It also offers a marvellous view of the West Vancouver waterfront.

At the Raincity Grill, near English Bay, the menu changes according to whatever fresh, local ingredients are on hand. Wine is available by the glass from an extensive, award-winning wine list. The West Coast theme is upheld by a duo of hotel restaurants as well. The Five Sails at Canada Place presents a menu that also focuses on imaginative presentations such as pan-seared halibut crusted with fine herbs and a watercress emulsion. To top it off, diners enjoy a spectacular harbour view. Diva at the Met optimizes an airy, natural space with multi-tiered seating, and out of its Waldorf-style open kitchen come both stylish, contemporary items such as potato-crusted wild salmon, cinnamon-smoked duck and perhaps the best desserts in the city by internationally-recognized pastry chef Thomas Haas.

The Fish House at Stanley Park has an enviable

ABOVE: SMOKED BLACK ALASKA COD FROM SEASONS RESTAURANT IN QUEEN ELIZABETH PARK BOTTOM: THE TEAHOUSE RESTAURANT IN STANLEY PARK

location, surrounded by trees, tennis courts, and lawn bowling greens in one of the world's best urban parks. Flaming prawns are one of the most popular dishes, and Chef Karen Barnaby's ahi tuna steak Diane with mashed potatoes has become a classic.

Bishop's location streetside in Kitsilano, away from the harbour and the beach, lets you fully appreciate master host John Bishop's superlative standards of service and cuisine. Should your attention stray to the modern Canadian art gracing the walls, the

C Restaurant

smoked sablefish with truffle brandade cake and herb horseradish sabayon or the crème brûlée (which may be cappuccino, roasted pear, or sun-dried cherry) will easily recapture your interest. The Pear Tree in Burnaby lures Vancouver visitors and residents out to the suburbs with the promise of Scott Jaeger's reasonably priced and inventive menu, which might, for example, offer a braised lamb shank with seared scallops and roasted pear risotto.

In the midst of all the West Coast innovation, a bit of tradition stands firm. Patrons at the Sequoia Grill (at the Teahouse Restaurant) at Ferguson Point in Stanley Park won't allow traditional favourites such as the Teahouse's stuffed mushroom caps off the menu. Seasons Hilltop Bistro, in Queen Elizabeth Park, also has a conservative menu which focuses mostly on fish and poultry. The restaurant overlooks a beautiful quarry garden, the mountains and the Vancouver skyscape.

UPSCALE AND HOTEL DINING

West recently received a gold award as restaurant of the year by *Vancouver Magazine*'s Critics' Poll for its outstanding decor, food, service and deep wine list. Try Chef David Hawksworth's foie gras and chicken liver parfait, but be sure to leave room for original and beguiling desserts. At Lumière, talented chef Rob Feenie has found the perfect balance between classic French and contemporary presentations. Feenie introduced tasting menus to the city. His

West Coast halibut

vegetarian tasting menu is superb. The restaurant was recently remodeled into two distinct areas: the Tasting Bar and the Dining Room. Next door is Feenie's, a casual dining bistro. C, located on the downtown perimeter, has extravagant caviars, a private wine cellar and a patio with a million-dollar marina view. C's chef creates distinct dishes that taste as intriguing as they sound: seared octopus, bacon-wrapped diver

Texas Flank Steak at Bin 941

scallops and any of the items from their menu tasting.

Some of the city's best restaurants are ensconced within downtown hotels, including the Five Sails and Diva at the Met (see Pacific Northwest). Fleuri may be tucked away at Sutton Place, yet it is widely known for its Chocoholic Bar, afternoon teas, Sunday brunch, seafood buffet and ever-changing, always excellent, menu. Chartwell, inside the Four Seasons Hotel, is a classic choice for Vancouverites and their visitors. The dining room's rich wood panelling and fireplace are as conducive to successful business dealings as they are to soothing dining. The Bacchus Restaurant in the small, exclusive Wedgewood Hotel is a beautifully and discreetly lit room that unfailingly delivers fine food.

SPECIALTY

The Hart House in Burnaby is remembered as much for its Tudor-style, heritage-home setting as it is for its service and food. Award-winning chef Carol Chow's cooking ranges from daring dishes like B.C. spot prawns with sauce provençal and citrus basmati rice to the more traditional rack of lamb with rosemary Yukon gold potatoes. The desserts have a traditional streak as well: a Belgian chocolate espresso mousse tower and a warm apricot-ginger cake.

Vegetarians and non-vegetarians seek out Habibi's for bargain-priced dishes of perfectly prepared traditional Lebanese home cooking, including falafels and vegetarian dishes. Hon's (see Asian) has a dedicated vegetarian cooking facility at its downtown Robson Street location and can fashion vegetarian versions of dim sum and almost any dish you can think of, even vegetarian goose (actually bean curd skin rolls filled with dried Chinese mushrooms). Planet Veg, close to Kitsilano Beach and Vanier Park, cooks up East Indian, Mexican and Mediterranean vegetarian fast foods. Lineups are fairly frequent but takeout is always an option. Order ahead or at the door (no home delivery available). There's no vegetarian fare at Memphis Blues Barbeque House on West Broadway and Commercial Drive. All the favourites — pulled pork, ribs, beef brisket and their signature cornish game hens — are beautifully prepared with sides of baked beans, coleslaw and cornbread.

Tapas are served at Bin 941 downtown, a warm, close room where the tasting bowls are generously filled and reasonably priced. A similar concept operates at Bin 942. The room is larger, but has much the same atmosphere and offers repeats of many of the menu items.

For many families, Earl's, which has several Vancouver locations, is the restaurant of choice. The service is fast and the food is fresh and healthy. It has an enviable wine list, and many of the locations have patios. For even faster service, look for White Spot Triple O's for fries, milkshakes and Vancouver's favourite burgers with the legendary Triple O sauce. Tomato Fresh Food Café distinguishes itself from other diners with healthy, colourful comfort food such as BLTs, turkey sandwiches, tomato and pesto sandwiches and vegetarian chile. On Commercial Drive, or "The Drive" as its universally known, Waazubee Café is casual and upbeat. The very hip Subeez with its 30-speaker sound system fits in well with its Yaletown neighbours. Don't miss the killer fries with garlic mayo, chicken and brie burger or any of the vegetarian dishes.

The Dockside Brewery on Granville Island fuses a casual restaurant with a micro-brewery and pub. In summer, the smashing outdoor patio is open for business. The large open kitchen is versatile, alternating between pub grub and up-market fare. The lounge offers a full bar of spirits and a range of lagers and ales from their highly regarded brewery. However, some say the best beer in town flows from the custom-designed taps at Steamworks, an extraordinary Yaletown brew pub with a wide-ranging brunch, lunch and dinner menu.

Patisserie Lebeau (near Granville Island) has fine Belgian waffles, delicious pastries and a selection of French breads and croissants for pâtisserie-purists. A few doors down at Les Amis du Fromage, mother and daughter team Alice and Allison Spurrell supply you and many top chefs with more than 400 cheeses at affordable prices. Comfort food takeout is also available from their freezer. Solly's Bagelry, at Main and E. 28th Avenue, is worth the bus ride for the best cinnamon buns in town.

Two newcomers to the scene deserve note. In Gastown, The Irish Heather is the delight of owners Sean and Erin Heather's eye, and many others. A multitude of brews, as well as single malt and Irish whiskeys tickle the taste buds, washing down homemade bangers 'n' mash and beer-battered cod in a fish 'n' chips combo. And for some of the freshest fish in town, Go Fish! is a takeaway on the waterfront near Granville Island. The fish is truly fresh, having come directly from the fishing boats docked nearby.

STEAMWORKS BREWERY

SHOPPING

PATRICIA FRASER

Stand at the corner of Granville and Georgia streets and you'll find yourself at the centre of Vancouver life with skyscrapers above and the SkyTrain below. This is the heart of cosmopolitan Vancouver. It's also the starting point for some serious shopping. No matter which direction you take, you'll find malls (the Pacific Centre and Sinclair Centre), shopping promenades (such as Robson Street), boutiques specializing in locally designed fashion in Gastown, and home décor and designer baubles in Yaletown.

GEORGIA AND GRANVILLE

On the northeast corner of Georgia and Granville streets is the Hudson's Bay Company, known as "the Bay." Established in 1824 as a network of fur-trading posts, the Bay is a Canadian tradition, and a handy stop for quality goods from scarves to soup plates. The other corners of Georgia and Granville streets hold the downtown Sears and Vancouver's own London Drugs, an institution in its own right.

Head downstairs through the Bay to the underground Pacific Centre Mall. Running north from Georgia Street, this attractive mall holds chains such as the very posh Canadian store, Holt Renfrew, as well as the Gap, Club Monaco, Banana Republic, Fairweather, Eddie Bauer Outdoor Outfitters, and Jacob.

ROBSON STREET AT NIGHT

Back above ground, walk west along Georgia and you'll pass the Vancouver Art Gallery, with a gallery shop stocked with unique arts and crafts, books and games. Keep going west until you come to Burrard Street. You could go underground again to the Royal Centre and Bentall Centre malls, or turn south for a block and head up to Robson Street.

ROBSON STREET

Once a quiet street known as Robsonstrasse for its European-style delis and coffee shops, Robson is now an urban carnival of youth-oriented chains such as the Gap and Gap Kids, Roots, Banana Republic and Mexx, interspersed

TOP: ITEMS AT THE VANCOUVER ART GALLERY SHOP
MIDDLE: DESIGNER SHOPS ON ROBSON STREET

with a special blend of coffee shops. Designer shopping bags swing off youthful arms amidst an up-tempo mix of well-heeled international travellers. Walk further west along Robson to Denman Street and you're deep into the West End. The shopping area here is more residential than Robson Street, with flower stores and framers, fish-and-chip shops and beachwear (being minutes from English Bay).

GASTOWN AND LONSDALE QUAY

WATER STREET

Built after the Great Fire of 1886, the Gastown area is chock-a-block with tourist shops and restaurants in refurbished heritage buildings along the waterfront. The former Canadian Pacific Railway station is now the terminus for the SkyTrain and connecting station for the SeaBus to the North Shore. Take the SeaBus for a 12-minute waterborne jaunt across Vancouver harbour to the dock at Lonsdale Quay Market. Treat yourself to lunch, purchase a hand-crafted souvenir, then head back on the handy, frequent SeaBus.

GRANVILLE ISLAND

Granville Island, on the south side of False Creek, is a former industrial peninsula reclaimed by the city and reborn as a shopping and arts centre. The huge Granville Island Market is a collection of vendors of gourmet food items, fresh produce and handcrafted jewellery and gifts. In the Net Loft, another large

building packed to the gunwales with boutiques, find Edie Hats (a Vancouver fashion landmark), Paper-Ya's decorative handmade papers, Beadworks' collection of 30,000 jewelry beads, and a multiplicity of artists' studio shops, galleries and gift stores. The Kids Only Market, a reconverted warehouse complex at the entrance to the island, is home to 28 individual sellers for children.

ANTIQUES AND COLLECTIBLES

Vancouver loves antiques. Shops and galleries are concentrated in three areas: West 10th Avenue by the University of British Columbia (Folkart Interiors and others); Granville Street between West 6th and West 14th avenues (Small Comforts Antiques, William Robert Antiques, Hampshire Antiques, Farmhouse Collections); and Main Street between 12th and 29th avenues (Second Time Around, Ages Ago and Baker's Dozen).

BOOKSTORES

If you've seen the movie *You've Got Mail*, you know about the battle of the bookstores, between the mega-stores and the little corner shops. The big guys are represented by three Chapters bookstores (downtown, on South Granville and at Metrotown mall), each with its own Starbucks coffee shop, children's story times and comprehensive database of books in print. The little guys include Duthie Books and new-age Banyen Books on West 4th Avenue, and gay lit Little Sister's Book and Art Emporium in the West End. On West Broadway, Kidsbooks is a must-see for young readers.

KIDS ONLY MARKET ON GRANVILLE ISLAND

CANADIAN CLOTHING DESIGNERS

Western style starts here: First Nations fashion maven Dorothy Grant uses her Haida background as inspiration for clothing based on "button blanket" designs. Zonda Nellis on South Granville has developed a worldwide

following for her subtly coloured, elegant hand-loomed designer wear. Canadian RozeMerie Cuevas designs for Jacqueline Conoir, available at JC Studio on West 6th Avenue. In swank Kerrisdale, Margareta Design offers clothing that is conservative and classic. A-Wear is the house label for a team of local designers at swank Leone in Sinclair Centre. For hard-wearing, attractive travel wear, visit Tilley Endurables on South Granville.

Clothing for the well-dressed tot can be found at Bobbit's for Kids! on West 4th, Isola Bella in Kerrisdale and Please Mum on West Broadway. As for toys and games, check out Kaboodles on Granville Island

THE TOYBOX ON WEST BROADWAY

and West 10th and the Toybox and Toys R Us on West Broadway. As well, the Kids Only Market on Granville Island offers multiple shops under one roof, including one devoted to kites.

CHINA AND CRYSTAL

Apart from the Bay, which has everything, you can find what your heart desires at Atkinson's at West 6th and Granville. The whole store sparkles. Chintz and Company in Yaletown boasts "entertaining tablewares." W. H. Puddifoot & Co. is a favourite in Kerrisdale.

DESIGNER BOUTIQUES

You'll find favourite labels at Vancouver's many designer boutiques. Petites in particular will be pleasantly surprised at the selection. Nearly one-third of Vancouver's population is of Asian heritage and sizes are appropriately geared to the market. Most shops are temptingly close to major downtown hotels. On West Hastings, there's Chanel, Leone and Escada; there's the Gianni Versace Boutique at the Sinclair Centre; Enda B Fashions, Edward Chapman's Ladies Shop, Bacci's and Boboli are all on South Granville;

and Dyanna's Fine Clothing for Women is on Howe Street.

FIRST NATIONS ARTS AND JEWELLERY

Vancouver offers a fine selection of authentic First Nations art and jewellery. In Gastown, Hill's Native Art on Water Street (formerly Hill's Indian Crafts) stocks carved jewellery and chunky, virtually indestructible Cowichan sweaters. The Inuit Gallery, around the corner on Cambie Street, is a respected gallery for collectors of quality Inuit and First Nations carvings and prints. Marion Scott Gallery, a recent newcomer to Water Street, has renowned Inuit artworks. The Lattimer Gallery on West 2nd Avenue near Granville Island offers masks, jewellery, prints and drums. The Museum of Anthropology at the University of British Columbia has a good selection of jewellery, books, prints and sculpture, including soapstone, a traditional local material.

HOME FURNISHINGS

Cosmopolitan Vancouverites enjoy their interiors as well as their city's great natural settings. Near the corner of Broadway and Granville streets, decorators will find classic Jordan's on Broadway, rustic Country Furniture, and urbane Industrial Revolution. Upholstery Arts on Burrard Street near West 8th Avenue offers a huge selection of soft furnishings made to order. Yaletown's Bernstein and Gold sells fine Egyptian cotton linens, Italian bedding and tapestries, and Fortuni lighting in an elegant setting. Like most other stores, shipping is available on items.

GIFT SHOPS

You will find well-designed objects from pottery to jewellery at Circle Craft on Granville Island and the Vancouver Art Gallery, on Robson between Hornby and Howe. Obsessions Gift Shop in Yaletown is a clever store with intriguing personal and household designer items including local jewellery in sterling silver and precious stones. And for birthday/wedding/anniversary gifts for every budget and occasion, try Chachkas on Robson, and Moulé on West 4th and Park Royal Mall in West Vancouver.

JEWELLERY

In Vancouver, as in every other major Canadian city, the grande dame of jewellery stores is Birks, now presiding at the corner of Hastings and Granville. Long-respected jeweller Georg Jensen as well as Tiffany & Co. in Holt Renfrew, are both in the Pacific Centre. Other sparkling stars are Karl Stittgen for gold and precious metals in clean, modern lines and the internationally recognized Martha Sturdy for jewellery and home fashion accessories in unexpected materials and organic forms (both on South Granville).

LEATHER

Those who are, as they say, "into" leather will find a wonderful selection of ready-made and custom apparel at Mack's Leathers on Granville Street. More prosaic choices may be made at Castle Milano in the Sinclair Centre, Danier Leather in the Pacific Centre and on Robson, and Neto on East 4th Avenue.

MUSIC

Vancouver has some of the best CD prices in the world, and it's all due to A&B Sound's downtown and other locations. They keep the prices down, but they have plenty of competition. HMV is nearby on

HILL'S NATIVE ART IN GASTOWN

MACK'S LEATHER ON GRANVILLE

JOHN FLUEVOG BOOTS AND SHOES

BOBOLI ON SOUTH GRANVILLE

Robson. For those hard-to-find eclectic recordings, try Highlife Records on Commercial Street, and the Magic Flute and Zulu Records on West 4th Avenue.

MEN'S CLOTHING

High-end establishments well worth a visit include Boboli on South Granville, Harry Rosen, Boys' Co. and Holt Renfrew in the Pacific Centre, Leone in the Sinclair Centre, Mark James on West Broadway, Enda B. on 10th Avenue, S. Lampman in Kerrisdale, and for custom-mades, Chevalier Creations on Seymour Street.

For a sportier look, try Eddie Bauer in the Pacific Centre, Roots on Robson Street and Tilley Endurables Adventure Clothing on Granville. In Yaletown, Vasanji's progressive lines for men arrive weekly from Los Angeles, New York and Italy. Look for the latest in trend-setting styles plus a good Italian shoe selection.

SHOE STORES

Save your shoe leather for a walk along Robson Street, where you'll find Salvatore Ferragamo and Stephane de Raucourt. Over at the corner of Robson and Granville streets, the unique, funky style of internationally renowned shoemaker John Fluevog tempts those most willing to put an outré foot forward. The classic Ingledew's, also on Granville, offers quality dress, casual and walking footwear.

ENTERTAINMENT

SHAWN BORDOFF

Vancouver is well-known for entertainment, offering everything from big-name performers to talented amateurs. If you enjoy music, ranging from folk to classical, and live theatre or dance, you'll find events happening every night of the year. The after-hours scene is lively with many clubs open downtown in what is known as the Entertainment District. Vancouver clubs offer something for all ages and persuasions. Most performing arts productions sell tickets in advance. Ticketmaster has a monopoly in this area, with a telephone line dedicated to arts events.

COMMODORE BALLROOM

LIVE THEATRE

The Vancouver Playhouse (part of the Queen Elizabeth Theatre complex) is one of the best regional theatres in Canada. Plays presented here employ the top actors, directors, designers and craftspeople from across Canada.

The theatre has been home to the Vancouver Playhouse Theatre Company since 1962, a company that often premieres award-winning

Canadian plays.

In the 1930s, the Stanley Theatre on Granville Street near Broadway was the place for vaudeville. It later became an excellent movie theatre but eventually closed in the heyday of multiplex madness. In 1997, the Arts Club Theatre completed lengthy and difficult renovations to transform the dilapidated but distinguished cinema into a first-class professional theatre. Today it's a delightful 650-seat venue with a charming interior, home to many of Vancouver's most entertaining productions, including many smaller musicals. The plays are just as good at the Arts Club's 480-seat Granville Island Stage. A string of hits, including homegrown and international plays, contribute to the Arts Club's longevity. Having run the Arts Club since it opened in 1972, artistic director Bill Millerd is the most respected, and probably most decorated, theatre practitioner in the country.

If you thought that Granville Island was just for shopping, you'll be surprised at how many live theatres coexist here. Across the walkway from the Granville Island Stage is its 220-seat New Revue Stage. This cabaret-style venue hosts the Vancouver TheatreSports League, offering comic improvisation fine-tuned to a science. If you haven't seen a live improv show, catch one of the regular early-evening performances. Vancouver TheatreSports is suitable for the entire family. The Waterfront Theatre is another Granville Island venue, noted for performances of new Canadian plays.

For some adult comedy improvisation on the edge, Urban Well Kits Beach hosts hilarious shows every Monday night after 9 p.m. And if merely watching an improv is not enough and you want to get involved in a show, consider some interactive theatre. Since 1995, people have been raving about Hoarse Raven Theatre's production of Tony and Tina's Wedding, a dinner theatre show with a twist. You start off at a "church wedding" at St. Andrew Wesley's Church in the West End and end up flirting at the "dinner reception" a few blocks away. The audience member initially too embarrassed to respond to the actors usually ends up being the star of the show.

Constructed in a former fire hall, the Firehall Arts Centre on East Cordova is devoted to new plays, performance art and dance. Located just two blocks

NICOLA CAVENDISH AS MAE WEST IN *DIRTY BLONDE*

MIDDLE: FIREHALL ARTS CENTRE
BOTTOM: NICOLA CAVENDISH AND ALLAN MORGAN IN *DIRTY BLONDE*

from troubled Main and Hastings, the Firehall has a loyal audience for its multicultural productions. In addition to its professional theatres, Vancouver has several good community theatres. Presentation House in North Vancouver is as good as most professional venues. Metro Theatre in South Vancouver's Marpole area has mastered the art of dry British comedy. At the Jewish Community Centre's Norman Rothstein Theatre, a state-of-the-art auditorium seats 318 people in luxury.

If you're looking for a New York-style Broadway production at Vancouver prices, the Queen Elizabeth Theatre is the place to go. Throughout the year, large musicals with elaborate sets stop by to dazzle Vancouver audiences at the "QE." The City of Vancouver built the Queen Elizabeth Theatre in 1959 — by West Coast standards, that makes it a historical monument. Nevertheless, the building is perfect for Broadway shows. The stage is 23 metres (75 feet) wide with a proscenium arch; the seats are plush and the décor is elegant.

MUSIC

Vancouver has a strong musical history. The Vancouver Symphony Orchestra (VSO) has existed since 1919, and now performs more than 130 concerts annually. Over the years, the VSO has welcomed many outstanding artists including violinist Midori, singer Isabel Bayrakdarian, pianist Lang Lang, and the up-tempo Canadian Brass ensemble. You'll usually find the symphony at the historic Orpheum Theatre, built in

KATHLEEN BRETT AND THOMAS GERTZ IN *LA BOHÈME* AT THE VANCOUVER OPERA

1927. The Orpheum, like the Stanley Theatre, opened as a vaudeville house. At the time, it was one of the largest and most impressive theatres on the West Coast. Later, it dwindled into a movie house. In 1977, after five years of extravagant renovations, the City of Vancouver reopened the Orpheum as home to the VSO. It still impresses with its classic ambiance of old-time elegance.

Like the symphony, the Vancouver Opera grew out of historic roots, with the first opera performances in the city in the late 1880s. The Vancouver Opera company was launched in 1960, with a performance of Bizet's Carmen. Today, Vancouver Opera is one of the largest performing arts organizations in BC, with a

LA BOHÈME, VANCOUVER OPERA

strong commitment to the development of Canadian talent. While the opera hires principle singers of international fame, preference is given to Canadians. The company also employs its own orchestra and chorus made up of local musicians and singers. There is plenty for the traditional opera fan, from Don Giovanni to Madama Butterfly. All performances are at the Queen Elizabeth Theatre.

One of Vancouver's newest musical venues is the Chan Centre for the Performing Arts at the University of British Columbia. This 1,400-seat facility was designed to have optimum acoustics. The UBC Opera Society performs here a few times a year, as does the Vancouver Symphony Orchestra. If you want to hear something really special, look for the Vancouver Cantata Singers performing at the Chan Centre. This 40-voice award-winning choir is recognized as one of Canada's foremost ensembles.

One of the most enjoyable places for an informal concert is the Commodore Ballroom on Granville Street downtown. Once a fancy black-tie room, the Commodore gradually deteriorated into little more than a beer hall. For years, the main attraction remained its bouncy, horsehair-sprung floor. The floor eventually gave out from years of hard dancing. In the mid-1990s, the club closed, was renovated and reopened. Although the floor was repaired, there is still a bit of bounce left in for fun. Check in advance to see who's playing because the Commodore is very eclectic. Artists include national and international musicians of every genre.

For jazz, try the intimate Seb's Market Café and The Cellar Jazz Club, both on E. Broadway. A casual spot for lively local bands is the long-running Backstage Lounge on Granville Island. For rocking blues, the Yale (near the Granville Bridge on the downtown side) boogies on in one of the oldest buildings in Western Canada. When the Yale was built in 1889, it was a place for miners and loggers to get a drink. They still serve beer, but it's now one of the best blues bars in the world. Dress casually and enjoy.

DANCE

For modern dance, the Vancouver East Cultural Centre on Venables is BC's most diverse performance space. "The Cultch" opened on October 15, 1973, with a two-week run of the locally based Anna Wyman Dance Theatre. Today the Cultch offers a marvelous array of unique dance performances and performing arts. Beware of the balcony though. It's terrific to look at but not a good place to sit. Sight lines

ACACIA SCHACHTE AND EDMOND KILPATRICK IN BALLET B.C.'S PRODUCTION OF *THE WINTER ROOM*

are best from front row centre on the lower level. You may want to keep an eye out for Kokoro Dance, an innovative troupe that performs here and at various other venues throughout the city. The long-running Judith Marcuse Projects creates multi-disciplinary dance and theatre productions at various city-wide locations.

For classical and modern dance, Ballet British Columbia has built an international reputation for artistic excellence. The company first performed on April 11, 1986 and was quickly recognized for its combination of talent and creativity. You can see the ballet at the Queen Elizabeth Theatre.

SANDRINE CASSINI AND EDMOND KILPATRICK IN BALLET B.C.'S PRODUCTION OF *CARMEN*

CLUBS

For star watchers, the bar of choice is the Gérard Lounge. Located on the first floor of the Sutton Place Hotel, the Gérard is one of Vancouver's trendiest lounges. It is also exquisitely furnished, luxurious, and the bar prices reflect the surroundings. It's not uncommon to spot some of Hollywood's most memorable faces here. Vancouver is known for its politeness, so please be discreet. If you're more intent on meeting someone available, attractive and of the opposite sex, Richard's on Richards is the place to go. The crowds at this big dance club tend to be in their late twenties and early thirties. On the weekend, the music leans towards hip-hop and house.

A few blocks from Richard's, you'll find one of the country's most sophisticated night clubs. Skybar, at the corner of Granville and Smythe streets, is Vancouver's new, exclusive, three-level dance club. AuBar nearby is the place to be seen. The club has a line outside most every night from Thursday through Saturday. Another place to

BAR AT OPUS HOTEL

PUMPJACK'S GAY LEATHER BAR

dress up for and be seen is the lounge at the new Opus Hotel in Yaletown. Gastown's Sonar dance club attracts a casual youthful crowd of more than 1,000 to a brick-walled warehouse space. Dance reigns supreme with hip-hop, Top 40, funk, and alternative and electronic music on various nights.

The biggest problem with Vancouver clubs are the lineups. Any place worth going to usually has a lineup after 9 p.m. Smoking is not permitted inside public buildings, so be prepared to smoke outside.

GAY AND LESBIAN

In Vancouver, the downtown clubs with the least amount of attitude are the gay clubs. Celebrities is the queen of clubs. Recently reopened after extensive renovations, it's not to be missed for its lighting and visuals, mod décor and state-of-the-art sound. Hot DJ's and performers get the crowd of gay, straight and bi-partygoers in the mood. The Odyssey, geared toward alternative dance music, has always been a popular club with a loyal gay crowd. Variety is dished up with drink specials, special DJ nights and gay bingo. Check out the city's only private outdoor patio garden bar, a popular spot in the summer for all gays and straights.

If you're looking to meet a gay man while you're in town, your best bet is Numbers. It's the gay equivalent to Richard's on Richards. PumpJack Pub is a gay leather bar where fetish enthusiasts come to play.

Vancouver is also home to Honey Lounge, a cool bar with a good percentage of Lesbian patrons. Next door to Honey is a women's-only nightclub called Lick, an "All-Girl-Operated Underground Queer Night Club." Patrons here enjoy the club's super sound system and drink specials. Thursday nights are harder-core tech nights.

The Davie Village in the West End between Burrard and Jervis streets is a 24-hour playground of clubs, bars, cafes, fancy restaurants, budget eateries, sex shops, bookstores, drugstores, groceries, furniture stores, banks and bakeries. Stop and enjoy the amenities before and after an evening out on the town.

GASTOWN AT NIGHT

GALLERIES

ANN ROSENBERG

In 1961, the New Design Gallery, operated by Alvin Balkind and Abraham Rogatnick, was the first contemporary commercial gallery in Vancouver, specializing in leading-edge Canadian contemporary art. Now, more than 45 years later, there are over 100 galleries in Greater Vancouver that sell contemporary work from many countries (including Canada) to ever more culturally diverse and increasingly sophisticated audiences. In the past, the artistic contributions of Canada's First Nations people went unacknowledged. Now, in downtown Vancouver alone, eight major venues specialize in Northwest Coast, Inuit and Plains art and artifacts.

MARCHESSAULT-ARCETRI-HIRES AT BAU-XI GALLERY

BURGERS' *BEYOND THE BOUNDS* AT BAU-XI GALLERY

SOUTH GRANVILLE

"The Row" is an impressive strip of 20 galleries on or near Granville Street in a section of the city known as South Granville. Akin to Soho in New York or Yorkville in Toronto, the cluster of exhibition spaces on the Row offers an insight into the range of the commercial art scene in the city. The Row begins at 16th Avenue with contemporary art at Catriona Jeffries Gallery and continues with many outlets on either side of Granville. At the far end is Uno Langmann's antique-oriented salesroom just before the entrance to the Granville Bridge.

Outlets between West 5th and West 7th

DIANE FARRIS GALLERY

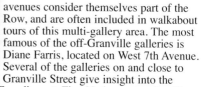

avenues consider themselves part of the Row, and are often included in walkabout tours of this multi-gallery area. The most famous of the off-Granville galleries is Diane Farris, located on West 7th Avenue. Several of the galleries on and close to Granville Street give insight into the history of Canadian art. First Nations art and artifacts may be discovered in Douglas Reynolds and Spirits of the North. The Heffel Gallery specializes in nineteenth-century and Group of Seven paintings. The Harrison and the Art Emporium show landscapes with rich colours that Tom Tomson would have enjoyed.

The Bau-Xi serves Canada's most senior artists, while Atelier represents contemporary art. The Equinox presents internationally known Canadian artists, including Gathie Falk and Tak Tanabe.

Monte Clark Gallery deals with younger art stars like Generation X's Douglas Coupland. Art by French-speaking Canadians is on display at Le Centre Culturel Francophone de Vancouver. Douglas Udell Gallery represents Prairie artists, including the popular, idiosyncratic Joe Fafard.

Flavours of the exotic may also be found on the Row at the Jacana. Simon Patrich's Latin American connections give his exhibition program a unique twist. The Kurbatoff exhibits works by international artists, often with Eastern European backgrounds.

JE T'AIME BY ANNA BONIFACHO AT BAU-XI GALLERY

Located far from the strip is the city's most important international commercial gallery of art and sculpture — the Buschlen Mowatt at 1445 West Georgia. It's worth a special trip.

GRANVILLE ISLAND

Vancouver's highly successful Granville Island is located just a few minutes from the Row. The site houses dozens of artists and artisan studios open to the public. Visitors can watch art in progress. An island favourite is "New-Small and Sterling" glass studio, with its crowd-pleasing demonstrations of glass blowing.

Charles H. Scott is the most important public gallery on Granville Island. It features a rotation of exhibitions designed to complement the Emily Carr Institute of Art and Design's curriculum. Malaspina Printmakers and the Dundarave Print Workshop show limited edition prints created by their members. Circle Craft Gallery and Crafthouse both exhibit juried selections of B.C. craftspersons' art in media as diverse

CHARLES H. SCOTT GALLERY

as knitted ware and original furniture. The Gallery of B.C. Ceramics exhibits, as you might expect, the best of the province's potters. In addition to shops where certain small items of Northwest Coast design may be purchased, the New Eagle Spirit Gallery offers ceremonial objects for sale.

Adjacent to Granville Island, closer to Burrard Street, is another cluster of attractive galleries. The Waterfall, designed by world-famous architect Arthur Erickson, encompasses four galleries. On West 2nd Avenue nearby, is the Leona Lattimer Gallery, which specializes in Northwest Coast art and limited edition prints. The Bjornson Kajiwara Gallery on West 3rd Avenue stresses experimental art by emerging artists.

SPIRIT WRESTLER ART

GASTOWN

The oldest intact commercial district in Vancouver is Gastown, an area of century-old buildings housing both elegant, established galleries as well as souvenir-type shops with t-shirts and works by less-experienced Canadian and First Nations artists. Vancouver's three most impressive showcases for Northwest Coast and Inuit artists and sculptors — Spirit Wrestler, the Inuit Gallery and the recently relocated Marion Scott Gallery — are found here. All stage museum-quality exhibits in heritage premises.

PUBLIC AND NON-PROFIT GALLERIES

In addition to the Charles H. Scott Gallery, there are several important galleries maintained by public institutions. Each contributes enormously to the city's exposure to art and art history.

Chief among these, of course, is the Vancouver Art Gallery, which proudly exhibits art from its ever-expanding collection of Canadian and international contemporary art. Also on exhibit are the greatly admired traditional works of Canada's Group of Seven as well as British Columbia's own Emily Carr. A rich exhibition schedule is amplified by so-called blockbuster shows where high-profile names like Rodin, Rembrandt, Chagall and Warhol draw large audiences. Serious students of art will always learn from the curated exhibits of this reputable institution, thanks to substantial support by the City of Vancouver.

SCULPTURE AT BUSCHLEN MOWATT GALLERY

The special programs of the Morris and Helen Belkin Gallery on the University of British Columbia campus and its satellite at 555 Hamilton Street bring artworks from other countries to Vancouver. Mid-twentieth century British Columbia art, however, is the focus of the majority of its shows. The gallery is also a centre for academic research into this period of local art.

Small-scale artist-run centres and non-profit venues include the Access, Artspeak and Gallery Gachet, all in Gastown. Also on the list are the Contemporary Art Gallery on Nelson, the Or on Richards and Centre A on Homer. Further afield is the grunt on East 2nd Avenue. All have the mandate to exhibit challenging art, video, performance, photographs and electronic works by up-coming artists. Visit these galleries to find out about the newest, freshest art that is being produced today.

Parks and Gardens

Marg Meikle

VanDusen Garden
(top and bottom)

It will come as no surprise to visitors that gardening is currently the number one outdoor leisure activity in Vancouver. It has always been in the top five — and it shows. The combination of a mild climate, plenty of precipitation and very diverse immigration to this area makes for a wide variety of gardening styles. From the abundant crops of the Chinese vegetable gardens around Chinatown to the amazing tomatoes and grapes of the Italian community around Commercial Drive, from the seemingly out-of-place palm trees on Beach Drive in the West End to the colourful perennial borders in many other neighbourhoods, there is much to enjoy around here. Vancouver is also one of the few cities in the world blessed with two botanical gardens: VanDusen Botanical Garden and the University of British Columbia (UBC) Botanical Garden are both superb living research libraries.

VanDusen Botanical Garden

Lush VanDusen is a 22-hectare (55-acre) garden conveniently located on the edge of Shaughnessy, a well-heeled, historic section of Vancouver. But remarkably, the lush, mature VanDusen Botanical Garden was only built on a former golf course in the early 1970s. At any time of the year you can find plants, trees and shrubs in bloom. This garden also contains many theme areas, including the Chinese Medicinal Garden, Children's Garden, Fragrance Garden, Meditation Garden, Rose Garden and a Sino-Himalayan Garden. There's also a maze, a

rhododendron walk, a Canadian Heritage garden and a fern dell.

Many popular special events are held here including the Festival of Lights at Christmas, the VanDusen Plant sale in April, the VanDusen Flower and Garden Show in June and various other club shows and sales throughout the spring and summer. There is a lovely gift shop, a fledgling plant shop and a very civilized restaurant called Shaughnessy's.

RHODODENDRON IN FULL BLOOM AT VANDUSEN GARDEN

UBC BOTANICAL GARDEN AND OTHER UBC GARDENS

The UBC Botanical Garden sits on the ocean edge of the campus, overlooking the Strait of Georgia. Open to the public for wandering, breathing in that fresh sea air and those gorgeous scents, this 28-hectare (70-acre) theme garden is also used for teaching and research. The various gardens include: Alpine Garden, Asian Garden, Winter Garden, B.C. Native Garden, Physick Garden (herbs), Food Garden and Perennial Borders. The 25-hectare (61-acre) David C. Lam Asian Garden has a huge variety of woody Asian plants, maples, clematis, roses, rhododendrons, azaleas, magnolias and rare Oriental plants. In addition to a wide variety of outdoor experiences available, the Shop-in-the-Garden offers a good selection of gardening books and a particularly great nursery, including plants developed through the UBC plant introduction program and unusual plants propagated by

BELOW: MAZE AT VANDUSEN BOTTOM: POND AT VANDUSEN

members of the Friends of the Garden.

Of special interest at UBC is the classical Japanese Nitobe Memorial Garden designed, with a very West Coast view, by Japanese landscape architect Kannosouke Mori. He used many native trees and shrubs, training and pruning them in traditional Japanese fashion. Within this one-hectare (2.5-acre) garden are many more: the Tea Garden with a Tea House, the Nightingale Fence, the Tenth Bridge, several water crossings and a stroll garden.

QUEEN ELIZABETH PARK AND BLOEDEL CONSERVATORY

Second only to Stanley Park, Queen Elizabeth Park is located on Little Mountain, the highest point in Vancouver. It offers a terrific view of the city and the North Shore's Coast Mountains. June is a particularly showy month for the 52-hectare (130-acre) Queen E. Park, as the locals call it, because the roses are in full bloom. But any time is worth a wander through the Quarry Garden at the peak of the mountain. It was created in the 1960s and there are similarities to Butchart Gardens near Victoria, which was created 60 years earlier, also in a quarry.

QUEEN ELIZABETH PARK

INSIDE THE DOME AT QE PARK

There is public art of note throughout Queen Elizabeth Park. A Henry Moore sculpture, *Knife Edge-Two Piece*, is close to the Bloedel Conservatory. The conservatory is a huge climate-controlled Plexiglas dome that holds a large variety of tropical, desert and exotic plants as well as more than 100 tropical birds. It is a particularly great destination on a rainy day, for inside this very warm and dry dome is a jungle of palms, banana trees and orchids, among other species.

DR. SUN YAT-SEN CLASSICAL CHINESE GARDEN

The Dr. Sun Yat-Sen Classical Chinese Garden, opened in 1986, is the first authentic full-sized classical Chinese garden built outside China. In a serene environment behind a wall in the middle of Chinatown, you will find tranquil ponds, natural rock sculptures, courtyards and an interesting variety of plants. The garden reflects the Taoist philosophy of accentuating harmony in contrasts. Every stone, pine and magnolia flower in the garden has been placed purposefully and carries a symbolic meaning. The garden offers guided tours, which provide perspectives on Chinese culture, life during the Ming dynasty, architecture and plants. A popular program offered at the garden is the Enchanted Evening series in July and August. Visitors sip a cup of complimentary tea, enjoy a one-hour Chinese music program and then stroll through the garden. This is an especially nice place to go on a rainy day, as the walkways are covered and the tips of the eave tiles are designed to let the drops fall from them in a particularly gentle way.

DR. SUN YAT-SEN CLASSICAL CHINESE GARDEN

STANLEY PARK

STANLEY PARK'S GARDEN DELIGHTS
The 404-hectare (1,000-acre) heavily wooded Stanley Park has many attractions, including a variety of gardens. Of special interest in June and July is the Rose Garden, which features hundreds of roses divided in beds by colour. Also noteworthy, particularly in April and May, is the Ted and Mary Grieg Rhododendron Garden containing not only rhododendrons, but also camellias, magnolias, maples and azaleas. The park boasts many trails throughout the forested area. (See Stanley Park map, page 6)

CYCLING IN STANLEY PARK

CENTURY GARDENS AT DEER LAKE PARK

If you like rhododendrons, Burnaby's official flower, this is the place to see a lot of them. Located on the grounds of the Burnaby Art Gallery, this garden was created in 1967 for Canada's centennial. The garden, which overlooks Deer Lake, also has a good collection of roses and azaleas.

PARK & TILFORD GARDENS

Created in 1968 by a privately owned distillery, these North Vancouver gardens have been preserved despite rezoning and other changes in the area. The owners and merchants of the nearby Park & Tilford Shopping Centre now fund the gardens, which consist of separate theme gardens or outdoor rooms devoted to roses, herbs, rhododendrons and West Coast native plants as well as the White Garden (perennials), Asia Garden, Townhouse Garden, Yellow Garden, annual display gardens, hanging baskets, a Victorian greenhouse and a Florentine pergola covered in vines.

BELOW: STANLEY PARK

The gardens display plants suitable for the West Coast climate and are developed with organic methods and integrated pest management. Park & Tilford works with Capilano College's horticultural students and staff to create a unique, hands-on experience.

TREES GALORE

Vancouver has more flowering trees than any other city in Canada. Trees have been the lifeblood of the economy and define this place. Vancouverites are truly passionate about their trees. Tens of thousands of flowering cherry, plum, magnolia and dogwood trees make spring a delight throughout the city. As well as the tree collections in the public gardens listed here, consider a free tour of the Riverview Lands Davidson Arboretum. This collection of about 1,800 trees on the 99 hectares (244 acres) of the Riverview Hospital grounds contains more than 150 varieties. It was one of the first arboreta in Canada, created around 1905.

In the Shaughnessy area is a round park in the

middle of "The Crescent," one of the most prestigious addresses in town. This park has a collection of unusual trees, some of which are more than 100 years old. See if you can spot the Japanese Snowbell, Winged Euonymus, Pyramidal Blue Lawson Cypress or Eddie's White Wonder Dogwood, the latter developed right here in Vancouver. For a complete map, a listing, and much more on trees, see Gerald Straley's *Trees of Vancouver*.

ACTIVITIES AND SPECTATOR SPORTS

BOB MACKIN

Vancouver is North America's four-season recreation destination. Where else can you start the day on a golf course, race through gnarly trails on a mountain bike at midday, hit the ski slopes or marina before sunset, and then unwind at a professional hockey or football game? Both weekend warriors and armchair admirals will find plenty to see and do. One of the best parts is that so many of the outdoor activities come without a hefty price tag.

OUTDOOR ACTIVITIES

SUMMER

Beaches

Vancouver's beaches are ideal for relaxing or getting sweaty in the summertime. Kitsilano and English Bay are the most popular, which means space is at a premium on the best days. Downtown beaches include Second or Third Beach at Stanley Park, or venture westward toward the University of British Columbia to Jericho or Spanish Banks. If you can do without clothes, Wreck Beach, steps below the university, is always an alternative. Another good bet is Ambleside, over the Lions Gate Bridge in West Vancouver. All are good for swimming, but the best pool for laps and laughs is the 137-metre (450-foot) Kitsilano Pool, open

mid-May to September.

Indoors, you'll be pleased with the Vancouver Aquatic Centre on the north side of English Bay under the Burrard Street Bridge or the University of British Columbia's aquatic centre. Suburban Richmond and Coquitlam built modern pool facilities in the 1990s.

BC LIONS

Water Sports

Water, water everywhere. Though you may not want to sip the saltchuck, it is ideal for canoeing, kayaking or windsurfing. Deep Cove and Howe Sound are good spots for these activities, but False Creek, Kitsilano, Jericho Beach and Ambleside are also viable options. Watch out for commercial vessels. Vancouver is paradise for ocean kayakers and has many rivers for those looking for that downstream rush. The Capilano River is the easiest to reach.

Windsurfing's best local venue is English Bay, where rental equipment and lessons are available. Experts head to the blustery north end of Howe Sound in Squamish (an hour's drive north of Vancouver) for some of North America's finest conditions.

Cycling

TOUR DE GASTOWN CYCLING RACE

The City of Vancouver and its suburbs have slowly made streets and bridges more bike-friendly. In Vancouver, an extensive network of routes dedicated to cycling. The Lions Gate Bridge was overhauled to include wider, smoother sidewalks with cyclists in mind. The ride may be windy, but the view from the top of the bridge is magnificent.

A favourite bicycle route is the Richmond dyke system on Lulu Island, which passes

through the fishing village of Steveston. Another popular route is the False Creek to Point Grey waterfront path. The Pacific Spirit Regional Park near the University of British Columbia has a wealth of trails for all abilities. Whistler is also a cycling magnet, with accessible free cross-country trails and a paid course for downhill and freeride experts on Whistler Mountain. Cypress Mountain in West Vancouver followed suit with a course designed by North Shore mountain biking legend Todd "Digger" Fiander. The undisputed champ for popularity and accessibility is the Stanley Park seawall. Rent your bike near the entrance to Stanley Park. Don't forget a helmet: it's the law to wear one while cycling.

VANCOUVER CANUCKS

In-Line Skating

If you'd rather have wheels on your two feet than two wheels and a seat, try in-line skating. Helmets, gloves, knee and elbow pads are highly recommended. The Stanley Park seawall isn't just for bikes. In fact, in-line skaters outnumber cyclists on some summer days. Skate rentals are located near the entrance to Stanley Park.

For a more serene skate, try the wooded wonders of North Vancouver's Lower Seymour Conservation Reserve.

HASTINGS RACECOURSE

FURRY CREEK GOLF COURSE

Golf

Some people wouldn't take a walk in the park without a club, balls and a tee. Luckily, there are many places to do that in Vancouver. The area boasts a variety of public, private and semi-private golf courses. For the novice, there are pitch-and-putt courses at Stanley Park and Queen Elizabeth Park. The University Golf Club, and Langara and Fraserview courses are among the closest to downtown. Richmond's Mayfair Lakes offers plenty of water hazards on what was once a farm. En route to Whistler, the Furry Creek course spills down a mountainside, providing unique challenges and an unbeatable view of Howe Sound. Whistler's smorgasbord of four courses includes ones designed by the likes of Jack Nicklaus, Arnold Palmer and Robert Trent Jones Jr.

Hiking

Hiking is another popular activity on the West Coast. You don't have to go far to get away from the hustle of city life. In Vancouver, visit Pacific Spirit Regional Park at the University of British Columbia and Stanley

BEACH VOLLEYBALL

Park downtown. In nearby Richmond, the dyke system is flat and close to the Gulf of Georgia and the Fraser River. On the North Shore, Seymour and Cypress provincial parks offer a multitude of trails, as does the Lower Seymour Conservation Reserve and Lynn Canyon park. Lighthouse Park in West Vancouver is another option. The most challenging of all is the Grouse Grind, a 2.9-kilometre (1.8-mile) hike up Grouse Mountain in North Vancouver. Depending on the avalanche/landslide risk, it's open from April through October. Summer hiking at Whistler offers spectacular views. When climbing or hiking in any of B.C.'s mountains, always be prepared with the proper footwear, equipment and clothing. It's best to hike with a buddy. Even on the sunniest days, the weather can be unpredictable.

WINTER

Skiing and Snowboarding

Vancouver is known for its abundance of rain. Luckily, on the Coast Mountains that equals tempting winter snowfalls. On the North Shore, where it's higher and colder, winter sports enthusiasts will find a variety of recreation options. Grouse Mountain, Cypress Mountain and Mount Seymour all offer top-quality downhill and cross-country skiing and snowboarding. Grouse adds sleigh rides and outdoor ice skating. Cypress and Seymour are

CYCLING AT WHISTLER

similarly popular with those who ski, snowboard and use toboggans and inner tubes. Grouse is the most accessible, with direct public transit service and a breathtaking eight-minute aerial tram ride, the Skyride, from its parking lot. Cypress is tabbed as host of the 2010 Olympic and Paralympic Winter Games' snowboarding and freestyle skiing events. Whistler Mountain gets the marquee downhill events.

Snowmobiling

For those who like motorized action, there's snowmobiling in Whistler less than a three-hour winter drive from Vancouver. Canadian Snowmobile Adventures provides tours on Blackcomb Mountain. An alternative way to tour the trails is on the company's snowcat, a large enclosed vehicle that seats 19 people. In the summer, the company offers all-terrain vehicle tours.

Family-oriented Winter Sports

Grouse Mountain has turned part of its ski area into a winter wonderland with an ice skating and hockey rink and sleigh rides. It's also one of a number of mountains that offer snowshoeing, the fastest-growing winter sport in North America. It's fun for the whole family and you don't need lessons. Just strap on the shoes and go. Rent them at Grouse, Seymour and Cypress.

TUBING AT CYPRESS MOUNTAIN

EXTREME SPORTS

Highway 99, also known as the Sea-to-Sky Highway, leads the way to challenging outdoor activities. The town of Squamish is called the outdoor recreation capital of Canada, and the name is well-deserved. Whistler also offers a multitude of choices, from glacier skiing to death-defying downhill mountain biking.

Climbing

If it's cold enough and the water freezes (which doesn't happen every

VANCOUVER SUN RUN

year), there's ice climbing at the 300-metre (985-foot) Shannon Falls. A few minutes north of the falls is the legendary Stawamus (Squamish) Chief. The big granite rock that looms above the Squamish townsite at the end of Howe Sound was first conquered by climbers in 1961. It's been a provincial park since 1997 and a popular hiking spot, but it's not recommended for rookies. Rock climbers and newbies can practice their technique at a variety of indoor rock climbing centres in the suburbs. The Chief is the second largest granite monolith in the world at 700 metres (2,300 feet) high. It's also a popular nesting habitat for the peregrine falcon, which sometimes forces closure of climbing routes.

Soaring and Skydiving

The Vancouver Soaring Association operates in the Fraser Valley at Hope Airport from spring to early autumn on the longest turf airfield in Canada. The sensation of motorless flight is amazing. Club members are only too glad to take interested newcomers for a ride. If you'd like to free fall, with a parachute strapped to your back, of course, then Pitt Meadows airport is the place to go.

Whitewater Rafting

IN-LINE SKATERS ON THE SEAWALL

The water is cold and fast-flowing, but that's part of the rush of whitewater rafting. There is prime rafting

on the Chilliwack River in the Fraser Valley and the Cheakamus River off the Sea-to-Sky Highway.

Zip-trekking and Bungee Jumping

Ever wanted to fly through a forest like a bird or jump from tree to tree like a squirrel? The next best thing is zip-trekking in Whistler. And for those who like the rush of jumping off high objects with nothing attached to them but a giant elastic band, the sport of bungee jumping is still going strong above the Cheakamus River near Whistler.

SPECTATOR SPORTS

Baseball

Nat Bailey Stadium is one of the oldest ballparks in North America (built in 1951) and home to the University of British Columbia Thunderbirds during late winter and spring. The Vancouver Canadians of the single A Northwest League return to action every June through September with a 38-game home schedule. It's the first chance to see tomorrow's Oakland Athletics' stars.

Football and Soccer

There's been one constant since B.C. Place Stadium opened in 1983: the B.C. Lions of the Canadian Football League have played there. The season runs from early July to October. The stadium's latest distinction is to host the opening and closing ceremonies of the 2010 Olympic and Paralympic Winter Games. Summer tours of the interior are available.

The Vancouver Whitecaps soccer team plays outdoors at Swangard Stadium. There's nowhere better to be on a summer night than at Swangard among the tall trees just a corner kick from Vancouver on Boundary Road and Kingsway. The men play April to September, while the women's team has an abbreviated May to August season. Unlike the rest of Vancouver's sports franchises, nearly all the players are homegrown. Many have played internationally.

Hockey

Vancouver has two hockey teams. The National Hockey League's Canucks play at GM Place downtown. The team has twice played in the Stanley Cup finals, but is still trying for its first championship. The Giants of the Western Hockey League (WHL) play in the Canucks old home, the Pacific Coliseum. The Chilliwack Bruins are the newest WHL franchise, debuting at Prospera Centre in the Fraser Valley in 2005.

ZIP-TREKKING IN WHISTLER

Horseracing

Hastings Racecourse on the Pacific National Exhibition grounds is more than 116 years old. Its scenic view is the best of any Canadian track, with Burrard Inlet and the North Shore's Coast Mountains in the distance. Thoroughbred racing runs April through November. Hastings' valley cousin is Fraser Downs in the Cloverdale area of Surrey, 45 kilometres (28 miles) from Vancouver. Harness racing runs September to May.

ANNUAL EVENTS

The TELUS World Ski & Snowboard Festival in Whistler is winter's last blast in April. The all-out sports and music bash features on-going parties, films, concerts and adventure zones. The top professional skiers and snowboarders and some of the latest buzz bands come to play.

The Vancouver Sun Run in mid-April is the second largest 10-kilometre (6-mile) footrace in North America and threatening to become the biggest. In 2005, more than 48,000 people walked or ran from Burrard and Georgia streets to B.C. Place Stadium. The first Sunday of May is traditionally Adidas Vancouver International Marathon day in the City of Vancouver.

The False Creek waters near Science World host competing dragon boat teams in the latter half of June. The Dragon Boat Festival is a weekend-long celebration of the city's ethnic diversity, with teams representing a number of nationalities and causes.

The cobblestoned streets of Gastown were a stop on bicyclist Lance Armstrong's long voyage to winning six consecutive Tour de France titles. He won the criterium race in Gastown in 1991. After a lengthy absence, the Tour de Gastown is back and bigger than ever. Look for it in late July.

Nobody gets bored in Vancouver, but people come here to "get board." The Slam City Jam in late August at B.C. Place Stadium is the North American pro-skateboarding championship.

TELUS WORLD SKI & SNOWBOARD FESTIVAL

KIDS' STUFF

MARIAN GILMOUR

Children of every age, and those who are simply young at heart, can choose from a variety of interactive cultural activities or sample second-to-none outdoor experiences.

If it should happen to rain, head for indoor venues such as Science World, the H.R. MacMillan Space Centre or the Vancouver Aquarium Marine Science Centre. The films shown at the CN IMAX Theatre at Canada Place and the Alcan OMNIMAX Theatre at Science World offer big-screen opportunities. The size and intensity of these productions may be overwhelming for younger children. Check with venue staff before taking the family.

Some of the attractions mentioned throughout this guide are seasonal, others are once-a-year special events. It is always wise to call ahead for hours, admission prices and travel directions.

CAPILANO SUSPENSION BRIDGE

OUTDOOR ATTRACTIONS

Hold on to your kids for a spectacular walk across the swaying 140-metre (450-foot) wood and cable footbridge of the Capilano Suspension Bridge. This popular North Shore attraction spans the Capilano River gorge and hangs 70 metres (230 feet) over the raging river's waters. New to the park is Treetops Adventure, a walk through the towering treetops on swaying bridges. Also on the North Shore, Lynn Canyon Park hosts an Ecology Centre and another

LYNN CANYON ECOLOGY CENTRE

swinging footbridge above Lynn Creek.

The VanDusen Botanical Garden is home to an Elizabethan hedge maze that kids will love to get lost in. The hedge is about 1.5 metres (five feet) high. There are wooden steps throughout so shorter folk can climb up to see they are not really lost.

Stanley Park offers numerous attractions spread throughout its 404 hectares (1,000 acres). Kids of all ages will want to ride the miniature train that travels about 1.5 kilometres (almost a mile) through a Pacific Northwest rainforest. The Children's Farmyard features barnyard animals. Lower Brockton Oval offers a display of totem poles of various BC First Nations.

Another place for children to experience birds and animals is the Greater Vancouver Zoo in Aldergrove. Its park-like 48 hectares (118 acres) are home to 194 species of animals, including tigers, wolves, zebras, rhinoceroses, hippos and camels. The zoo is 48 kilometres (30 miles) east of Vancouver and is open year-round. North Vancouver's Maplewood Farm is a two-hectare (5-acre) petting farm of barnyard animals including rabbits, goats, cows, horses, donkeys, sheep and lots of ducks, geese and chickens. The farm also features seasonal special events.

Playland, open from April to the end of September, offers 35 outdoor rides ranging from the traditional wooden roller-coaster and Ferris wheel to the Ring of Fire and the Rainbow. There are also games, attractions and, of course, cotton candy and foot-long hot dogs. Playland is located on the Pacific National Exhibition grounds on East Hastings Street. Call for times and days.

WATER PLAY

PLAYLAND AT THE PACIFIC NATIONAL EXHIBITION GROUNDS

Depending on the time of the year, Vancouver's 11 sandy ocean beaches offer fine swimming. Lying in tidal pools, digging holes, or building sandcastles and driftwood structures can be a lot of fun. Lifeguards are

on duty from Victoria Day through Labour Day at Second Beach and Third Beach in Stanley Park, and at English Bay, Sunset Beach, Kitsilano Beach, Jericho Beach, Locarno Beach and Spanish Banks.

Kitsilano Pool is a huge outdoor heated pool and its graduated slope makes it excellent for small children. It's open from Victoria Day to mid-September. Second Beach Pool, in the heart of Stanley Park, is another favourite outdoor destination. After exhausting the pleasures of the pool's three small water slides, check out the children's playground that boasts a real fire engine.

The Granville Island Water Park and Adventure Playground offers water cannons (ground-level spouts that gush water), a safe waterslide and shallow wading areas. The park is supervised in season and parents can sit on the grass and enjoy the excitement. The Stanley Park Water Park, just north of Lumberman's Arch, offers much of the same action but also has equipment suitable for children with physical disabilities.

VANCOUVER MARINE ANIMAL SCIENCE CENTRE

MAPLEWOOD FARM

CHILDREN'S CULTURE

Vancouver's premiere event for kids is the Vancouver International Children's Festival. Vanier Park becomes a festival village for this one-week event, which begins in late May. Outstanding international and top-notch local talent present fine-quality performing arts. The purchase of show tickets includes admission to the festival site. Check out the box office at the festival gates for often-available rush tickets. Otherwise, a small fee allows

77

you on-site to enjoy the roving entertainers, face painters and the multicultural community stage. Young readers take a place of honour at the

THIRD BEACH

Vancouver International Writers (& Readers) Festival. Held in October at various Granville Island locations, the festival dedicates three days to children's events. Twelve months of the year, head for the lower level of the Vancouver Public Library at Library Square. The area is devoted to children. If you're buying books, Vancouver's Kidsbooks on West Broadway treats kids as serious readers. They hold readings, book launches and book signings.

HISTORY AND LIVING CULTURE

The Cedar Cottage/Trout Lake Pow Wow held at Trout Lake Community Centre on Mother's Day weekend

AT SECOND BEACH PLAYGROUND

offers a glimpse into the rich cultural traditions of Canada's First Nations people. This event features

intertribal dancing and drumming, hoop dancing, a princess pageant, and arts and crafts displays.

Take a walk into the past at the Burnaby Village Museum and Carousel. More than 30 authentically restored buildings and a costumed staff recreate a 1920s village. There is also a beautifully restored C.W. Parker Carousel, circa 1912. Open seven days a week from late April to September and in December. The Fort Langley National Historic Park marks the site of a reconstructed Hudson's Bay Company post. Children can see and sample life as it was in the last century.

The B.C. Sports Hall of Fame, located at

Gate A in B.C. Place Stadium, is more than a collection of medals, trophies, personal mementoes and photographs. High-energy kids get a workout in the Participation Gallery, climbing a rock wall, testing their pitching arm or sprinting against the clock.

ANNUAL EVENTS

GAIL BUENTE

Vancouver is a city of hale-and-hearty outdoor types who spend their leisure time communing with nature. These rugged individualists are also fiercely loyal to their festivals and cultural events.

WINTER

On New Year's Day the notorious Polar Bear Swim attracts upwards of 2,000 shivering participants into the icy waters of English Bay. Another outdoor tradition, the Brackendale Winter Eagle Festival and Count takes place along the Squamish River in the Squamish-Brackendale area 74 kilometres (46 miles) north of Vancouver. An eagle count is taken each January.

SPRING

Spring starts with the week-long Vancouver International Wine Festival, a fundraiser for the Vancouver Playhouse.

By May, the festivals are truly in bloom. One bright May morning, thousands of runners arrive for the Adidas Vancouver International Marathon, Canada's largest marathon.

Kids have a festival all their own in late May. Featuring dance, theatre, music, puppets and clowns, the Vancouver International Children's Festival is one of the high points of the spring season.

In June, False Creek welcomes the annual Alcan Dragon Boat Festival. Each brightly painted 12-metre

PAINTED DRAGON PROWS

SNOWSHOEING AT WHISTLER RESORT

DRAGON BOAT RACE

(40-foot) boat is powered by a team of twenty, all paddling in unison.

SUMMER

Summer in Vancouver is a non-stop festival. Leading off the season is the TD Canada Trust Vancouver International Jazz Festival, embracing samba, free jazz and blues, to name a few musical styles.

Throughout the summer, Bard on the Beach takes over Vanier Park in Kitsilano. Productions are staged in a backless tent, so viewers can enjoy the play with a backdrop of mountains.

In July the Vancouver International Folk Music Festival takes over.

July also brings the HSBC Celebration of Light Fireworks Festival to downtown Vancouver. Countries compete over three nights with a fourth night devoted to the winning displays.

During the first two weeks in August, Festival Vancouver's remarkable array of classical, jazz and world music concerts feature top-notch local and touring artists.

The final fling of summer is the Pacific National Exhibition (PNE), the grand-daddy of Vancouver festivals during the last two weeks of August. Visitors ride the roller coasters and chow down on corn dogs and mini-donuts.

FALL

Summer officially ends with Labour Day weekend, but visitors can come inside for the Vancouver Fringe Festival in September, a theatre event for those who enjoy the new and sometimes outrageous.

JAZZ FESTIVAL IN DAVID LAM PARK

Next comes the Vancouver International Film Festival, with an emphasis on films from Canada and Pacific Rim countries.

Taking place on Granville Island in October, the Vancouver International Writers & Readers Festival is a week of readings by the most exciting writers from around the world and around the corner.

VANCOUVER
NEIGHBOURHOODS

DOWNTOWN

BARBARA TOWELL

DOWNTOWN WINTER NIGHT LIGHTS

Vancouver is a relatively new city. In 1884, William Van Horne, the influential general manager of the Canadian Pacific Railway, visited what was then the logging village of Granville. He made two recommendations: that the tiny village of approximately 100 buildings become the terminus of the first cross-Canada railway, and that it be renamed Vancouver. In spite of the Great Fire of June 13, 1886, which totally destroyed the new city, a boom was on. By 1889, more than 10,000 people lived here. The Greater Vancouver area today numbers more than 2 million people.

Throughout its brief history, Vancouverites have fought hard to preserve the city's heritage buildings. Downtown Vancouver is proof of some success. A walk in the area

STREET ARTIST

reveals a satisfying mix of old and new. Old here means buildings from the late nineteenth century and early twentieth century. New is as recent as the Vancouver Public Library's central branch, which opened in 1995.

Vancouver's history can be traced through the architecture of its downtown core, which encompasses West Georgia Street to the south, Burrard Street to the west, Cordova Street on the waterfront to the north (look for the mountains) and Cambie Street to the east. It's fair to say that politics, business and faith shaped the city. The result is an eclectic mix of buildings, starting from the château-like Fairmont Hotel Vancouver at Georgia and

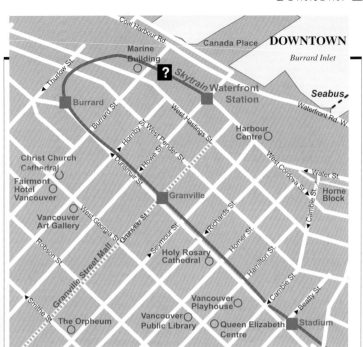

DOWNTOWN

Burrard Inlet

Burrard and ending with a Roman coliseum-like library further east on Georgia Street. Although the number of permanent residents in the area is miniscule compared to the West End, Gastown or Yaletown on False Creek, downtown Vancouver does not empty out at night. Because of the many hotels, restaurants and entertainment venues in the area, the streets of the inner core remain fairly busy until midnight.

FAIRMONT HOTEL VANCOUVER

FAIRMONT HOTEL VANCOUVER

First came the Canadian Pacific Railway (CPR), then came progress. Our walk begins at the corner of Georgia and Burrard where, in 1928, construction began on the Hotel Vancouver. This grand hotel, designed by the CPR in the impressive style of its Château Lake Louise and Banff Springs Hotel, would convince travellers that Vancouver was not a damp parochial backwater but a glistening modern metropolis. The next year, the stock market crashed and construction came to a standstill. For nearly a decade, the hotel's unfinished steel skeleton stood as a reminder of grim economic times. Only the impending royal visit of King George VI in 1939 brought

Christ Church Cathedral

about its hasty completion.

In the intervening period between start and completion, tastes changed. Ideas of tradition gave way to faith in the modern. As a result, the lower arcade, lobby and VIP suites were finished in an Art Deco style rather than the original classical approach. When Hilton took over management in the 1960s, much of the interior was redecorated yet again in a more classical form. Today's updated interior is a glamorous journey into a more luxurious past. Memorable exterior features of the Fairmont Hotel Vancouver remain its steep green copper roof and its sly, slightly impish gargoyles.

Christ Church Cathedral

Across the street from the Fairmont Hotel Vancouver is the lovely and vibrant Christ Church Cathedral (690 Burrard Street), seat of the New Westminster Anglican Diocese. Designed by C.O. Wickenden, churches in this Gothic-revival style thrived in Canada in the nineteenth century, with each denomination mounting its own modifications (compare the Catholic Holy Rosary Cathedral noted later). The austere lines and interior atmosphere of Christ Church speak of its ties to Britain. Christ Church was built to serve the growing population of the city's West End, but initial funds were sparse. The inaugural service on October 6, 1889, was held in the granite basement, the only finished part of the building. In the aptly named "Root House," 52 parishioners were warmed by a coal-fire boiler. To raise

Waterfront Station

money, parishioners purchased stock in the church's construction company. Within six years, the sandstone structure was complete, with additions in 1909 and 1940. The interior boasts an impressive ceiling with beams of Douglas fir. Of the church's 29 stained-glass windows, three are by William Morris. They were acquired in 1984 on permanent loan from the Vancouver Museum and can be seen on the north-facing wall on the west side. The first organ was installed in 1895, employing an organ blower at the rate of five dollars a month. The pipes of the second organ can be seen in the church, though they are no longer functional. Be sure to check out the regular musical events taking place here. Information is available at the church or on their website at www.cathedral.vancouver.bc.ca.

As with many of Vancouver's older buildings, the cathedral was threatened with demolition in modern times. In 1976, after five years of lobbying, the building was named a "Class A" heritage site by the municipality.

MARINE BUILDING

A five-minute walk north along Burrard Street towards the mountains brings you to the spectacular Marine Building (355 Burrard). Erected in the Art Deco style, its construction cost its Toronto-based developers $2.5 million in 1929. By 1930, the developers were broke and offered the building to the city for $1 million. When legislators refused to pay, Britain's Guinness family spotted a bargain and stepped in, purchasing it for much less. The same fiscally astute family built the Lions Gate Bridge in 1938, and ran it as a toll bridge until it was sold to the B.C. government in 1963.

The Marine Building's architects, McCarter and Nairne, suggested a design reminiscent of a "great crag rising from the sea, clinging with sea flora and fauna, tinted in sea-green, touched with gold." Indeed, no other Vancouver building is more finely finished. No visit to the Marine Building would be complete without a venture inside, through its extraordinary front door with bronze grills and Art Deco zigzags. The lobby's walls include terra cotta friezes depicting the history of transportation and the colonial discovery of the Pacific Coast. The building was restored in 1989.

MARINE BUILDING

MARINE BUILDING EXTERIOR DETAILING AND INTERIOR (BELOW)

WATERFRONT STATION

Crossing over to West Cordova, proceed to Canada Place with its five white "sails" built for Expo '86. A stroll on the promenade is in order before moving on to Waterfront Station, built by the Canadian Pacific Railway (601 West Cordova) in 1914. Two earlier stations stood on the spot, a timber structure in 1887 (where the first passenger train arrived on May 23, 1887) and a château-style station in 1898-99. Waterfront Station was the only building in Vancouver designed by the firm of Barott, Blackader and Webster. In the words of architectural historian Harold Kalman, their creation is the most "self-consciously pompous building type [made] in the early part of the century." It is indeed a grand terminus with an expansive column façade and pilastered waiting room. It now serves as an entrance to both SkyTrain and SeaBus public transit systems.

Shops fill the former waiting room, but the public aspect of the site has eroded, as there are no longer public washrooms and seating is scant. Paintings on the upper walls depict Canadian landscapes set in the West. The building was restored in 1976-77.

SINCLAIR CENTRE

SINCLAIR CENTRE

Crossing Cordova, you can enter the Sinclair Centre from its rear entrance or head a block up the hill to its main entrance at 757 West Hastings Street. The building was completed by the department of public works in 1910 to house the post office and other federal offices. In 1939, an extension was added at 325 Granville Street. The two "faces" of the Sinclair Centre reflect very distinct economic periods.

The original building was executed in an Edwardian Baroque style that married architectural influences from both the French and English. Built for $600,000, its rusticated granite basement continues up to smooth columns reaching past the second and third floors. The fourth floor includes dormer windows. The entire structure is finished off with an impressive clock tower. The granite exterior hides an early example of a fireproof steel frame.

King George VI was kept busy on his royal visit to Vancouver in 1939. He not only opened the Hotel Vancouver but also the extension to the post office. The addition could not be more contrary to the design and intent of the original building. The first building was erected during Vancouver's construction and land speculation boom. As a result, it is highly ornate, expressing optimism in the future wealth of the country. The extension, on the other hand, was finished at the tail end of the Depression. Its exterior walls are bereft of decoration except a minimal application of pilasters used to harmonize with its predecessor. Interestingly, it was the original building, not the extension, that was occupied in 1935 by 750 unemployed men, as it more aptly captured the spirit of federal power. Their demands for relief led to a violent backlash from police and a number of the protesters were hospitalized.

The Sinclair Centre is now an elegant shopping mall, retaining many of its original architectural and decorative highlights.

HARBOUR CENTRE AREA

HARBOUR CENTRE TOWER

Exit the Sinclair Centre on Hastings Street and walk east to Simon Fraser University's Harbour Centre at 515 West Hastings Street. There is usually a small but interesting art show in its impressive modern lobby. The view of the harbour from the adjoining ceiling-high window is impressive. Downstairs is a good bookstore and a food fair. The Harbour Centre Tower is home to the Lookout!, a visitor attraction. Not notable architecturally, the tower does offer one of the finest views in the city.

A block away, at 342 Richards Street, the Century House is worth a peek. Designed by J.S.D. Taylor and completed in 1912, it is noteworthy not because of its classical style (there are other, finer examples to be found), but for a particular detail that is best described as magic realism: the building is crowned with a pair of winged beavers. One can only wonder how contemporaries viewed these particularly whimsical little creatures, which are part beaver and part bird. The best view is from across the street.

Continuing south along Richards to Pender Street, note

the neon waterfall of the former Niagara Hotel, now Ramada Inn (435 West Pender). Fifty years ago, Vancouver was ablaze with neon, winning it the title of the neon capital of North America. It's hard to imagine a landscape where the Ramada Inn's sign could be considered modest, but in neon's heyday there was one neon sign for every 18 residents. Suburban expansion in the 1960s linked neon with urban decay. Modernization of the downtown core proved to be the demise of neon in Vancouver, although the artform is now experiencing something of a comeback. The Vancouver Museum features a sampling of Vancouver's neon history.

WINGED BEAVERS ON CENTURY HOUSE

HOLY ROSARY CATHEDRAL

Back on Richards Street, you can't miss the Holy Rosary Cathedral (646 Richards). In 1900, when most of Vancouver's buildings were no higher than three stories, the cathedral's 21-storey peak must have cast an impressive shadow. Built during a period of considerable church debt, some parishioners questioned the sense of the monumental Gothic-revival structure. The building was dubbed McGuckin's Folly after the priest whose efforts made construction possible.

HOLY ROSARY CATHEDRAL

Built of Gabriola Island sandstone with granite foundations, the church's asymmetrical towers are its most prominent visual feature. The cathedral bells are of particular auditory interest. In the east tower, eight bells are tuned to a full octave, producing up to 5,000 different sequences. Inside the cathedral, granite-encased marble columns support an arched ceiling. Among the many stained-glass windows are eight depicting biblical scenes. Visitors are welcome.

LIBRARY SQUARE

Continue south a few more blocks to Georgia Street, then head east to Library Square, the home of the Vancouver Public Library's central branch (350 West Georgia). Described as a rectangle within an ellipse, the controversial design by Moshe Safdie & Associates with Downs/Archambault and Partners resembles a Roman coliseum. Opened in 1995, the nine-storey-high structure houses the library, an adjoining office tower and retail shops on the lower level concourse. Library Square includes two outdoor plazas, which often host special events. The concourse, with its six-storey-high view of the internal workings of the library, is a great place to catch your breath over an excellent cup of coffee, a slice of pizza or an ice cream cone. Sit, sip and do some serious people watching.

LIBRARY SQUARE

WEST END

JAMES OAKES

DAVIE STREET

The West End is Vancouver's original residential neighbourhood, occupying the western half of the city's downtown peninsula. Once home to blue bloods living in stately mansions surrounded by gardens and quiet streets, the area has evolved into a remarkably diverse community — home to single parents, upwardly mobile singles, gays and lesbians, foreign students, recent immigrants, senior citizens, low-income transients, condo owners and wealthy retirees. The West End, in short, is a success story of urban livability that is the envy of cities across North America.

BOUNDARIES

The West End is the most densely populated square kilometre in Canada. Zoning maps show Georgia and Burrard streets as the northern and eastern boundaries, while Stanley Park and English Bay create the western and

MANHATTAN BUILDING

southern extremes. Laid out on a simple grid pattern, the main streets of the West End running east/west are Beach, Davie, Robson and Georgia. The main north/south streets are Denman, Thurlow and Burrard. Included within the West End's boundaries are three distinct commercial zones, running along Robson, Davie and Denman streets. Public transit

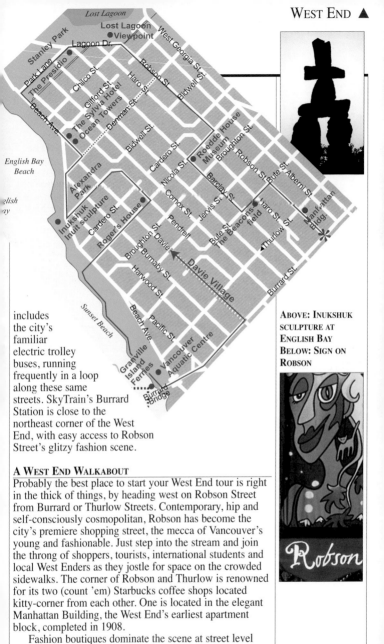

includes the city's familiar electric trolley buses, running frequently in a loop along these same streets. SkyTrain's Burrard Station is close to the northeast corner of the West End, with easy access to Robson Street's glitzy fashion scene.

A WEST END WALKABOUT

Probably the best place to start your West End tour is right in the thick of things, by heading west on Robson Street from Burrard or Thurlow Streets. Contemporary, hip and self-consciously cosmopolitan, Robson has become the city's premiere shopping street, the mecca of Vancouver's young and fashionable. Just step into the stream and join the throng of shoppers, tourists, international students and local West Enders as they jostle for space on the crowded sidewalks. The corner of Robson and Thurlow is renowned for its two (count 'em) Starbucks coffee shops located kitty-corner from each other. One is located in the elegant Manhattan Building, the West End's earliest apartment block, completed in 1908.

Fashion boutiques dominate the scene at street level along the next block of Robson, overlooked by an excellent selection of upstairs restaurants, including Tsunami Sushi, Moxies, and CinCin. You can continue along the high-energy Robson stroll for several more blocks, but try venturing into the heart of the residential West End by taking a left at Bute Street. You'll soon come to a leafy little park complete with benches and flower beds. Overlooking it is the Beaconsfield, a stately, if somewhat run-down, stone and brick structure. This is one of the West End's oldest remaining apartment buildings.

Three blocks further on (take a right at Barclay Street

ROEDDE HOUSE MUSEUM

and proceed down the hill to Broughton Street), you'll come to the Roedde House Museum (1415 Barclay), another architectural treasure of the West End. Roedde House stands among a collection of restored, late nineteenth century wood-frame houses in Barclay Heritage Square. Carefully restored with period furnishings and décor, the museum is a journey back in time to the height of Victorian and Edwardian elegance.

After soaking in the atmosphere, head back out to Robson Street and continue west down the hill towards Stanley Park. Although the lower end of Robson is being gentrified with upscale shops and condominiums, it has the friendly atmosphere of an urban village with green grocers, pizza shops, video rental outlets and a 1960s-style Safeway.

On the far side of Denman Street, in the exclusive area known to locals and realtors as "West of Denman," Robson becomes strictly residential for its final two blocks until it merges with Lagoon Drive. Here, on a slope overlooking Lost Lagoon, visitors are greeted with one of the best city views, a 180° panorama of Stanley Park, Coal Harbour and the North Shore mountains.

Admire the view while walking south along Lagoon Drive, but when you reach Nelson Street take a moment and look upwards at the row of high-rises bordering the park. Standing among the conventional 1960s and 1970s towers is the post-modernist Presidio, designed by Vancouver architect Richard Henriques, who in turn was inspired by Austrian architect Adolf Loos' Villa Karma near Montreaux, Switzerland. Many of the Presidio's multimillion dollar suites were purchased in the early 1990s by offshore buyers who reportedly enjoy their residences for only a few weeks every year. Once you've come back to earth, follow the pedestrian path running along the edge of the park until you come to Beach Avenue and the shores of English Bay.

ENGLISH BAY JOGGER

THE SEASIDE

Swimmers began flocking to English Bay when the West End was first developed in the 1890s. By the turn of the twentieth century, summertime crowds travelled to the popular bathing beach on the newly opened Robson and Denman streetcar line. Today, the Brighton-style pier has long since disappeared, but the holiday-resort atmosphere along the beach is as strong as ever. At the first sign of a sunny day, the area is invaded by sunbathers, beach lovers, dog walkers and windsurfers.

The ivy-clad Sylvia Hotel on Beach Avenue, overlooking English Bay, still offers visitors perhaps the best accommodation location-wise for the money. It was built in 1911 as the Sylvia Court Apartments before the Depression forced the owner to rent it out as a seamen's hostel. After the war, it moved upscale and branched out into the liquor business, opening the city's first cocktail bar in July 1954. A recent renovation has transformed the bar into a smartly sleek spot to admire the view of the bay over a cocktail.

THE SYLVIA HOTEL

Next door to the Sylvia, at 1835 Morton Avenue, stands the Ocean Towers, a jazzily shaped apartment building dating from 1957. Across the street, at the intersection of Denman and Davie, a cluster of imported palm trees completes the exotic "British California" ambiance. Take a brief side trip along Denman Street, which offers beachwear, bicycle rentals, cappuccinos, a fresh juice bar and an amazing variety of international cuisine. Pedestrians like to think they rule the street and traffic moves by at a crawl.

ALEXANDRA PARK
BANDSTAND

Don't forget that English Bay is also an evening destination. Locals and visitors come out to walk along the seawall promenade, listen to musicians and watch the sunset beyond the anchored freighters and the mountains of Vancouver Island. During the annual Celebration of Light fireworks festival in July and August, upwards of 300,000 people gather around the bay to watch the spectacular international displays.

At the eastern most end of the English Bay beach, you'll find an Inuit "inukshuk" sculpture by Alvin Kanak. Commissioned by the Northwest Territories for Expo '86, the large granite blocks represent a human figure with welcoming, outstretched arms. More recently the work inspired the logo for Vancouver's 2010 Winter Olympics.

From here, cross Beach Avenue at the pedestrian light to the lovely Alexandra Park, named after the consort of King Edward VII. It boasts a pretty wooden bandstand constructed in 1914 for outdoor concerts, as well as a marble fountain adorned with a brass plaque honouring the city's beloved Seraphim "Joe" Fortes. Generations of children learned to swim from this Barbadian immigrant,

GRANVILLE ISLAND FERRIES

who acted as lifeguard and special constable at English Bay until his death in 1922.

From the northeast corner of the park, walk north on Bidwell to Davie Street, turn left, and head up the hill until you come to the impressive Roger's House at 1531 Davie. One of the last survivors of the West End's age of opulence, this elegant mansion-turned-restaurant was designed by Samuel Maclure, one of the most prolific architects of well-heeled Vancouver society, for local sugar magnate Benjamin Tingley Rogers.

To continue exploring the West End's southern flank, return to the seashore via Nicola Street and then stroll toward the Burrard Street Bridge until you arrive at Sunset Beach. This marks the end of the English Bay Seawall and the entrance to False Creek. At the foot of Thurlow Street stands the Vancouver Aquatic Centre, which houses a 50-metre pool, a children's pool and a diving tank, among other indoor recreation facilities. Behind the Aquatic Centre you'll find the West End landing of the Granville Island ferries. The little passenger ferries run regularly from dawn until dusk, serving English Bay, Vanier Park in Kitsilano Point and Granville Island.

ROGER'S HOUSE

THE 24-HOUR VILLAGE

Our final destination, what's becoming known as Davie Village, is bit of a hike back up on the West End's central plateau. Just follow the pedestrian path across from the entrance to the Aquatic Centre, which leads to the north end of the Burrard Street Bridge. From there, walk north along Burrard Street for three blocks then hang a left when you come to a pair of gas stations at the corner of Davie Street.

Here's where you'll find the locals going about their daily routines: picking up the dry-cleaning, checking their e-mail at the corner Internet café, buying groceries at the

DAVIE VILLAGE

24-hour supermarket, getting a prescription filled at the mega-drugstore, or having a meal at one of the many reasonably priced ethnic restaurants along the street.

And just in case you hadn't noticed the profusion of rainbow freedom flags along the street, Davie Village is also the traditional core of Vancouver's gay community, with clubs, bookstores, and cafés located close by. The busy Gay and Lesbian Centre on Bute Street houses a drop-in centre, lounge and library. By night, Davie supports a lively social scene. Gay bars like Numbers, the Fountainhead and Pumpjacks are usually packed. Several all-night eateries are open to all. For midnight snacks, try the Fresco Inn, Hamburger Mary's, or the Oasis, a relaxed piano bar where unrepentant smokers can still enjoy a puff on the outdoor patio. It's all part of life on the wild side in Vancouver's swingin' West End.

GASTOWN

LEANORE SALI

Stand in Maple Tree Square looking west along Water Street. The red brick streets of Gastown are bustling with people. Local residents stop to chat with their neighbours, international students rush to their classes, business people dodge the throngs to make their luncheon appointments and visitors from around the world wander through the shops and restaurants, stopping en route to pose for photographs by Gastown's world-famous steam clock. In Gastown, residents and tourists have learned to enjoy life in the streets in much the same way Europeans do.

The handsome façades of the brick buildings reveal a mix of antique stores, boutiques and street-level galleries that contain a broad selection of Canadian First Nations art. In restaurants housed in former warehouses, diners are offered a variety of cuisine and price ranges. The nightlife is lively with a selection

COFFEE SHOP IN GASTOWN

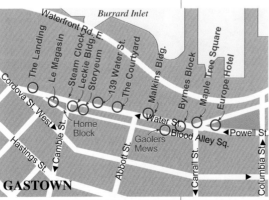

GASTOWN

93

STEAM CLOCK

of nightclubs, cabarets and pubs that cater to every age group.

Although Gastown still remains a favourite location for architectural firms, design companies, music promoters and advertising agencies, it is also beginning to attract other young urban professionals.

GASTOWN'S HISTORIC PAST

The original name of the small settlement around which Vancouver grew was unofficially known as Gastown. The first settler was Captain John "Gassy Jack" Deighton, a Yorkshire man who'd been a sailor, prospector, steamboat pilot and saloonkeeper. Gassy Jack arrived at Burrard Inlet in the fall of 1867, opened his Globe saloon and prospered. Almost immediately others came to join him.

By the 1870s, Gastown was a multicultural community of saloons, hotels and grocery stores catering to mill workers, lumbermen, ships' crews and whalers. During the next decade, the community underwent a growth spurt following the announcement that it would be the site of the Canadian Pacific Railway terminus. By 1886, it had 1,000 buildings and 3,000 residents. On April 6 of that year, it was officially renamed Vancouver.

Shortly after, on June 13, 1886, a brush-clearing fire blazed out of control and burned the town to the ground. While destroying the old town, the Great Fire spurred the biggest building boom in West Coast history. The area prospered until Vancouver's economic boom collapsed in 1914. From the 1930s to the 1950s, Gastown, once the heart of Vancouver, became a virtual backwater.

Gastown remained in decline until the early 1960s when a few enterprising merchants and property owners, recognizing the architectural heritage underneath the grime of the old buildings, began to put some money into

EUROPE HOTEL

restoring them. City Hall joined in the cause. New street lamps were installed, streets and sidewalks were bricked, and the meandering courtyards and mews were left intact. In 1971, the Province of British Columbia designated Gastown a historic district.

GASTOWN TOUR

Start your tour at Gassy Jack's statue in Maple Tree Square. Facing east, you'll see the Europe Hotel, built in 1908 by Angelo Calori. A flatiron-shaped building, built to fit the triangular-shaped lot, the Europe was the earliest reinforced concrete structure in Canada and the first fireproof hotel in Western Canada.

The building directly behind Gassy Jack's statue is the Byrnes Block (2 - 8 Water Street). Built in 1886 by George Byrnes, a former sheriff of the Cariboo

STORYEUM

during the gold rush days, this was one of the first brick buildings in Vancouver. It once housed the Alhambra Hotel, one of the city's fancier establishments at the time.

Take the entrance off Carrall Street to the central courtyard known as Gaolers Mews. This is where the town's first jail and the home of Gastown's first constable were located. Vancouver's first city council meeting was held here. The site later housed the city's first post office and later the city's first fire hall. The building was renovated in 1974 to create the interior courtyard and office and retail complex.

Exit onto Water Street. As you stroll west along Water, take the time to browse through the many galleries and shops along the way. Many galleries specialize in West Coast and Inuit art, offering the largest selection in Western Canada and representing internationally renowned First Nations artists.

GASTOWN SHOPPERS

On the north side of the street you'll see a large building housing the Old Spaghetti Factory Restaurant (55 Water). It was built in 1907 as the warehouse and headquarters for Malkins, one of B.C.'s main food wholesalers. The upper floors were renovated in 2002 to accommodate live-work studios.

Continue along Water Street crossing to the north side at the corner of Water and Abbott streets. As you continue your stroll west along Water, notice the courtyard, built in 1974 and designed to blend in with its older neighbours. Just west of the courtyard is 139 Water Street, built in 1898 as the first warehouse for Malkins wholesale grocery business. Renovated in 1996 into apartments, this building is an excellent example of Gastown living today.

Across the street, a new and innovative attraction opened in 2004. Called Storyeum, the 9,290-square-metre (100,000-sq. ft) indoor venue showcases the colourful history of Canada's West Coast. Live actors and multimedia effects are combined on impressive underground stages.

At the corner of Water and Cambie streets is Gastown's famous steam clock. Although built in 1977, the movements of the steam clock are based on an 1875

WATER STREET

design. A continuous supply of steam feeds the clockworks from the steam vent beneath the street.

Cross over to the south side of the street. The red-brick building on the southeast corner of Water and Cambie is known as the Leckie Building. It was built in 1910 by the Leckie family as a shoe and boot factory. Renovated in 1990 for office and retail use, the Leckie Building is an excellent example of the timber construction used in early Gastown buildings.

Stroll south on Cambie to Cordova Street. Turn right at the corner and meander west along Cordova. The buildings along this strip of Cordova Street once housed merchants outfitting gold seekers headed for the Klondike. Today, this area is an emerging fashion district offering designs by Vancouver's up and coming fashion designers.

The building on the northwest corner of Cambie and Cordova was built in 1888. It was known as the Masonic Temple, as it housed the Masonic Grand Lodge. Next door is the Horne Block, built by land investor and city politician J.W. Horne. Designed by Nathaniel Stonestreet Hoffar, the city's first important architect, the Horne Block was the mid-1880s most exquisite venture into the Victorian Italianate style of architecture.

At the entrance to the alley off Cordova is the Le Magasin building. Check out the face ornaments on the fibreglass frieze. These face ornaments are life masks of notable entrepreneurs from Gastown's 1960s revival and the individuals responsible for the revitalization of the area during the 1970s. Take the back entrance of Le Magasin and walk through the building to exit onto Water Street. On both sides of street you will see the best examples of 1890s architecture still standing in the city.

Cross over and continue west along Water Street until you get to the Landing (375 Water). This converted warehouse, built by the Kelly Douglas grocery company in 1905 from profits made from outfitting Klondike gold seekers, reflects the general history of wholesaling in Gastown. The building was renovated in 1988 as a retail and office complex. Enter the building and walk over to the large window overlooking the harbour. From here you get a spectacular view of Vancouver's port and railway system, the catalysts that started it all.

THE HORNE BLOCK

CHINATOWN

JOANNE POON

Vancouver's Chinatown is the third-largest in North America, a bustling community encompassing Chinatown proper as well as neighbouring Strathcona. Back in the early 1880s, the then-swampy Chinatown land was on the edge of False Creek. Geographically, Chinatown stretches from Gore Avenue east to Carrall Street, and west on Pender and Keefer streets. This historic area began to grow in the late nineteenth century after the completion of the Canadian Pacific Railway. Many Chinese railway workers stayed in Canada, moving to the "Saltwater City" for jobs.

CHINATOWN
NEIGHBOURHOOD

The majority lived in Chinatown. A predominantly male society, the workers contracted for seasonal jobs in canneries and lumber mills. They lived alone, far from their families in China, unable to bring them to Canada because of the repressive head tax and a closed-door immigration policy introduced

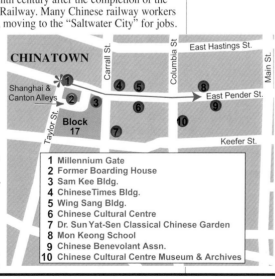

1 Millennium Gate
2 Former Boarding House
3 Sam Kee Bldg.
4 Chinese Times Bldg.
5 Wing Sang Bldg.
6 Chinese Cultural Centre
7 Dr. Sun Yat-Sen Classical Chinese Garden
8 Mon Keong School
9 Chinese Benevolant Assn.
10 Chinese Cultural Centre Museum & Archives

in 1885. Chinese entrepreneurs like merchant Chang Toy and Canadian Pacific Railway Chinese agent Yip Sang were precursors of Chinatown's commercial development.

CHINATOWN TOUR

The epicentre of historical Chinatown is the intersection of Carrall and East Pender streets. Stand on the corner and look around. The southwestern block of the intersection was known as Block 17. It was here, at 87 East Pender, that a seven-storey boarding house complex once stood. Built by a group of Chinese merchants, the complex included stores on the ground floor and residential quarters on the upper floors. The majority of the residents were the Chinese "married bachelors" who came to Canada alone. After the anti-Asian riot in 1907, when 2,000 members of Vancouver's Asiatic Exclusion League stormed Chinatown and Japantown, an iron gate was erected at the building's main entrance to protect its residents from attack. At night, the gate was locked for security purposes. More recently, the building housed SUCCESS, a major community and immigrant services agency (now relocated to new headquarters at 28 West Pender Street). Shanghai and Canton alleys also ran off Block 17. They were once busy with stores, restaurants, barbershops and Chinese opera theatres. When Dr. Sun Yat-Sen visited Vancouver in 1910, he drew an audience of 1,000 to one of the theatres. Both alleys were demolished in the 1940s when non-Chinese industries began to move into the area. Look for the street plaques commemorating their history.

The Guinness Book of Records calls Block 17's Sam Kee Building (8 West Pender) the narrowest building in the world. The Sam Kee Building belonged to a wealthy Chinese merchant, Chang Toy. When he bought the land in 1903, it was a standard-sized lot. In 1912, the government decided to widen Pender Street and expropriated 24 feet from the front of the lot, leaving only six feet on which to construct a building. Which is what Chang Toy did to spite the officials. Although narrow, the 1913 building included a bathhouse in the basement for the use of the married bachelors living upstairs. As there were no bathroom facilities in the building, the residents had to

SAM KEE BUILDING

pay to use the bathhouse. The building is now owned by Jack Chow Insurance.

Across the street (116 East Pender) stands a building that belonged to the Chinese Freemasons (Cheekongtong). It was the office of the *Chinese Times*, one of the first locally printed Chinese newspapers. When Dr. Sun Yat-Sen visited Vancouver to raise funds for the 1911 Revolution in China, he stayed here. To support the revolution, the Freemasons mortgaged the building.

The location of the Chinese Cultural Centre (50 East Pender) and Dr. Sun Yat-Sen Classical Chinese Garden (578 Carrall) was the site for Vancouver's Jubilee Celebration in 1936. For the festivities, the entire area was lit up and decorated with a Chinese arch and pagoda. In 1980, the Chinese Cultural Centre was built. Stop in at the centre's museum and archives (555 Columbia) to view exhibitions on Chinese arts and the history of Chinese-Canadians. Two bronze inscriptions near the entrance commemorate historic passages in B.C. history. One recognizes the industry and sacrifices of Chinese railroad workers, thousands of whom died building the Canadian Pacific Railway, Canada's first transcontinental line. The other honours the efforts of Chinese-Canadian Second World War veterans to gain voting rights for Chinese people living in Canada, a goal accomplished in the province in 1947.

Across from the Chinese Cultural Centre stands the Wing Sang Building. Constructed in 1889, it is both the oldest building and the first brick building in Chinatown. It was built by Yip Sang, a successful Chinese merchant with four wives and 23 children. The entire family lived here and Yip ran his import-export business, the Wing Sang Company, on the ground floor. If you look up, you'll note the inscription "1889" on the original building. As the family and the business grew, Yip Sang expanded with a bay-windowed addition and a six-storey building on the back. He linked the front and back buildings with a staircase on the third floor. One of the interesting architectural features is the door on the second floor facing Pender Street. Since the swamps of False Creek still extended to the area, the door was used for loading and unloading goods.

TOP: **Chinese Cultural Centre Museum and Archives**
MIDDLE: **Sculpture at Dr. Sun Yat-Sen Classical Garden**
ABOVE: **Bust of Dr. Sun Yat-Sen**

Millenium Gate

STORES AND ASSOCIATIONS

Walking towards Gore on Pender, you enter another section of Chinatown. Here, you might be attracted at first by the different storefronts, including herbal outlets, jewellers, restaurants, and arts and crafts companies. When you look up, you'll be amazed to see the historic buildings around you. All share similar features: a slender shape, decorated with Western-style pillars and Chinese-style recessed balconies. Balconies like these were common to the buildings in South China. The pillars and the pediments supporting them were heavily influenced by Western architecture. This combination of Chinese and Western styles is a characteristic of Chinatown architecture.

Many of these buildings are now the offices of Chinese associations. They are surname associations, for example the Lee, Wong and Chin associations. Others were formed with people from the same village in China. All played a significant role in the life of early Chinese immigrants. Associations offered help and financial aid to members in need, and places to gather socially and share news from home. Today, members still visit their associations to play mah-jong, meet friends, practice Cantonese opera and celebrate Chinese festivals.

The Chinese Benevolent Association (108 East Pender Street) was formed at the turn of the century and the building erected in 1901. After the Second World War, the Chinese Benevolent Association, together with other associations and individuals in the community, successfully lobbied for the vote and the repeal of the Chinese Exclusion Act of July 1, 1923, which had effectively suspended Chinese immigration to Canada.

The Wong Association, one of the largest surname associations in the area, founded the Mon Keong School (123A East Pender) in 1925, mainly for children of the Wong clan. Children attended Chinese-language classes after school, which was one of the ways Chinese parents ensured language proficiency for their children. The school is still in operation.

TOP: HISTORIC BUILDING ON PENDER STREET
MIDDLE: AT THE MARKET
BOTTOM: MON KEONG SCHOOL

One newcomer to Chinatown is the summertime night market held Thursdays through Sundays. Several streets are closed to traffic, attracting throngs browsing for bargains on everything from clothing and antiques to handbags and delicate glass figurines. Another newcomer is the purple, red and gold Millennium Gate arching over Pender Street near Taylor. It symbolizes the area's rich history and enduring presence.

There are many other historic buildings to visit in Chinatown. Why not take one of the popular walking tours offered by the Chinese Cultural Centre to learn about them?

COMMERCIAL DRIVE

GARY MCFARLANE

Everyone calls it "the Drive," but the best way to experience Commercial Drive is a leisurely walk past its diverse array of shops, cafés, parks and community and cultural centres. Like much of Vancouver, the area was densely wooded late into the nineteenth century. The Salish Indians once hunted elk here. Long-gone forests fed the historic Hastings lumber mill. The first homes were built in the working-class suburb of Grandview in the early years of the twentieth century. If you wander through the streets east of the Drive you can easily imagine Vancouver as it was in 1910. Grant Street, Lakewood Drive, Rose Street, Salsbury Drive and Napier Street, among others, retain many of these grand and eccentric buildings, some decaying rustically, others lovingly restored.

ITALIAN NEIGHBOURHOOD

Following the First and Second World wars, waves of Italian immigrants settled in the area. Commercial Drive is still an excellent place to shop for prosciutto, sausages, great rounds of cheese and biscotti at the numerous bakeries, delis and produce markets. During soccer season, sitting in Caffé Roma Sports Bar is a sensation not unlike Milan at rush hour. Sip an espresso under a reproduction of the Sistine Chapel at Calabria Bar, rub elbows with Roman sculptures and peruse portraits of Italian stars. Check out the First Ravioli Store (1900 Commercial) for the best fresh pasta in the city. Then stand in line for fresh gelato at Gelateria

101

Dolce Amore (1598 Commercial).

While it has retained its Italian flavour, the Drive in recent years has been a landing place for successive waves of immigrants from Asia, Latin America, the Middle East, and Eastern Europe, each bringing a legacy of culture and food. The Drive has great restaurants, most very gentle on the wallet.

COFFEE AND CULTURE

Social life on the Drive centres on tiny cafés. Coffee is taken very seriously here, and not only by Italians. Local Ethiopian eateries feature a ritual that includes coffee beans roasted at the table; Harambe Café is said to be the best. Vegetarians throng to Sweet Cherubim, Yogi, or Juicy Lucy's. Dutch Girl Chocolates serves up exquisite homemade truffles. Havana Restaurant features an art gallery, dance lessons and Cuban cigars on the menu — but this being Vancouver and not Havana, they can't be smoked on-site. Whether you're in the mood for sushi, tapas, pupusas, or pho, you'll find them and more on the Drive.

Quirky specialty shops abound. Worth browsing are the hundreds of magazines at Magpie Magazine Gallery, Highlife Records for world music, and Beckwoman's, a curiosity shop crammed to the ceiling with clothing, beads and political posters. One-of-a-kind crafts by Vancouver artisans fill Dr. Vigari Gallery.

Local cultural meccas include the Vancouver East Cultural Centre, also known as "the Cultch," located in a former Methodist church. Catch jazz-with-your-tapas at the Latin Quarter, or an eclectic mix of jazz, alt-country and Middle Eastern music with a Turkish menu at Rime. The funky Waazubee Café has turntabling DJs on many evenings, and Café Deux Soleils has rock and alternative acts as well as on-tap selections from the acclaimed Storm microbrewery located nearby.

BOTTOM: HAVANA RESTAURANT

YALETOWN

BRIAN BUSBY

Yaletown is at once one of Vancouver's oldest and newest neighbourhoods. The original residents were railway workers from the Fraser Canyon town of Yale who, quite literally, picked up their houses and moved to the area after the completion of the transcontinental railway. During the early years of the last century, most homes were replaced by dozens of timber, brick and concrete warehouses. The rail yards remained until the 1980s when the land was cleared for Expo '86, the world exposition. During the past decade, Yaletown has experienced dramatic upward growth: dozens of tall residential towers, built in the aftermath of Expo '86, now overlook False Creek. The new buildings, in combination with an extended seawall and a series of new parks, attract a varied population, making Yaletown a neighbourhood much admired by urban planners.

URBAN FARE

A WALK THROUGH YALETOWN

An appropriate place to begin exploring Yaletown is at Emery Barnes Park located on the northwest corner of Davie and Richards streets. A U.S. Olympic athlete and professional football player, Barnes arrived in Vancouver in 1957 to play for the B.C. Lions football team. He later became a dedicated social worker and for 24 years served as the local member of the provincial legislature. Barnes was one of the first two Black Canadians elected to the legislature and was the first to take on the role of Speaker. A narrow, mosaic-bottomed stream running between a

EMERY BARNES
PARK

THE OLD CANADIAN
LINEN COMPANY
BUILDING

small artificial waterfall and a large fountain bisects the park, which is one of the newest in the city.

Crossing to the southeast corner of the intersection, you'll find the old Canadian Linen Company Building. Now housing a grocery store, this modern-style structure is a remnant from the time when Yaletown served as the city's garment district. Heading one block east, at the

corner of Davie and Homer, you'll encounter the Gray Block. Completed in 1912, this is just one of the Yaletown buildings built by brothers Donald and Russell Gray. The Gray Block is typical of many of the older Yaletown structures in both architecture and the fact that it has been converted into shops and residential lofts. Continuing eastward along Davie, you'll find yourself descending a small hill. At the base is the Opus Hotel, Vancouver's first boutique inn and the hotel of choice for many in the film and music industries.

The next intersection is Pacific Boulevard, a wide thoroughfare made possible by the lands cleared for Expo. As you cross Pacific, you'll notice a large glass pavilion displaying Canada's most historic locomotive. On May 23, 1887, Canadian Pacific Railway Engine 374 pulled the first transcontinental train into the city, thus completing the National Dream. Appropriately, the pavilion is attached to the old CPR roundhouse, at which the locomotive was

CANADA'S MOST
HISTORIC
LOCOMOTIVE

serviced during its many visits to the city. The renovated roundhouse was used during Expo and has since been converted into a community centre. The old turntable is still in place, forming the focal point of a large semi-circular courtyard. Directly across the street is Urban Fare, a gourmet food store that also features a cafeteria-style restaurant and a

coffee shop. The tables outside the store provide a
favourite perch for people watchers.

THE SEAWALL

The block ends in a roundabout, which is, in fact, the
beginning of Davie Street. You'll notice an odd-looking
structure displaying photographs from Vancouver's past.
Each image becomes clear at a different angle — best keep
your eye on traffic as you cross the street. A description of
each photo is engraved on the structure's concrete
foundation. You are now on the seawall. Gazing to the left
provides a nice view of Yaletown's new residential towers,
a good indication why renowned Generation X author

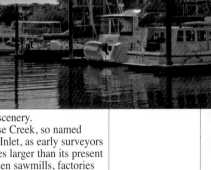

Douglas Coupland refers to
Vancouver as the "City of
Glass." Straight-ahead is the
Yaletown Aquabus ferry
terminal, allowing
pedestrians easy access to
Granville Island and other
destinations around False
Creek.

Head to the right along
the seawall. Be aware that the
pedestrian portion of the
route runs parallel to that set
aside for cyclists and those
on roller-blades. Although the
lanes are clearly marked, it is
easy to become sidetracked by the scenery.

You are now walking along False Creek, so named
because it does not lead to Burrard Inlet, as early surveyors
had expected. Once nearly five times larger than its present
size, much of the creek was lost when sawmills, factories
and the railway moved into the area. For much of the last
century, its shores served as the polluted industrial heart of
the city. In the past few decades, False Creek has become
largely residential: more than 15,000 people now live along
its shores.

Following the seawall leads to David Lam Park. A real
estate developer and philanthropist, Lam was the first
Chinese-Canadian to serve as a lieutenant-governor. The
park features two children's playgrounds, tennis and
basketball courts. It is dominated by a large playing field
most often used for soccer and ultimate Frisbee.

As you pass by the playing field, look to your right.
Notice the twin waterfalls hugging what appears to be a

TIME CAPSULE

glass-door garage. This is the False Creek Pump Station, which supplies water to Vancouver's fire hydrants. Anything but utilitarian in design, the pump station features two of the more welcoming public washrooms in the city.

Walking up the stairs on either side of the pump station leads to the roof, which affords a dramatic view of False Creek. You are now back on Homer Street, the closest intersection being Homer and Pacific. Crossing Pacific, you'll come upon a series of red wedge-shaped structures. They are, in fact, time capsules. Unlike most time capsules, the contents are conveniently listed on each: "a woman's left boot, a woman's right boot (non-matching), not too many men's black plastic combs…" It is no coincidence that the capsules are interspersed with identically shaped trash receptacles.

Having passed all three capsules, you'll be at the corner of Homer and Drake, starting point of the Great Fire of Vancouver. On June 13, 1886, a fire set to clear brush ran out of control and swept toward the city. In less than an hour, the City of Vancouver, which had been incorporated just two months prior, was all but destroyed.

OLD YALETOWN

Cross the street and walk a short block east on Drake. You're now at the corner of Drake and Hamilton. Turning left on Hamilton leads to the older area of Yaletown. Once-neglected warehouses dominate this collection of narrow streets. Restored and converted to mixed use, they maintain their original elevated brick-paved loading docks. The large cantilever canopies, once unique to Yaletown, are emulated throughout the city.

Continue on Hamilton to Davie Street. As tempting as it might be to scoot across the street, it is best to use the crosswalk, just a bit to your right. This will lead to Mainland Street. Within two blocks is a rich, eclectic mix of clothing boutiques, furniture stores, hair salons, kitchen

YALETOWN'S RESTORED WAREHOUSES

showrooms, a shop devoted to cookbooks, a beer microbrewery, and a car dealership.

The end of this retail strip is Nelson, historically the northern border of Yaletown. Turn left, walk a few dozen paces, and left again to return to Hamilton. Mainland and Hamilton are in some ways twins, each featuring unique and interesting shops. What's more, both streets offer a number of cafés and a wide variety of restaurants, one of which is certain to be the perfect place to rest tired feet and eat a well-deserved meal.

GRANVILLE ISLAND AND FALSE CREEK

ALMA LEE

Before Granville Island was built, there were two sandbars at this location used as a fish enclosure by First Nations people before European contact. As Vancouver grew, the sandbars' proximity to False Creek made them the ideal site for industry. After many failed attempts to reclaim the sandbars, the newly formed Vancouver Harbour Commission gave the go-ahead in 1915 for them to be turned into an island. Until just after the Second World War, the area was choked with sawmills and factories manufacturing everything from barrels to boilers and from chains to cement. By the 1950s, the area was a toxic wasteland. Something had to be done. In 1972, a group of young architects and urban planners known as "The Barefoot Gang"

GRANVILLE ISLAND FERRY

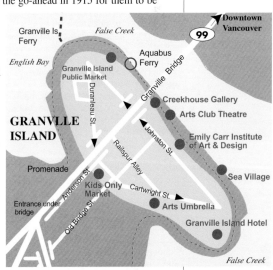

BURRARD BRIDGE FROM GRANVILLE ISLAND

brainstormed the redevelopment of Granville Island. Their vision, scoffed at by many, created the unique environment it is today.

A UNIQUE URBAN TRANSFORMATION

Although the grimy industries are gone, Granville Island remains a place where people work. These are merchants from all walks of life and cultural backgrounds. The butcher, the baker, the candlestick maker would be an apt rhyme to describe the island. In the Granville Island Public Market, it's fun to get to know the folks who are so incredibly knowledgeable about their products, whether it's fresh fruit from the Okanagan, exotic fish from the

Southern Hemisphere or fine cheeses from around the world. A favourite spot is the bakery and French specialty foods store La Baguette et L'Echalote.

Get to the island by Aquabus ferry, False Creek

PUBLIC MARKET MERCHANT

Ferry or TransLink bus (the #50 bus, False Creek South on Granville to the entrance), on foot, by bike or in-line skates. Free parking on the island is limited to three hours and closely monitored but paid covered parking is fairly copious. If you prefer a little exercise, park off-island in the day lot at Lamey's Mill Road and The Castings and walk west along the False Creek seawall for the flavour of the terraced residences and their lovely gardens. Nearby is the new Go Fish!, a sidewalk takeout kitchen serving up the tastiest snacks of inexpensive wild salmon, halibut, and oysters fresh from the adjacent Fisherman's Wharf (1505 West 1st Ave).

The view of the city and the mountains from here is spectacular. The walkway takes you north onto the island at the False Creek Community Centre, close to the children's water park. This free water park is a good choice if you have younger children. Sit and rest while you watch them play in safety. Check out the Kids Only Market next door to the Crystal Arc. In the adjacent pond, look for turtles basking on stones in the summer. Across the street is the Granville Island Brewing Company, where you can stop and sample their product.

Pick up a map at the Information Centre (1398 Cartwright Street), to help you circumnavigate the island. If you get lost, don't worry — you just might stumble onto a little-known treasure. After I'd worked on the island for six or seven years, I walked into Dig This, a gardening shop, and exited by the back door to find two or three hitherto unknown great little shops and a tiny café. One special off-the-beaten-track spot is the mound at the far east end of the island, a great place to take in the tranquil view of boats moored on False Creek, to say nothing of the view of Mount Baker on a clear day.

A TOUR OF THE ISLAND

To make a circle of Granville Island, head east on Cartwright Street. You'll pass Arts Umbrella, a facility for young aspiring artists, dancers and musicians. At the end of Cartwright is the Granville Island Hotel, a boutique hotel with an excellent patio restaurant, brew pub and many charter boats moored close by. Walking west on Johnston Street, Sea Village on the north side is an eclectic mix of float homes with impressive container gardens on the decks. Continue along to the Emily Carr Institute of Art & Design. Drop in and see what's on at the Charles Scott Gallery. As you stroll on, you can't miss Ocean Cement, one of the island's last industrial tenants. You'll remember that the industrial nature of Granville Island still exists when you dodge cement trucks or pass a shop that makes nails. Notice that many of the islands' buildings are constructed from corrugated metal, retaining the industrial look. Next to Ocean Cement, the Creekhouse Gallery is home to a mix of shops, galleries and offices. Nearby on Old Bridge Street is the New-Small and Sterling Studio Glass workshop and glass gallery. From the sidewalk, you

BLACK STONE PRESS

BLACK STONE HAND PRESS

can watch glass-blowing in progress.

As you walk past the Granville Island Stage and the New Revue Stage, both run by the Arts Club Theatre, you'll come to the star of the site, the Granville Island Public Market. From the vivid bouquets of flowers outside to the locally grown fresh fruit and vegetables inside, it's a feast for the eyes and taste buds. Best advice: nibble your way through the market; there are often free samples.

Leaving temptation behind, check out the Net Loft across from the public market. In the past, fishers repaired their nets here; today, it's yet another surprise of little shops. On the water nearby, you'll find Vancouver's love affair with the water continues with boat builders, boat repairers, chandlers, boat charter rentals, kayak rentals, fishing boats and live-on moorages. You'll pass Granville Island Museums, a fascinating three-in-one spot with excellent collections for anglers, rail enthusiasts and ship-lovers.

Every day, visitors to Granville Island travel around the world with the music of the buskers, whether they're flute players from the Andes or a piper from Scotland. Stand-up comics and magicians entice you to stop, take a break and laugh at their antics. The arts come to life as you watch artisans at work at Black Stone, David Clifford's hand press (1249 Cartwright); at Paper Ya, purveyor of handmade paper, in the Net Loft; and in the Diane Sanderson weaving studio (#15-1551 Johnston). Festivals are an ongoing attraction, including a new play festival in May, comedy and jazz festivals in June, a folk music festival in July, a wooden boat festival in August and the Vancouver International Writers & Readers Festival in October. In December, the Christmas Carol Ships form a convoy to dazzle onlookers along False Creek with a myriad of sparkling lights. As a visitor, you might even plan a special holiday to enjoy one of these annual events.

ART IN THE PUBLIC MARKET

Granville Island is justifiably famous. And famous people come here to visit. You never know whom you'll see, from superstar Canadian authors to superstar actors busy filming in Hollywood North (please, no autographs!). You can do practically anything on Granville Island — exchange money, buy books, learn how to scuba dive or kayak, even live there. Anything to do with the outdoor West Coast style is pretty much available here. Granville Island is the kind of place that invites you to explore again and again.

KITSILANO

TRUDE LaBOSSIERE HUEBNER

Cross Burrard Bridge from downtown and you are in a world set apart. High-rises are replaced by wood-framed houses, business suits by bathing suits. The views from the beaches strung along the south side of English Bay are unmatched, especially at sunset. Often simply called Kits, the area's very name derives from the Squamish chief Khahtsahlano. In 2005, Kitsilano celebrated its centennial. Today, diversity is the essence of every aspect of the neighbourhood.

4TH AVENUE, THE HEART OF KITSILANO

Once over the bridge, continue several blocks along Burrard to 4th Avenue. Turn right and you are in the heart of Kits, with its population of singles, families and seniors and an overall higher-than-average education level. Housing ranges from small apartments to lovingly refurbished heritage homes. Kitsilano is an outdoor playground for its residents, who cycle, run, in-line skate, swim, and play tennis and beach volleyball.

Continue on 4th Avenue to Cypress Street. Turn left and head south to 6th Avenue. At the intersection of Cypress and 6th, one of Vancouver's many attractive community gardens grows in abundance. Flowers and vegetables cover the boulevard each summer. Turn right and continue west

KITSILANO NEIGHBOURHOOD

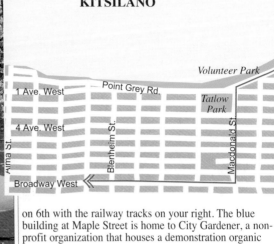

Burrard Inlet

KITSILANO

Volunteer Park

1 Ave. West — Point Grey Rd.

Tatlow Park

4 Ave. West

Alma St.

Blenheim St.

Macdonald St.

Broadway West ≪

**VANIER PARK
CYCLISTS**

on 6th with the railway tracks on your right. The blue building at Maple Street is home to City Gardener, a non-profit organization that houses a demonstration organic garden.

Continue walking on 6th until you reach the Arbutus Real Food Market. This is a convenient spot for some freshly baked goodies and a washroom break inside the market's rustic wood structure. Then head north along Arbutus, back to 4th Avenue. Cross 4th to Sophie's Cosmic Café, a funky Kitsilano landmark since 1987.

Walk east along 4th Avenue back to Cypress Street, one of the city's many designated bicycle routes. Turn left, check out the small village, then continue to Cornwall Avenue. Here you can begin to explore the fabulous and famed Kitsilano waterfront.

KITSILANO POINT

Cross Cornwall and continue south several blocks to Kitsilano Point. You'll know you're there when you reach a 30.5-metre (100-foot) totem pole, a replica of one given to Queen Elizabeth II in 1958 to commemorate B.C.'s centennial. Carved by famed Kwakiutl carvers, the totem is

**TOTEM POLE IN
HADDON PARK**

a fitting reminder that this area was originally a Squamish village called Sun'ahk.

Turn right at Whyte Street, cross Chestnut Street, and head past the Vancouver Museum on your left. Pause to admire its Haida hat-shaped roof and the crab fountain sculpture out front. A visit to the museum opens doors to local history. Next door is the H.R. MacMillan Space Centre and Planetarium with its ever-popular space shows.

Head into Vanier Park. You can't get lost, as there are few trees on the site, which makes it ideal for kite-flying. Walk along the park shore heading west. Vanier Park is the summer home to Bard on the Beach, an annual Shakespeare festival. More than 80,000 people attend the evening performances each year.

A few steps further west is the Vancouver Maritime Museum. Inside the A-frame building

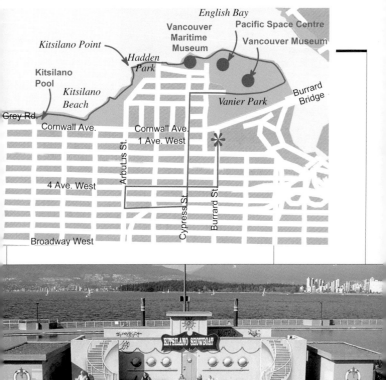

is the famed Royal Canadian Mounted Police vessel *St. Roch*. The *St. Roch* was the first ship to sail the Northwest Passage from both east to west and west to east, and to circumnavigate North America. You are now in Haddon Park, named after millionaire property developer and philanthropist Harvey Haddon, who died in 1931.

KITSILANO SHOWBOAT

TATLOW PARK

KITSILANO BEACH

Walking west along the shoreline, you approach Kitsilano Beach. Waist-high logs in orderly rows in the sand form ideal backrests and informal seating for a multitude of sunbathers. The tower, situated where the sand meets the lawn, houses the city-wide lifeguard command centre for Vancouver's dozen beaches. Refreshments and washrooms are available here. It's no wonder that this is a favourite spot for many Vancouverites. It's also a great place to meet the locals.

Nearby is the 137-metre (450-foot) Kitsilano Pool, an outdoor summer classic overlooking the ocean. The pool opens early for brisk morning swims. The Kitsilano Showboat, an institution since 1936, is located above the pool. Showcasing amateur performers during the summer months at no charge. This is also a wonderful spot to view the four annual Festival of Lights fireworks events on English Bay in July and August.

From Kitsilano Beach, it's an easy walk along Cornwall to the foot of Macdonald Street. Two parks are located here. On the north side, Volunteer Park provides a path down to the rocky shoreline.

BRIDGE IN TATLOW PARK

On the south side, Tatlow Park is tucked in behind the tennis court. Cornwall Street becomes Point Grey Road, leading to some of Vancouver's priciest waterfront homes.

Enter Tatlow Park with its picturesque wooden bridge. Beneath it is a salmon-spawning stream. Look closely: you may spot some fish. Beside it is an apartment complex built on the former palatial estate of Killarney, once the gathering place for the city's elite. Mrs. Jessie Hall, its hostess, was the first child of European descent born in the Cariboo. Leaving Tatlow Park, walk along Macdonald Street to 4th Avenue. Cross to the south side, where you'll find the Naam Restaurant, founded in the 1960s. The food is vegetarian, the patio open-air, and the décor features West Coast cedar and plants.

Kitsilano has a variety of housing, with very few high-rises — a by-law prevents more. For typical Vancouver architecture, wander the neighbourhood streets and avenues. Streets run north and south, avenues run east and west. Many of the original stately homes have survived.

Shopping? In the 1960s, West 4th Avenue was known as a haven for hippies and artists. Today, the avenue bursts with eclectic shops and artisan bakeries from Burrard to Balsam.

Continuing south on Macdonald, head for Broadway Avenue (which is also 9th Avenue) five blocks away. In the early years, Kitsilano expanded southward to Broadway, a major east-west connector route. Today, it is a thriving residential and business district. Browse the jewellery stores, ethnic food outlets, clothing boutiques and bookstores (including Kidsbooks, the city's best children's bookstore). When you need a break, choose from the many fine dining and casual restaurants, cafés and coffee shops.

The #99 B-Line express bus as well as the #9 regular bus run frequently along Broadway. If you're taking the bus, both connect to other bus routes as well as the SkyTrain's Broadway Station. The #22 Macdonald bus also goes downtown.

UBC

CHRIS PETTY

On any given day in the academic year, upwards of 45,000 students, faculty, staff and visitors arrive on the campus of the University of British Columbia to work, study and enjoy the ambiance of Canada's third-largest university. Perched out on the end of Point Grey, some 20 minutes from the city centre, UBC boasts one of the prettiest campuses in the country. With its forest setting, landscaped gardens and spectacular views across the Strait of Georgia and Howe Sound, visitors can often be heard to mutter, "How the heck do they get any work done around here?"

The new University Town, an eight-neighbourhood housing development for students, faculty, staff and off-campus purchasers, is set to attract an additional 20,000

TOP LEFT: CHAN CENTRE
TOP RIGHT: THE IONA BUILDING AT THE VANCOUVER SCHOOL OF THEOLOGY, UBC

MAIN LIBRARY

people to the university's core. As a small city, UBC has all the amenities: concert halls, restaurants (from greasy spoons to fine dining), theatres, sports facilities, bars and shops. As a university, it has the vitality that goes along with a population skewed towards the younger end of the scale. UBC is a walker's paradise. Gardens, wide boulevards, outside eateries, stunning architecture, gorgeous viewpoints and quiet, off-the-beaten-path spots for rest and reflection draw visitors throughout the year.

HISTORY

UBC became a degree-granting institution in 1915. Originally housed in old warehouses and church basements near Vancouver's City Hall, the plan was to move UBC to Point Grey, but the First World War stopped construction. "The Great Trek" in 1922, in which students, faculty and alumni marched in demonstration from downtown to Point Grey, was the culmination of a noisy campaign to get the government of the day to resume building the campus. It worked. The Great Trek, and the sense of intrepid adventure shown by the marchers, has become a working metaphor at UBC, and is celebrated at every opportunity. The Point Grey campus opened in 1925.

Those first buildings remain some of the most remarkable on campus and are quite wonderful examples of neo-Gothic architecture. Main Library, just off Main Mall, features superb stone masonry, stained-glass windows and brass fittings. Look for the two little stone monkeys on the front wall. Each holds a book, one saying "Funda," and the other "Evolut," reflecting the Scopes Monkey Trial controversy that raged at the time. Main Library has one of the most spectacular study rooms in the country, called the Learning Commons. Have a seat in a comfortable leather chair, bask in the sunlight shining in through 30-foot-high stained glass windows, and wish you could enrol. Main Library, like most other buildings on campus, is open during daytime hours and is fun to wander through.

BELKIN ART GALLERY

A TOUR OF UBC

The university offers free walking tours daily from May to August, starting at the Student Union Building (SUB), with orientation to the main campus amenities and academic facilities. You can also pre-book group

tours. But the best place to start your own tour is at the Rose Garden. Drive onto the campus via Chancellor Boulevard (an extension of 4th Avenue), until you get to the Rose Garden parkade. You can park here all day for a few dollars. Take the elevator up from the parkade and look north towards the mountains. You're on the Flagpole Plaza above the actual Rose Garden. The view from the Rose Garden — Howe Sound and the North Shore's Coast mountains fading off into the distance — stretches before you like a travel poster. The garden itself is spectacular and in bloom from early spring until well into fall.

As you contemplate the great view, remember that the world-class UBC Museum of Anthropology is just across the road and to the left. The museum, along with the Nitobe Memorial Garden and UBC Botanical Garden, should not be missed. With one of the top First Nations art collections in the world, the Arthur Erickson-designed building is a wonder on its own.

MUSEUM OF ANTHROPOLOGY

MAIN MALL

Main Mall stretches the length of the university from the Flagpole Plaza to Thunderbird Stadium. Short side trips from the mall bring you to virtually all the university's features. The Chan Centre is nearby (that big, round building that looks like a giant industrial widget), as is the Belkin Art Gallery, Frederic Wood Theatre and the UBC School of Music. The Chan Centre auditorium, which seats 1,400, is said to have the best acoustics in town. In addition to ticketed performances, free recitals by local and international performers, as well as practices by the UBC School of Music, are often held here. For tickets, free tours and free events, check with the box office. The Belkin Gallery just across the way shows travelling art exhibits as well as the university collection. It is open daily. Check, too, the program at the Fredric Wood Theatre, home to UBC's theatre program.

C.K. CHOI BUILDING

Continue along Main Mall to the huge library plaza and the Koerner Library. The state-of-the-art building is called the "green jewel" of the campus by its architect. Locals think it's either beautiful or horrifying, but all agree the Koerner stands out. Take the elevator up to the top and look east to the Main Library and the Coast Mountains in the distance.

117

KOERNER LIBRARY

SITES OF INTEREST

UBC has many great buildings. One of the most interesting is the C.K. Choi building west of the Koerner Library on West Mall. It's the most environmentally atuned building on campus and is built out of recycled materials from the Old Armouries (demolished a few years ago). It's also probably the only new building in Vancouver that has chemical toilets.

South on West Mall is another UBC wonder, the First Nations Longhouse. Built to house First Nations programs, it also serves as a gathering place for First Nations students. Enter and note the huge sculpted log poles and other pieces of First Nations art. Outside, follow the cool sounds of a waterfall to one of the most relaxing (and little-known) hideaways on campus.

From the Longhouse walk east on Agricultural Road, past Main Library to East Mall and the Student Union Building. That building and the nearby Aquatic Centre (indoor and outdoor pools), War Memorial Gym and Student Recreation Centre, make up the most active non-academic area of the campus. UBC has the largest intramural sports program in Canada. A visit to any of the latter three buildings shows why. The facilities are first rate.

The UBC Bookstore, the largest university bookstore in Canada, is located across the bus loop from the SUB. It has a huge selection of academic books, a well-stocked fiction and magazine section, as well as gifts, clothing, computers, art supplies and electronics.

Back on Main Mall heading south is the dome of the Astronomical Observatory, just beside the UBC Geophysical Observatory (which monitors earthquake activity) and the Geological Museum. All these facilities are open to the public.

UBC BOOKSTORE

Perhaps the most interesting building at UBC appears just before Main Mall descends into parking lots and athletic fields. The lobby and study areas of the Forest Sciences building are nothing short of a post-modern forest glen. Huge beams made of Parallam (which looks like popsicle sticks glued together) spread up to the roof three storeys above. Everything in the building shows off the quality and beauty of wood construction, and the whole thing has the delightful odour of a cedar chest.

NORTH SHORE

ROCHELLE VAN HALM

It's the Coast Mountains that anchor Vancouver's majestic setting: the North Shore comprises a wilderness just 30 minutes from downtown Vancouver. Residents enjoy a beautiful community well-endowed with recreation opportunities, excellent shopping and the beauty of nature best explored from the hiking trail. While some residents still see black bears and deer in their backyards, there are plenty of big-city attractions in the communities of West and North Vancouver.

AMBLESIDE PARK

LIGHTHOUSE PARK

WEST VANCOUVER

After crossing the Lions Gate Bridge, the first exit takes you into West Vancouver, one of Canada's richest communities, evidenced by the visible presence of luxury import cars on the roads. Like its residents, the municipality takes pride in its appearance. Every year, it plants 30,000 spring flowering bulbs, tends 180 hanging flower baskets and creates major floral displays. Follow Marine Drive between the two sides of Park Royal Shopping Centre, a home for fashion mavens. Next comes Ambleside Park, boasting beaches, a playground, skateboard park, duck pond, Ambleside Par 3 Golf Course and an off-leash dog park. The West Vancouver Sea Walk begins along the shoreline, one of the community's best-used facilities. Dogs are relegated to their own path on the other side of the fence, between 18th and 24th streets. Seals bob in the distance, salmon leap, summer cruise ships pass nightly and savage winter storms toss logs high onto the shore.

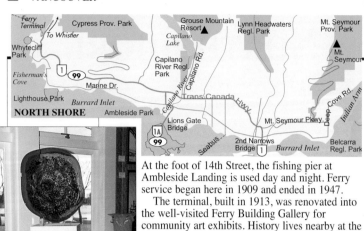

Ferry Terminal | To Whistler | Cypress Prov. Park | Grouse Mountain Resort | Lynn Headwaters Regl. Park | Mt. Seymour Prov. Park

Whytecliff Park · Capilano Lake · Capilano River Regl. Park · Capilano River · Capilano Rd. · Mt. Seymour

Fisherman's Cove · Marine Dr. · Trans Canada Hwy. · Deep Cove Rd. · Indian Arm

Lighthouse Park · Burrard Inlet · Ambleside Park · Mt. Seymour Pkwy.

NORTH SHORE · Lions Gate Bridge · Seabus · 2nd Narrows Bridge · Burrard Inlet · Belcarra Regl. Park

FERRY BUILDING GALLERY

WEST VANCOUVER MUSEUM

At the foot of 14th Street, the fishing pier at Ambleside Landing is used day and night. Ferry service began here in 1909 and ended in 1947.

The terminal, built in 1913, was renovated into the well-visited Ferry Building Gallery for community art exhibits. History lives nearby at the West Vancouver Museum and Archives, housed in an old ballast-stone house built in 1940 by Gertrude Lawson, daughter of John Lawson, who is known as the father of West Vancouver. The floral clock at the foot of 15th Street — considered ill conceived by some residents — occasionally tells the correct time!

After strolling Bellevue Avenue, lined with fashionable shops, follow Marine Drive to West Vancouver's Memorial Library, which has the highest per capita circulation of any library in Canada. Across Marine Drive is Memorial Park, where large rhododendrons bloom each spring. Follow the path over the bridge to the playground by the stream, where the historic Village Walk begins. Nearby is the new geothermal-heated Aquatic Centre with an ozone-treated leisure pool, waterslides and hydrotherapy.

In the 2400-block of Marine Drive, the village of Dundarave blooms with hanging baskets and a summer flower boulevard. The shops include an old-style hardware store with whatever you might need; plus antiques, art and gelato. Capers is the choice for an organic lunch on the deck overlooking the ocean. In late summer, the annual

SEYMOUR MOUNTAIN LOOKOUT

country-and-western hoedown fills the street with square dancing and kids' pony rides.

Another pier at the foot of 25th Street marks the end of the Sea Walk, along with playgrounds, an interesting sculpture of a girl on a turtle, a sandy beach for swimming and lunch from a concession stand with architectural merit and a stunning English Bay view. The Beach House at Dundarave Pier offers upscale dining in a building finely restored from its 1912 beginnings. The restaurant offers a heater-warmed patio to allow diners to enjoy their meals long after the sun sets into the Pacific. Marine Drive meanders westward, past grand estates with multimillion-dollar cliff-hanging homes and a few original seaside cottages from the 1920s and 1930s. In the 3700-block of Marine Drive, the once-treacherous Suicide Bend allows room to pull over for a photo of the ocean, Point Grey beyond, and a closeup look at freighters anchored in the bay. Explore local beaches with their own natural attractions at West Bay (public access off Radcliffe Avenue), Sandy Cove (at Rose Crescent) and Stearman (off Ross Crescent).

BELOW: SEA WALK
BOTTOM: MEMORIAL PARK

The government's Fisheries and Oceans laboratory (4100-block of Marine Drive) now studies salmon on the site where the Great Northern Cannery packed fish from 1891 until 1967. Outside the Cypress Park Market (4360 Marine Drive), historic photos show the neighbourhood of years ago. Watch for Piccadilly Road South, and take a left turn into lower Caulfeild, the English-style village designed by

SEAVIEW WALK

Francis Caulfeild in the 1920s. The neighbourhood celebrates on the village green in front of St. Francis-in-the-Wood Anglican Church, a favourite for weddings.

Returning to Marine Drive, turn left at Eagle Harbour Road to visit a small neighbourhood beach, watch local children learn to sail and Eagle Island residents use a cable ferry to haul themselves and their groceries home, a stone's throw from the mainland.

From Marine Drive, turn north onto Cranley Drive for Seaview Walk, part of the TransCanada Trail. The path leads from Nelson Creek to the old rail bed, overlooking hundreds of boats moored in Fisherman's Cove and leading to the Gleneagles Golf Course. The municipally-owned 18-hole course provides ocean views from the greens. Retrace your steps and continue west on Marine Drive, snaking up the rocky hillside.

NORTH VANCOUVER

Follow the signs to Highway 1 East/Highway 99 South, known locally as the Upper Levels Highway, for a quick trip east with views of English Bay, Burrard Inlet and Vancouver. When the skies are clear, you can see as far as Vancouver Island and Mount Baker. Take Exit 22 and follow Mount Seymour Parkway to the Parkgate Village Shopping Centre, then turn left at Mount Seymour Road. Halfway up Seymour Mountain, you'll find a lookout point

VIEW FROM DEEP COVE CULTURAL CENTRE

from which to view Simon Fraser University, Indian Arm and the wilderness beyond. Hiking trails begin farther up where the road ends in the top parking lot.

Returning downhill, turn left at Mount Seymour Parkway and watch for the close-up view of Indian Arm, nestled in mountains shrouded in mist. Turn left onto Deep Cove Road for the short drive

into the forested cove. This franchise-free town offers unique cafés for lunch or coffee, where you'll meet the locals when you take a break from your sidewalk stroll. At the Deep Cove Cultural Centre, residents are invited to participate onstage or backstage. The Seymour Art Gallery features local artists, and the Shaw Theatre, the Deep Cove Heritage Association and Arts in the Cove provide opportunities for artists of all ages and aspirations. From Deep Cove Lookout at the foot of Gallant Avenue, see weekenders stocking up for a cruise up Indian Arm. Join them on a rental paddle from Deep Cove Canoe and Kayak Centre and view waterfront homes on Panorama Drive. A public footpath follows the shore to Panorama Park where live music fills summer evenings. The Baden Powell hiking trail begins just north of the park. This 48-kilometre trail links Deep Cove to Horseshoe Bay across the North Shore mountains.

North Vancouver is well-equipped for local culture. Live theatre is offered at Presentation House. Upstairs, the Presentation House Gallery is renowned for its photography exhibitions. North Vancouver Museum and Archives focuses on the local history of logging, shipbuilding and early community development and features a walking tour of historic houses. Just down the hill is Lonsdale Quay Market where you can buy live crabs, whole salmon or just a sandwich, fresh pasta, vegetables, flowers and Italian deli specialties. Children can blow off steam in the upstairs ballroom. The Lonsdale Quay Hotel overlooks the Cates tugboat operation and the SeaBus, a commuter ferry, links Lonsdale Quay with downtown Vancouver. The Lower Lonsdale area is undergoing redevelopment from its shipyard past. At the foot of Lonsdale Avenue, visit the Pacific Great Eastern railway station, built in 1913. It retains elements of the past, as well as information about walking tours and a proposed walk-through of the underbelly of a giant ship.

TOP: LONSDALE QUAY MARKET SIGN
MIDDLE: LYNN CANYON PARK SUSPENSION BRIDGE

OUTDOOR FUN

Lighthouse Park (off Beacon Lane at Marine Drive, West Vancouver) offers trails through an old-growth forest of giant Douglas firs, pines, hemlocks and arbutus trees that look as if they're peeling rust-red bark. Stroll to Point Atkinson lighthouse, built in 1912 and still operating. When fog rolls in, the foghorn is very loud. The rocks are a great vantage point to view the freighters and sailboats in English Bay.

SEABUS

Whytecliff Park offers rocky views to Bowen Island and the passing ferries, plus picnic sites and a climb up Whyte Islet, accessible at low tide. The stony beach is popular for divers as marine life is protected in an underwater reserve.

POINT ATKINSON LIGHTHOUSE

Porteau Cove, 25 kilometres (15 miles) north of Horseshoe Bay off Highway 99, is one of the few places you can camp alongside Howe Sound. An artificial reef of shipwrecks at the cove makes this a favourite dive area. Walking trails lead through the picnic area to a small hill with a lookout.

During winter, skiing and boarding are no more than 30 minutes away from downtown Vancouver at three different mountains. From Highway 1, take Exit 8 and follow Cypress Bowl Road to Cypress Provincial Park for downhill and cross-country skiing, snowboarding and snowshoeing day and night. The 75-year-old rustic Hollyburn Lodge serves homemade chili, bakes its own bread and during ski season, packs the house with Saturday night bluegrass or folk music. Whatever the season, the Highview Lookout provides a tremendous view of the City of Vancouver, the Fraser Valley, Richmond, the Strait of Georgia and the Gulf Islands beyond. Summer hiking on Cypress Mountain ranges from Yew Lake Trail, an easy interpretive loop that is wheelchair and stroller accessible, to the rugged 30-kilometre (18-mile) Howe Sound Crest Trail.

Grouse Mountain offers excellent downhill skiing and snowboarding on 22 runs. Sleigh rides through alpine meadows, outdoor skating, snowshoeing and the latest, showshoe running, are also offered. Hiking in the summer includes the Grouse Grind, a steep climb up beneath the Skyride. At the top, Grouse offers guided walking tours and paragliding for the ultimate view.

Mount Seymour provides natural terrain that's ideal for learning to ski or snowboard. There are snowshoe trails and snow tubing as well.

In North Vancouver, Lynn Canyon Park is a wilderness not far from civilization, with an informative Ecology Centre. The Lynn Canyon Suspension Bridge, less well-known than its well-promoted cousin, the Capilano Suspension Bridge, is just as spectacular in a more natural setting. Few, however, can resist the Capilano Suspension Bridge with its adrenalin-pumping, swaying pedestrian bridge across the deep Capilano River gorge. The site's new Treetops Adventure activity, in the old-growth forest across the bridge, takes visitors high into the canopy to walk between century-old trees on narrow footbridges.

WHYTECLIFF PARK

VICTORIA

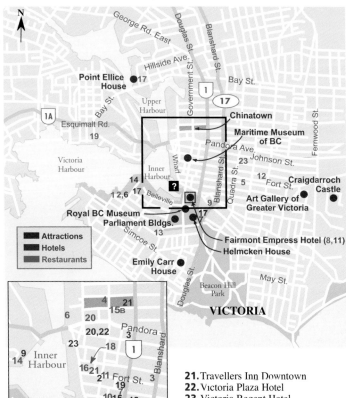

Hotels

1. Admiral Inn
2. Bedford Regency Hotel
3. Best Western Carlton Plaza
4. Best Western Inner Harbour
5. Chateau Victoria Hotel
6. Coast Victoria Harbourside Hotel and Marina
7. Crystal Court Motel
8. Days Inn on the Harbour
9. Delta Victoria Ocean Pointe Resort Hotel and Spa
10. Executive House Hotel
11. Fairmont Empress Hotel
12. Harbour Towers Hotel
13. Hotel Grand Pacific
14. Laurel Point Inn
15. The Magnolia Hotel and Spa
16. Quality Inn Downtown
17. Queen Victoria Hotel and Suites
18. Ramada Huntingdon Manor
19. Strathcona Hotel
20. Swans Suite Hotel
21. Travellers Inn Downtown
22. Victoria Plaza Hotel
23. Victoria Regent Hotel

Restaurants

1. Barb's Fish 'n' Ships
2. Blue Crab Bar and Grill
3. Bond Bond's
4. Brasserie L'Ecole
5. Café Brio
6. Canoe Brewpub
7. Daidoco
8. Empress Room
9. Fire and Water Fish and Chophouse
10. Hugo's Grill and Brewhouse
11. Irish Times Pub
12. J & J Won Ton Noodle House
13. James Bay Tearoom and Restaurant
14. Lure
15. Noodle Box (2 locations)
16. Paradiso di Stelle
17. Point Ellice House
18. Rebar Modern Foods
19. Spinnakers Brewpub
20. Swans Brewpub
21. The Temple
22. Victoria Harbour House
23. Zambri's

EXPLORING VICTORIA

D. C. REID

With the mildest climate in Canada, Victoria deserves its title as "the Garden City." In February, residents count the flowers for the benefit of the rest of the snowbound country, recording well over one billion blooms some balmy winters. Every summer, it lines its streets with 3,000 overflowing hanging floral baskets.

KABUKI CAB

Compact and pretty, Victoria lies at the southern end of Vancouver Island. Vehicle traffic arrives at Swartz Bay's ferry terminal 30 minutes north of the city as well as at the Inner Harbour terminal, with scheduled ferry arrivals from Seattle and Port Angeles. Air travellers land at Victoria International Airport and take the scenic Pat Bay Highway. Others arrive on one of several daily helicopter flights from downtown Vancouver or the Vancouver International Airport, landing at the Helijet terminal within minutes of Victoria's city centre.

Once settled into your downtown hotel, Victoria is a walker's delight, with many of the main attractions mere minutes from one another. For variety, hitch a ride in a human-powered Kabuki cab, or lounge in a horse-drawn carriage. Double-decker English buses whisk patrons to the world-famous Butchart Gardens. Historical interest trips leave from the Inner Harbour bound for Beacon Hill Park, Chinatown, and surrounding neighbourhoods. For something completely different, head to the Oak Bay Marina, where you can feed wild seals by the docks.

The centrepiece of the city lies at the corner of Belleville and Government streets. The ivy-covered Fairmont Empress Hotel opens onto the causeway and the Royal British Columbia Museum. Famed for its exhibits of natural history, aboriginal lore and gold-rush paraphernalia, the museum ranks high with visitors. Completing the corner are the grey granite Parliament Buildings with green-weathered copper domes. At night, the Parliament Buildings are spectacularly lit with 3,300 tiny lights.

A few blocks away, Bastion Square marks the site of the original Fort Victoria. On the square, the 1889 Supreme Court building is now home to the Maritime Museum of British Columbia, the site of the city's first gallows and said to be haunted. There are small ferries in the Inner Harbour, and you can take a pleasant walk along the Songhees boardwalk and by the Dungeness crab displayed at Fisherman's Wharf.

If you don't know where to begin, phone Tourism Victoria at (250) 953-2033 or visit their office at 812 Wharf Street, across the street from The Fairmont Empress Hotel. Alternatively, there are several sightseeing companies in the city to take you on guided bus, carriage, or walking tours.

A BRIEF HISTORY

D. C. REID

THE FAIRMONT EMPRESS HOTEL

In 1843, James Douglas arrived aboard his ship, the *Beaver* to become chief factor for the Hudson's Bay Company. His new Fort Victoria owed its origin to American territorial ambitions. At the time, Great Britain and the United States disputed control of the Pacific Northwest. Shrewdly judging that the 49th parallel ultimately would become the border between the two nations, the Hudson's Bay Company sent Douglas from its Columbia River depot to set up operations on Vancouver Island's southernmost tip, thereby solidifying trade in beaver and sea otter pelts.

Douglas wrote, "The place itself appears a perfect Eden in the midst of the dreary wilderness." Through the Hudson's Bay Company, he leased the entire area of Vancouver Island for a mere seven shillings a year. This move forestalled American expansionism.

THE GOLD RUSH

The 1858 Fraser River gold rush transformed Victoria from a sleepy village of 500 inhabitants to a bustling, brawling settlement of 25,000 gold seekers. Seeking to keep Victoria ahead of Vancouver in development, Douglas declared the town a free port and taxed all traffic in goods.

When British Columbia joined Canada in 1871, Confederation Day marked a glorious binge in taverns and streets with speeches and naval guns saluting. In the same year the quintessential B.C. artist Emily Carr was born. At the time, her stark, savage style earned nothing but hostility.

Victoria's growing prosperity proved short-lived. The gold rush crash resulted in plummeting land values and the population shrank to 1,500 souls. Amor de Cosmos, the

AMOR DE COSMOS

West's first radical newspaper baron, railed against the government, criticizing the law-and-order-prone James Douglas as a species of cockroach. When Arthur Kennedy succeeded Douglas as governor, de Cosmos won a seat in the House of Assembly.

ECONOMIC CHANGE

Matching the theatricality of its new Legislature, Victoria's free port status conferred control over all B.C. trade in mining, lumbering, fishing, land sales, brewing and shipbuilding. By 1900, Victoria's population had tripled to 20,000 and business boomed. Francis Mawson Rattenbury, soon to become the province's most famous architect, designed the erroneously named British Columbia Parliament Buildings (in reality the Provincial Legislature) in 1898 and the Empress Hotel soon after.

FIRST PEOPLES MASK

But, again, the good times were short-lived. A fire during the First World War devastated the city core. The collapse of the seal hunt resulted in financial ruin for 80 per cent of Victorians. Salmon canneries and shipbuilding factories were moved to Vancouver. The Canadian government outlawed the opium trade. Victoria's economics changed from business and finance to government and tourism.

TOURISM

ROYAL BC MUSEUM

Fortunately Victoria's lingering financial demise received a restorative tonic: prohibition was declared in the United States. In the 1930s, whiskey from downtown factories moved through Smugglers Cove at night and sped to nearby American ports.

After the Second World War, retirees discovered Victoria, bringing with them over $50,000,000 per year. Construction of new Legislature wings, banks, law courts, power authorities, retail space and a refurbished City Hall altered the skyline for good. Along with the arrival of old money came the stability of the government payroll and the expanding tourist trade.

Capitalizing on Victoria's tourist potential, the renowned Royal British Columbia Museum opened in the early 1970s. Its four impressive galleries now focus on what visitors love best about the province: its climate, forests and oceans, First Peoples, and pioneer history. And visit they do: *Conde Nast Traveler* voted Victoria the best city in the Americas and Vancouver Island as best North American island in 2003.

TOP ATTRACTIONS

LESLEY KENNY

THE PARLIAMENT BUILDINGS	**THE PARLIAMENT BUILDINGS**

The name of this Victoria landmark overlooking the Inner Harbour is a misnomer. The only Canadian House of Parliament is in Ottawa, the nation's capital. In Victoria, the Parliament Buildings (named after a bill that was passed in the 1890s) actually house the Provincial Legislature, where the members of the legislative assembly sit. Free 45-minute tours run every day in the summer. When the house is in session, visitors can sit in the galleries and watch the ad-libbed performances.

In 1856, Governor James Douglas, the first governor of the colony of Vancouver Island, issued a proclamation to elect a House of Assembly. Seven members were elected from four districts. Governor Douglas didn't believe that the common folk should have much to say about how they were governed so he added a catch: all voters had to own at least 20 acres (8 hectares) of land. In the first so-called democratic election, only 40 people were allowed to vote for the seven representatives. All of the elected reps had ties to the Hudson's Bay Company. Three of them just happened to be enemies of Governor James Douglas.

GOVERNOR JAMES DOUGLAS

The first legislative assembly had little power. The only source of money was through the sale of liquor licenses. The Hudson's Bay Company was the legislative assembly's rival for authority, with vast amounts of money at its disposal from trading profits and land sales. In the beginning, the assembly was basically a place for public criticism of the heavy-handed Douglas administration. The assembly didn't have money for much-needed roads, nor did it have the authority to levy taxes or give grants. Meanwhile, the downtown core of Victoria was expanding, largely because of the gold rush, which attracted immigrants from around the world.

The original government buildings were designed by a German immigrant, Herman Otto Tiedemann, and built between 1859 and 1864. They were dubbed the Bird Cages for their unusual design. After Confederation with Canada in 1871, the first parliament of British Columbia met in the Bird Cages. Most of these structures were demolished to make way for the stone and marble buildings of today.

The new Parliament Buildings were designed by Francis Mawson Rattenbury, a 25-year-old architect from Leeds, England. Building began in 1893 and ended in 1898, all for less than $1 million. The stones were cut locally. The slate for the roofs came from Jervis Inlet off Vancouver Island. Inside, the marble in the assembly hall was imported from Italy, while the marble in the rotunda was from Tennessee.

The diamond jubilee celebration of Queen Victoria was scheduled before the completion of the Parliament Buildings. To show its appreciation, the government honoured the anniversary by hooking up thousands of tiny lights to the outside of the buildings. The lights were used for special occasions until 1956. But since that time, the lights have been turned on every day at dusk and turned off at midnight. There are more than 3,300 bulbs outlining the buildings, giving them a Disney-esque look.

But there's more behind this manicured façade than meets the eye. Soon after he designed the Parliament Buildings, Francis Rattenbury became the Canadian Pacific Railway's architect in the West. He designed the Fairmont Empress Hotel and numerous banks and mansions in Victoria and Vancouver. But his affair with Alma Pakenham, 30 years his junior, resulted in rejection by polite Victoria society. He left his wife and moved to England with Alma. It was there that Alma's new lover, George Stoner, an 18-year-old chauffeur, bludgeoned the famous architect to death in 1935. Stoner was sentenced to death, but after a public outcry, was given life in jail. Alma, thinking that her lover was going to be executed and realizing that her life in society was over, committed suicide.

THE PARLIAMENT BUILDINGS AT NIGHT

THE INNER HARBOUR AND FISHERMAN'S WHARF

Victoria's picturesque Inner Harbour is just a few steps from the Parliament Buildings. Walk down the steps either from Government or Belleville streets, and you'll find an eclectic group of buskers and artisans offering their talents and wares. After a day's shopping, sit on one of the benches or stone steps and watch the boats come into dock or small aircraft taxi along the water for a mid-harbour launch. Or enjoy a harbour view from the window at Milestone's restaurant on Wharf Street.

Walk around the dock and look at privately owned boats. On occasion, a meticulously restored sailboat or a reproduction of a historic explorer's ship is moored here. If the urge to get on the water overtakes you, try a Harbour Ferries tour or a shorter, 10-minute ferry ride to the West Bay Marina in Esquimalt. From there, walk back along a boardwalk beside the ocean. You'll pass by Spinnakers, one of Victoria's fine micro-breweries and pub, with patio seating that looks out at the Inner Harbour.

All around the Inner Harbour on Government and Belleville streets, horse-drawn carriage rides are available, as well as double-decker bus tours. Nearby, the *Coho* ferry docks on its way to and from Port Angeles, Washington, as well as a speedier catamaran destined for Seattle. On the Dallas Road end of the Inner Harbour is Fisherman's Wharf, a commercial fishing boat dock. Making the most of the fresh fish available here, Barb's Place Fish 'n Ships sells tasty lunches from a floating dock. No matter which way you face, the Inner Harbour is within a five-minute walk from major tourist attractions or the many boutiques along Government Street.

THE FAIRMONT EMPRESS HOTEL

Probably one of the most photographed Victoria landmarks, the Fairmont Empress

Hotel overlooks the Inner Harbour. The hotel was originally one of a series of château-style luxury hotels built by the Canadian Pacific Railway to attract cross-country travellers. Designed by Francis Rattenbury (architect of the Parliament Buildings), it was built in 1908 for $1 million. In the late 1980s, the hotel was restored to the tune of $45 million, closed for six months and completely gutted. The grand-style hotel, its towering brick walls partly covered in ivy, has 477 rooms and 34 suites on eight floors. There are 80 different room configurations, some with vaulted ceilings, others with interesting nooks. On a typical summer day, the Fairmont Empress Hotel registers 1,000 visitors.

The Queen of England doesn't stay here, but she does come for tea when she's in town. In fact, afternoon tea is open to everyone willing to pay the rather hefty fee. In summer, reservations are required for the five daily seatings. After tea, consider a walking tour of the hotel's public areas, including the archives with its collection of pictures, menus, silver settings and political cartoons.

Double-decker bus tours leave from the front of the hotel on Government Street. Boutique shops in the downtown core are just a block away. The concierges at the front desk are well-versed in tours and travel plans.

CHINATOWN

The two blocks that make up Victoria's Chinatown may seem small, but once you pass through the arched Gate of Harmonious Interest at Fisgard and Government streets, you could easily spend an entire afternoon browsing, shopping and eating. It is Canada's oldest Chinatown. Until the late 1800s, it was the largest Chinese settlement north of San Francisco. At one time, this "forbidden city" covered several blocks and bustled with more than 100 businesses, three schools, a hospital, two churches, five temples and two theatres.

The elaborate red-and-gold-tiled archway was the first permanent Chinese arch in Canada. In 1981, it was dedicated to the spirit of cooperation between the two cultures. Two hand-carved stone lions stand guard over the entrance, a gift from Victoria's twin city, Suzhou, China.

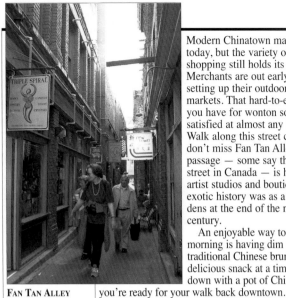

FAN TAN ALLEY

SHRINE AT THE ART GALLERY OF GREATER VICTORIA

Modern Chinatown may be smaller today, but the variety of food and shopping still holds its appeal. Merchants are out early each morning, setting up their outdoor vegetable markets. That hard-to-explain craving you have for wonton soup can be satisfied at almost any hour of the day. Walk along this street carefully so you don't miss Fan Tan Alley. This narrow passage — some say the narrowest street in Canada — is home to several artist studios and boutiques. Its more exotic history was as a home to opium dens at the end of the nineteenth century.

An enjoyable way to spend a Sunday morning is having dim sum. This traditional Chinese brunch is served one delicious snack at a time. Wash them down with a pot of Chinese tea and you're ready for your walk back downtown.

THE ART GALLERY OF GREATER VICTORIA

The only Shinto shrine outside Japan sits in the Asian Garden of the Art Gallery of Greater Victoria. Walk up Fort Street from downtown for 1.5 kilometres to Moss Street. The art gallery is tucked in just around the corner. The gallery's main base is Gyppeswick mansion, built by the Spencer family in 1889 and donated in 1951. Although the gallery has grown in size, the mansion is a significant part of the tour, from the tile painting of the Arthurian legend, Knights of the Round Table, to the large dollhouse in the wooden hallway. This dollhouse is perfect in more ways than one: because it's under glass, there are no dusting chores for its tiny occupants. Outside the mansion, the Asian garden is a peaceful spot, more subtle than colourful. A wooden Shinto shrine lends a reflective quality. This shrine was found abandoned in Japan and was rescued in 1987 and brought to the gallery.

There are now seven galleries including one entirely devoted to the work and writings of B.C. artist Emily Carr. Her passionate nature paintings are compared to those of Georgia O'Keeffe and Vincent van Gogh. A permanent exhibition entitled "In Her Own Words" features 20 works by Carr. Some seniors in Victoria remember that Emily Carr herself was a visitor of the Spencer family, in the very mansion that is now part of the

art gallery. Also in these galleries are the works of contemporary Canadian artists, North American and European historical artists, and traditional and contemporary Asian artists. One of the most recent gallery additions, the Lab, is devoted to original experimental projects. The gallery also hosts some 20 exhibitions per year.

The art gallery's permanent Asian collection of almost 17,000 items (the largest in the province), includes some of the finest examples of Japanese art in Canada. One of the permanent exhibitions is a fourteenth-century Buddha head. The City of Victoria's Ming dynasty bell was moved from Beacon Hill Park in 1990, perhaps because local kids of all ages figured out that if you curled your body up just right, and placed your hands and feet just so, you could hide inside the dangling bell.

Once a year, in July, the art gallery turns itself inside out for the Moss Street Paint-In. From the art gallery on Moss Street, all the way down to the beach at Dallas Road, artists line the sidewalks with their palettes and easels. Thousands of people turn out to watch them at work.

Guided tours of the art gallery are available upon request and for special exhibitions. There are lecture series throughout the year as well as workshops, art appreciation programs for children and a popular children's festival in September. Selected paintings are available for rent, private or business use, and some are for sale. There's also a gift shop with quality handmade décor items and jewellery. The gallery is open daily in the summer and extended hours on Thursday evening.

From here, it's a short walk to Craigdarroch Castle or the gardens at Government House (open to the public year-round).

135

HMS DISCOVERY

THE ROYAL BRITISH COLUMBIA MUSEUM

Adjacent to the Parliament Buildings, one of the most renowned museums in North America is open 363 days a year. The Royal British Columbia Museum, founded in 1886, sits on the corner of Belleville and Government streets. More than 100 full-time staff and 450 volunteers run the dozens of exhibits and four large galleries. The 2,420-square-metre (26,000 square-foot) building contains more than 7 million items that document the human and natural history of British Columbia (though only a fraction of these are on display at any one time).

The Royal B.C. Museum is designed to allow you to experience the province through your senses. Of course, you can read the printed materials, or take the time to study all the accompanying display legends and documentation, but even if you just strolled through each room and hall, looking and listening, you would pick it up by osmosis. Perhaps a good gauge of the museum's success and popularity is the evidence at the entrance gate: thousands of Victoria locals return each year, alone, with guests or with their kids, to see the latest exhibits.

The museum's four featured galleries lead visitors through realistic walk-through scenarios. The First Peoples Gallery opened in 1970 with the support of the local First Nations community. In this mesmeric space, enlarged images of early photographs, along with artifacts, video and audio, lead you through aboriginal history. Spend a contemplative moment in the impressive Big House, still used for ceremonial purposes. In fact, the Big House is owned by the local First Nations community. That gives it the unusual distinction of being the only space in the museum that isn't government property. At the side of the museum building, in Thunderbird Park, is a coastal longhouse, also used for ceremonial purposes.

GRIZZLY BEAR; LIVING LAND, LIVING SEA EXHIBIT

The Natural History Gallery introduces B.C.'s forests and ocean, and the history of settlement and development. The Modern History Gallery takes visitors on a tour of nineteenth-century Victoria, with a salmon cannery, cobblestone road, Chinese herbalist's shop and a dressmaker's studio. In the 20th Century Hall area, a living room scene has been replicated for each decade of the twentieth century, incorporating technological and design developments. Compare the history of the telephone, from a big

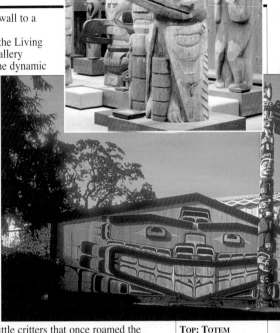

wooden box on the wall to a cordless phone.

In March 2005, the Living Land, Living Sea Gallery opened, exploring the dynamic connections between the earth, its climate and its life forms. At the entrance to the gallery, the museum's famous woolly mammoth greets visitors in a new and naturalistic environment.

From the tiny to the gigantic, the museum has something interesting or weird for everyone. For the bug collector, there are insect larvae and strange little critters that once roamed the territory where megastores now stand. Contrast these with the giant woolly mammoth, the museum's unofficial symbol and mascot, but don't embarrass yourself by asking who shot him. The woolly mammoth died in B.C. some 9,000 years ago.

TOP: TOTEM GALLERY, FIRST PEOPLES GALLERY BOTTOM: GIANT WOOLY MAMMOTH; LIVING LAND, LIVING SEA EXHIBIT

Quite fascinating is the tiny, intricately decorated Chinese slipper-shoe, once worn by a woman who had her feet bound. You can't help but wonder if she embroidered it herself. And, of course, history includes things that some folks actually remember, such as John Lennon's 1965 psychedelic Rolls Royce. It's owned by the museum, though it's often on loan.

The museum's National Geographic IMAX Theatre is a giant, six-storey screen adventure. The steeply pitched viewing room seats 400. The movies focus on family fare, such as nature or science, and run several times a day. A combined pass is available that includes the museum and the National Geographic IMAX Theatre.

Museum staff suggest you take three or four hours to experience all the galleries and exhibits available. After a trek through history, the café next door to the gift shop offers a respite.

137

THE
MARITIME
MUSEUM OF
BRITISH
COLUMBIA
(ABOVE AND
BELOW)

THE MARITIME MUSEUM OF BRITISH COLUMBIA

The Maritime Museum of British Columbia is on Bastion Square in the middle of downtown Victoria between Government and Wharf streets. Located in Victoria's original 1889 provincial courthouse, the museum is home to a collection of more than 5,000 artifacts that tell the story of the province's ocean-going history. Through its many precision-built models and antique nautical equipment, the galleries at this museum pay tribute to the Royal Canadian Navy from its early days. As well, they document the era of the elegant *Empress* steamship line, vessels of the same vintage as the *Titanic*. The economy-class version is represented in the paddle-wheelers that once steamed through the province's inland waterways.

Although most items are under glass, there are a few things to touch and operate. There's an 1864 torpedo and some other nasty hardware to play with (under supervision, of course). The old cage elevator, there since the building was the provincial courthouse, was installed for one of the rather portly judges. It seems that there was some doubt as to whether he could continue to walk up the three flights of stairs to his courtroom without risking a heart attack. Today, the elevator takes visitors to the third floor to watch a movie of a trip around Cape Horn from the perspective of a four-masted sailing vessel in a storm. When you return to

138

either the second or first floor, depending on the skill of the elevator operator, you may have to take a small step up, or down, into the room.

The courthouse on the third floor is still occasionally used for hearing cases when the new court on Broughton Street gets jammed. But be warned: ghosts of cases past may be haunting these rooms. The original gallows were just a short distance from the courthouse and the executed were buried in paupers' graves in the courtyard. The remains of nine such unlucky citizens have been found during upgrading, but it is believed that there are still three graves under what is now the museum.

Museum staff have invented a treasure hunt for kids. Written clues are scattered throughout the building and the winners are rewarded with a treat. This is nice for kids, and great for parents.

The museum's bookstore offers a comprehensive selection of maritime books on Vancouver Island, as well as other items you find in most museum gift shops. After your trip through the museum, walk across the square for a pint to talk about your own seafaring days and then wander down towards the water where you may just look at the Inner Harbour in a new light. The museum is open seven days a week, with extended daytime hours in the summer.

FIRST-FLOOR GALLERIES AT THE MARITIME MUSEUM

EMILY CARR HOUSE

A few short blocks behind the Parliament Buildings, at 207 Government Street, you'll find Emily Carr House, built in 1864. Emily Carr, Canada's first independent artist and writer, was born here in 1871, just a few months after British Columbia became the newest Canadian province. At the time, the house was located in a rural setting. The architecture of the artist's very Victorian-era family home is described as both San Francisco Victorian and English gingerbread. Tour the restored rooms and see some of Carr's own pottery and sculpture, as well as some of the family's original possessions.

Later in life, Emily Carr was an ingenious housekeeper at her boarding-house residence just around the corner from the family home. Carr rigged up a rope-and-pulley system and tied it to her sitting room chairs. When she didn't want visitors, she'd haul the chairs to the ceiling. Imagine, as well, her household menagerie, including her beloved pet monkey, Woo, and her griffon dogs.

In contrast to the Victorian artifacts, a modern convenience has been added. A computer terminal is available in the house for guests to look up information about the life and work of Emily Carr. One of the rooms is called the People's Gallery and is used to present the works of local artists. These changing exhibits can be viewed from May to September. Parking in this area is cramped at best, so the 10-minute walk from downtown is your best bet.

EMILY CARR HOUSE

HELMCKEN HOUSE

Helmcken House is the oldest house in British Columbia on its original site. It was built in 1852 for Dr. John Sebastian Helmcken, after he married the daughter of Governor Sir James Douglas. Dr. Helmcken was a surgeon with the Hudson's Bay Company who went on to become a statesman and helped negotiate the province's entry into Canada.

Originally, Helmcken House was a three-room log house. As the family grew, so did the house. Today, there are guided tours through the restored rooms, which are filled with many of the original Victoriana knicknacks and furniture pieces to make the house feel lived in. Although there are velvet ropes keeping you out of most of the rooms, you can sit on the reproduction sofa in the parlour, formerly the room where ladies entertained. Upstairs in the attic, there are old trunks and books and wooden toys you can examine. Dr. Helmcken's original nineteenth-century medical kit is on display on the top floor in the newest part of the house, which was added in 1883.

Helmcken House is right beside the Royal British Columbia Museum and adjacent to Thunderbird Park, where you can sometimes watch totem poles being carved.

POINT ELLICE HOUSE

In the middle of an industrial area, in what seems like the heart of a wrecking lot, there is a little oasis called Point Ellice House. Caroline and Peter O'Reilly owned Point Ellice House in the late 1800s. Both emigrated from England in the 1850s — Caroline after having spent some time in India looking for a British officer to marry. Instead, she married Peter O'Reilly in 1863 and spent the next few years in Victoria and on the mainland. After the birth of her second child, Caroline wanted to settle in Victoria to be near her own family. When she and Peter established their home at Point Ellice House, she was the quintessential lady of the house, organizing dinner parties and social events. Point Ellice House quickly became the place to be for local schmoozers.

HELMCKEN HOUSE

Peter O'Reilly, after emigrating to Canada at the age of 31, was employed as a justice of the peace, a magistrate, a gold commissioner, a collector of revenue, an assistant commissioner of lands, an Indian agent and a coroner. From 1864 to 1881 he served on the British Columbia Legislative Council as a magisterial appointee. In 1881, he retired as a judge.

The gardens at Point Ellice House have been restored according to the meticulous notes kept by the couple's daughter Kathleen O'Reilly. Some of

the heritage varieties of plants here are not often found in modern gardens. Today, the English-garden atmosphere is often used for private functions such as weddings, company parties and special anniversaries.

Inside the house, more than 10,000 original O'Reilly items have been catalogued by conservators and are on display, touted as the largest collection of Victoriana in its original setting. There is an audio tour of the house narrated by the "house boy," which no doubt makes Caroline O'Reilly turn in her grave.

Point Ellice House is located at 2616 Pleasant Street. If you travel west over the Bay Street Bridge and turn north on Pleasant Street, you'll see the large Point Ellice House sign. You can also get there from the Inner Harbour by taking a Harbour Ferry across the water.

CRAIGDARROCH CASTLE

The Gaelic translation of Craigdarroch is "rocky oak place." Certainly the Dunsmuir family, who built Craigdarroch, couldn't have imagined how apt this name would be.

Craigdarroch was built in the late 1880s. Robert Dunsmuir and his wife Joan emigrated from Scotland, but before moving to Victoria, lived in Nanaimo (a 90-minute drive north of Victoria today). In Nanaimo, Robert Dunsmuir began to make what became his fortune in mining. As mine superintendent for the Hudson's Bay Company, Robert discovered his own coal seam and started a company to export the coal to San Francisco. In 1882, the family moved to Victoria, where Robert served as the representative for Nanaimo in the provincial legislative assembly.

The stone mansion designed for the Dunsmuir family was built on the highest point in Victoria. Originally there was a lake, a bridge, streams, an orchard, tennis courts, a coach house, stables and a gazebo on the estate. All that's left today is the mansion, the south lawn and the original stone wall. Robert Dunsmuir died shortly before Craigdarroch was completed, but his wife moved in with some of her daughters (she had 11 children) and grandchildren. Presumably, they lived comfortably in the 39 rooms on four floors with 17 fireplaces. The mansion was equipped, even then, with gas lighting, electricity, plumbing and the new telephones.

The interior white oak panelling and woodwork were prefabricated and sent from Chicago. Inside the mansion is

CRAIGDARROCH CASTLE

the best collection of residential stained and leaded glass on the West Coast. In the grand entrance hall, the white oak staircase and sandstone fireplace greeted visitors to Craigdarroch, after they parked their coaches under the porte-cochère. On the second floor, Joan Dunsmuir's sitting room and two of the bedrooms are restored to their original Victorian state. In the Billiard Room, on the third level, you can stand on the Douglas fir floor and get a good view of the Strait of Juan de Fuca and the Olympic Mountain range in Washington State. But the best view is from the tower, with its blue dome ceiling and curved doors and windows with circular stained-glass windows fitted above the doors. From here you can have an unobstructed vista of the ocean and mountains.

Some years after Robert Dunsmuir died, his two sons began legal proceedings against their mother for control of their generous trust funds. When one son died, he left his estate to his brother, who continued to engage Mrs. Dunsmuir in a legal battle that made newspaper headlines across Canada. Some reports say that the formidable Joan Dunsmuir was a recluse during the last 18 years of her life, spending most of her time on the second floor of "rocky

DINING ROOM AT CRAIGDARROCH CASTLE

oak place." Craigdarroch Castle is open daily with extended hours in the summer. As the house is a historical museum, there are 87 stairs, but no ramps or elevator, and thus is not wheelchair accessible.

BUTCHART GARDENS
Butchart Gardens is not a botanical garden; it's just for show. But what a show it is. Located 21 kilometres (13 miles) north of Victoria,

halfway between the Swartz Bay ferry terminal and Victoria, the gardens began life as a rock quarry. Today, the 22 hecares (55 acres) of floral displays on the meticulously well-kept estate feature four main areas, the Sunken Garden, Japanese Garden, Rose Garden and Italian Garden. In 2004, the Canadian Government honoured Butchart Gardens with the designation of National Historic Site.

Original owner Robert Butchart was born in 1856, the oldest of 11 children in a Scottish family living in Owen Sound, Ontario. In his early twenties he formed a partnership with friends and began to manufacture Portland cement. The successful twist to his entrepreneurial idea was that Robert packaged and transported his cement in sacks, rather than the cumbersome barrels used at the time. As urban Canadian centres sprang up, the demand for cement increased, as did Robert Butchart's business. The young man went west.

THE SUNKEN GARDENS AT BUTCHART GARDENS

In 1902, Robert moved to Victoria, where a nearby limestone deposit at Tod Inlet provided him with the materials needed for his business: limestone, clay, fresh water and transportation by sea. Shortly thereafter he established the Tod Inlet Cement Plant, on the grounds of what is now Butchart Gardens. His Toronto-born wife, Jeanette Foster Kennedy Butchart, and their two daughters moved to the site and set up their home.

Mrs. Butchart was a certified chemist and sometimes worked in the cement factory — presumably for love and not money. To hide the unsightly factory from view, Jennie (as she liked to be known) planted trees and shrubs. When their formal residence was complete, she turned her hand to the construction of a Japanese garden, with the help of Japanese landscape artist Isaboru Kishida.

In 1908, the limestone supply from the quarry was exhausted and it was abandoned. The story goes that an offhand comment made to Jennie Butchart by a friend — "Even you would be unable to get anything to grow in there" — was the inspiration for the now famous Sunken Gardens. Jennie had tons of topsoil brought from nearby farms, and she used a bosun's chair to lower herself down the sides of the quarry, where she tucked ivy into the crevices, knowing it would one day cover the bleak walls. Rock gardens were made with the unearthed stones. A deep part of the 1.4-hectare (3.5-acre) quarry was lined and filled with water from a natural spring, forming a lake 20

143

BUTCHART ROSE GARDEN

metres (40 feet) deep in places. The Sunken Garden took nine years to make, and was completed in 1921.

The Italian Garden, the most formal of all the gardens, was completed in 1926. The bronze girl-and-dolphin statue in this garden was purchased by the Butcharts in Italy. The Rose Garden was completed in 1930, and here, too, the centrepiece wrought-iron wishing well was imported from Florence, Italy. As her gardens grew, Mrs. Butchart hosted hundreds and then thousands of curious guests, offering them tea and showing them around the gardens for free. In the 1930s, she and her husband were honoured with citizenship awards from the City of Victoria.

In 1939, 35 years after starting their garden work, the Butcharts gave the gardens to their grandson, Ian Ross, who continued to devote the same care to them until his death in 1997. It was Ian Ross who oversaw the illumination project in the 1950s to celebrate the gardens' 50th anniversary. At the time, it was one of the largest underground wiring projects in North America. Hundreds of miles of electrical cords were laid in the ground so that hidden lights would show off the gardens at night. Ross Fountain, at the far end of the gardens in the midst of a small lake, was built and named for Mr. Ross. The patterns made by the 21-metre (70-foot) fountain's spray continue for many hours before they are repeated.

Every year, approximately 250,000 new bulbs are planted by the 60 full-time gardeners. On summer nights, there is musical entertainment featuring local actors, singers and dancers, and on Saturdays, visitors are treated to a spectacular fireworks show choreographed to music. Throughout the grounds, teak benches are strategically placed for viewing the gardens. (Some of these benches were made from the decking of British sailing ships). Enjoy afternoon tea or an evening meal in what was the original Butchart residence, with two other restaurants on-site. If you prefer to eat and enjoy the scenery, pre-order a picnic basket for a lunch on the lawn. For a sweet tooth, there's the Gelateria ice cream takeaway in the Italian Garden.

If you're driving, follow Blanshard Street as it becomes Highway 17, and turn left on Keating Cross Road, about 21 kilometres (13 miles) north of Victoria. From there, follow the signs to the gardens. Public transit and private tour buses will also get you there.

BEACON HILL PARK

Centrally located Beacon Hill Park is across from the greatest soft ice cream drive-through in town (the Beacon Drive-In on Douglas Street). The combination of soft ice cream and the oldest and largest park in Victoria is difficult to resist. When the city was granted Beacon Hill Park in trust in 1882, the council introduced by-laws regulating the use of the park. To this day, it is illegal to graze cattle or discharge firearms in the park. Nor is it legal to use the grass to clean your carpets.

MING DYNASTY BELL

Beacon Hill Park seems to be made up of different rooms, each one with an ambiance of its own. Roll up your pant legs and splash at the water park on a hot day, or stroll through one of the more shady "rooms" and watch the ducks and swans from a wooden bridge arched over a stream. The swans have a royal pedigree, from the first ones shipped from the Royal Swannery on the Thames in the 1940s. About the park are exotic eucalyptus and palm trees and gnarled native Garry oaks.

Starting as early as February, daffodils and crocuses spring up everywhere. Their bright yellows and purples complement the blue-green plumage of the peacocks strutting on the walks. Bird watchers have recorded more than 150 species of birds in the park. Children enjoy the petting zoo (open in summer only) with goats and sheep, piglets, chickens and a pony. In the bandshell, free outdoor concerts are held, as are Shakespeare-in-the-park performances, and the harmonies of a tenor and his diva can be heard. On a Saturday morning, cricketeers play on the outskirts of the park. Beacon Hill Park is a non-commercial zone, so bring your own picnic lunch.

From the hilltop, there's a great view of the Olympic Mountain range just south of the border. It was on this hill that two beacons were set up in the mid-1800s to guide ships. Their presence led to the naming of the park by the Hudson's Bay Company. On the other side of the hill, towards Dallas Road and the ocean, is the official "Mile 0" of the Trans-Canada highway. Cross Dallas Road here and follow the scenic path along the cliffs or climb down the

JAPANESE GARDEN

steps to one of the beaches. Driving, biking or walking, the route along Dallas Road is probably the most spectacular in Victoria. Scenic lookout points along the ocean and some prize-winning neighbourhood gardens are found along the way.

Walking north, back towards downtown, stroll through St. Ann's Academy and grounds (corner of

Blanshard and Belleville). The former convent and girls school was built in 1871 and recently restored, with the majority of the building now housing offices. A portion of St. Ann's is open to the public. For a donation, take a self-guided tour of the interpretive centre and chapel. The 150-year old chapel is worth a visit. Patterned after Catholic churches in Quebec, it features a gilded altar, original oil paintings, exquisite gold-leaf detailing and a 1913 Casavant pipe organ. Now an interfaith chapel, St. Ann's hosts special events, including, of course, weddings.

OAK BAY

About 3 kilometres (2 miles) east of downtown Victoria lies the village of Oak Bay. Follow Fort Street, veering right onto Oak Bay Avenue to this British-style shopping district. Bookstores, gift stores, women's clothing stores as well as a mews with various eccentric items on both sides of the street (from galleries to sweet shops) are found here.

FOUNTAIN IN BEACON HILL PARK

At the corner of Oak Bay Avenue and Monterey, the Blethering Place is a cozy English-style teahouse. Amidst lace-covered tables and English memorabilia, treat yourself to a platter of crustless sandwiches, scones with cream and raspberry jam and black (or herbal) tea. The price is a fraction of afternoon tea at the Empress, though the atmosphere is a tad more modest. Nearby is an Italian deli and café that serves coffee and homemade Gelato ice cream. Half a block west is the Penny Farthing pub if a pint of beer is called for.

FORT STREET

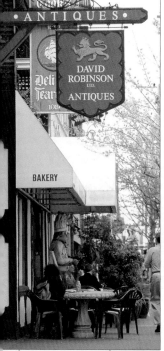

Along Oak Bay Avenue past the shops, curve to the right, take a left on Windsor Street to the Oak Bay Marina on Beach Drive. There's a decent coffee shop at the marina as well as in the more posh restaurant. Either gives you a view of the boats in the harbour through the large windows.

If you walk along the path beneath the restaurants, you have a good chance of getting up close and personal with one of the many seals that hang around waiting for scraps of fish from the daily catch.

Willows Beach is a short drive east along Beach Drive from the marina (turn right when you leave the parking lot). This sandy beach and children's play area is lively in the summer, especially if you're young and have the latest in fashion swimwear. Admire the great view of Mount Baker, a mountain and extinct volcano in the State of Washington. Turning left from the marina is the Oak Bay Beach Hotel on Beach Drive. Inside this Tudor-style hotel is the Snug, an English-style pub where a beer and a decent meal can be had. If there's room, sit on the patio overlooking the gardens and the ocean.

SHOPPING

MELANEY BLACK

Downtown Victoria, or Old Town Victoria, can be covered on foot in about an hour — a little longer if you stop at one of the many world-famous attractions nestled among fine examples of turn-of-the-century architecture. Lucky for you, one of these buildings, the Fairmont Empress Hotel, is also a good place to start your shopping tour.

MARKET SQUARE SHOP ON JOHNSON STREET

THE FAIRMONT EMPRESS/VICTORIA CONVENTION CENTRE

For most shoppers, Victoria begins here. The Fairmont Empress, a historic Canadian Pacific hotel, holds centre stage in Victoria's signature Inner Harbour. This elegant setting tempts travellers with objets d'art and designer clothes in shopping areas throughout the upper and lower hotel reception areas. Pewter and porcelain collectibles, fine jewellery, and sculpture are all part of the Fairmont Empress shopping experience. Aboriginal art and masks can be found in the Art of Man Gallery at the back of the hotel where it joins the Victoria Convention Centre. Among the convention centre stores on adjacent Douglas Street, you will also find Collections of Madison Avenue, a fine clothes retailer.

MERCHANDISE AT SYDNEY REYNOLDS

GOVERNMENT STREET

Moving up Government Street from the Fairmont

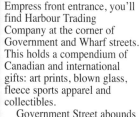

Empress front entrance, you'll find Harbour Trading Company at the corner of Government and Wharf streets. This holds a compendium of Canadian and international gifts: art prints, blown glass, fleece sports apparel and collectibles.

Government Street abounds with treasures for the discriminating shopper. For those with a penchant for chocolate, try Rogers' Chocolates or Purdy's Chocolates. Irish Linen Stores boasts a wide assortment of table linens and home goods, as well as some women's clothing. For lovers of fine British tweeds, British Importers has a complete selection of men's clothing and accessories. Similarly, W&J Wilson offers Aran and Payne sweaters and several lines of men's apparel.

If you love fine china, head for Sydney Reynolds for Spode, St. George, Royal Victorian and Brown Dorset. From here, you can stroll to Copithorne and Row, which features Waterford crystal and Wedgwood and Dresden figures. You'll also appreciate its Belleek and Swarovski china and quality giftware.

ROGER'S CHOCOLATES
MIDDLE: CHINA AT SYDNEY REYNOLDS
BOTTOM: GOVERNMENT STREET

No less than three Victoria stores are devoted exclusively to Christmas decorations and novelties, and two of these can be found on Government: the Spirit of Christmas and the Original Christmas Village. One block west towards the water is Christmas House. If you're looking for beautifully made decorations, ornate Christmas gift items and a variety of Christmas icons, these elves' workshops are open year-round.

A major landmark in Old Town Victoria is the very contemporary Hudson's Bay (now called the Bay) Centre Mall, a four-tiered shopping area built around a central courtyard, fountain and clock, spanning an entire block of Government Street from Fort Street to View Street. Those searching for the familiar will find it in La Senza Lingerie, Mariposa, Bentley, Aldo Shoes, Tabi International,

Boutique of Leathers and the Body Shop.

Across the street from the Bay is historic Munro's Books, nestled in a 1909 building. You'll find books for every interest. Next door is a B.C. icon, world-famous Murchie's Tea and Coffee, where you can buy Olde English and exotic teas, local coffee blends and gifts for caffeine connoisseurs. To complete the European flavour of the area, consider Crabtree & Evelyn for English toffee, soaps and scents and the finer things in life.

Wharf Street, one block west, primarily features restaurants that appeal to a variety of palates. If, however, you'd like to buy an interactive gift for those at home, you could have your pseudo-historical picture taken at Grandpa's Antique Photo on Wharf and Yates streets, choosing from a selection of costumes to suit your personality.

YATES STREET

If you appreciate and/or collect blown glass, shoppers can walk east up Yates to Broad Street and drop in on a live glass-blowing demonstration at Starfish Glassworks. Many of the artists sell their wares in the studio, where you will find everything from traditional forms to avant-garde expressions of the art in a myriad of colours.

Yates Street is also the place for those with a sweet tooth for British confections. The British Candy Shoppe teases taste buds with British toffee, biscuits and grocery items. A block farther up you'll find the English Sweet Shop, offering a similarly tempting array of English chocolates and sweets.

First Nations art is very popular in Victoria. While the Art of Man Gallery deals in large-scale art works on canvas or soapstone sculptures, the Cowichan Trading Company features locally designed, authentic Cowichan sweaters, small carvings and a wide assortment of less formal crafts. Hill's Indian Crafts sells gold and silver jewellery, as well as moccasins, carvings and Inuit art.

TOP: SHOP ON FORT STREET
ABOVE AND BELOW: ART AT SA-NUU-KWA GALLERY
BOTTOM: SWEATERS AT COWICHAN TRADING POST

MARKET SQUARE

Market Square, a collection of specialty stores built around a central courtyard, has something for all ages. Out of Hand features

149

MARKET SQUARE

the work of local artists, ranging from intriguing fountains to elegant objets d'art and framed acrylics, while Marigold Galleria is bursting with ceramic sculpture, glass and contemporary collectibles. For the young or the young at heart, try Foxglove Toys or sample the latest bestsellers at Griffin Books. There's even a store — Woofles, A Doggie Diner — for your favourite canine friend.

You'll find exotic gifts at Hoi Polloi and La Cache, and cafés to suit every taste. You can also sample the decadent pleasures of Fat Phege's Fudge Factory. Bricks of your favourite fudge flavours are created while you watch.

CHINATOWN

The Gates of Harmonious Interest at the corner of Government and Fisgard streets mark the entrance to the oldest Chinatown in Canada. Here you'll find an eclectic mix of east and west. Quonley's combines groceries and gifts in bamboo, wicker and brass. Nestled among the open-air markets, restaurants and exotic aromas on Fisgard is the Chinatown Trading Company, offering hand-painted ceramics, mats, bamboo, affordable gift items and housewares. Next to the Chinatown Trading Company is the entrance to Fan Tan Alley, a hodgepodge of storefronts

ANTIQUE ROW

that cater to more global interests. From musical instruments to artists' studios to African clothing and jewellery, these close quarters provide a unique shopping experience. Back on Fisgard beyond the alley is Fan Tan Gallery, a sensual array of textures and colours, batik, woods, glass and folk art from around the world.

ANTIQUE ROW

Packed into two city blocks on Fort Street, Antique Row draws those who appreciate the beauty of history. Each vendor has a particular specialty. Period furniture is found at Charles Baird and Faith Grant. Look for china, depression glass or pottery at the Glass Menagerie and the Old Vogue Shop. You'll find silver and jewellery at Maggie Dove and a little bit of everything at Recollections. Whatever you're looking for, Antique Row offers a rich assortment of pre-millennium artifacts.

DINING

GARY HYNES

Victoria is becoming known for its high concentration of quality restaurants, featuring cuisine based on the foodie mantra of "local, seasonal and organic." Which is not surprising since the city is located within one of the best food-growing areas in Canada. All the ingredients a chef could want are close at hand, with a near year-round growing season, spectacular seafood from the surrounding ocean, and wild food from nearby forests and mountains.

The Victoria dining scene is generally more laid-back and sedate than its trendy Vancouver cousin. An influx of younger chefs over the last few years, however, is proving it has more to offer than the places on the Inner Harbour tourist beat. The city now offers many good restaurants, bistros and cafés in every area. Neighbourhoods such as Cook Street Village and Antique Row are catering to an increasingly sophisticated crowd who demand quality food and good service at affordable prices.

Compared to other major Canadian cities, high-quality dining in Victoria is generally less expensive. Start your culinary tour in the city and take in the charms of the heritage buildings and colourful gardens. Then, if you're willing to take a drive into the country, you will find many top tables set amidst

SPECTACULAR VANCOUVER ISLAND DINING: SOOKE HARBOUR HOUSE

FRIED YELLOW ROCKFISH TAIL WITH STINGING NETTLE SPAETZLE

CAFÉ BRIO

spectacular West Coast surroundings. Dine at the Aerie Resort, high atop a mountain overlooking the long fiord-like Finalyson Arm, or make a pilgrimage to Sooke Harbour House, one of Canada's gastronomic treasures.

FINE DINING

Fine dining in Victoria in most cases means an emphasis on what is local and in season. The valleys and coastal areas of Vancouver Island are a haven for small farmers, many of them escapees from the big cities on the mainland. Many chefs scour the farm gates of the Cowichan Valley, Metchosin Valley or Saanich Peninsula, trying to outdo their rivals in sourcing out the most flavourful blackberries or the rarest heirloom tomatoes. Throw in a catch from the sea, such as local spot prawns, Dungeness crab, sablefish and a variety of wild salmon, and why would they want to cook with faraway global ingredients anyway?

In town, for four-star dining and impeccable service, there's Café Brio serving up some of the best food in town. The art-filled room may be noisy for some, but the kitchen sources its crispy salad greens from a local farm. The staff is warm and knowledgeable, and Greg Hayes' wine list always features a rare find or two. The cooking is contemporary Pacific Northwest and chef Chris Dignan creates wonderful multi-textured food combinations.

A new addition to the dining scene is the Rosemeade Dining Room. Located in the restored former home of architect Samuel McClure, stunning contemporary décor mixes with an edgy menu to create a dramatic and astonishing dining experience. Chef Richard Luttman

THE VIEW FROM OCEAN POINTE

creates new dishes such as kushi oyster with chile sake and lime gratin or Alaska scallops with bone marrow, dandelion greens and a fennel and vermouth purée. The servers are refreshingly keen and knowledgeable.

Downtown, the Temple is located in a historic bank building close to the waterfront. Chef Garrett Schack creates ethereal dishes that are deceptively simple in their presentation, but delightfully complex on the palate. The seafood is second to none. Within the new Marriott Hotel, chef Jeff Keenliside (formerly of Café Brio) has been garnering superlatives at the Fire and Water Fish & Chophouse. Gentle handling of local seafood, strong relationships with local farmers and producers, and a canny eye for just the right wine pairing make this a wonderful new entry in the downtown dining scene. For classic continental cuisine served by black-tie waiters in a cottage-like setting, reserve for dinner at Victoria Harbour House. The owner of more than 25 years is faithful to an enduring menu of seafood, lamb and steak. Dungeness crab is a specialty.

CHEF EDWARD TUSON AT SOOKE HARBOUR HOUSE

The most sumptuous restaurants, however, are to be found just outside of town. No one visiting Victoria should miss one of Canada's top restaurants, the Sooke Harbour House. Fredrica and Sinclair Philip started this country inn 19 years ago and have been receiving accolades ever since. Dazzlingly innovative and delightfully eccentric, the kitchen remains a crucible for modern Canadian regional cuisine. A close second is the Arbutus Grill at the Brentwood Bay Lodge and Spa. An award-winning wine list, a gorgeous West Coast-style dining room fashioned from native woods, and a menu filled with gastronomic treats make for a complete and exciting dining experience. Seafood is a restaurant specialty, with delights that include Juan du Fuca spot prawns with lipstick radishes or sockeye salmon grilled over arbutus coals and served with a lavender basil cherry salad. If time permits, the guided

Foraging Cruise is a great way to learn the secrets of the salmon run, lift prawn traps, or dig for clams.

At the Aerie Resort, perched high up on the Malahat, diners feast on the regionally inspired creations of Chef Letarde. Letard's French techniques give a refined twist to the local ingredients he adores. At the far tip of the Saanich Peninsula, near the ferries to Vancouver, chef Pierre Koffel of the Deep Cove Chalet has been turning out some of the most sophisticated dishes to be found in the province. There's fresh foie gras flown in from Quebec, truffle soup, scrambled eggs with caviar and a cellar full of vintage Bordeaux and Sauternes.

BISTROS, CAFÉS

Victorians are an outdoorsy lot and prefer not to dress up if they can help it. Therefore, the most popular destinations are the bistros and cafés springing up all over the city. A husband-and-wife team look after Paprika Bistro in the city's tony Oak Bay area. Here, George Szasz's Hungarian background combines with his ability to present light, yet vividly flavoured dishes to make a night out in this intimate room a pleasure. At Brasserie L'Ecole, chef Sean Brennan and wine sommelier Marc Morrison team up to present classic French bistro dishes using Vancouver Island ingredients. Devotees swear by the steak and frites, which are tossed with parmigiano and doused with truffle oil. The daily cheese board offerings are not to be missed. Casual modern restaurants are a hot category in Victoria. And no wonder. The prices are affordable, the food is well-prepared and contemporary, and the people-watching is the entertainment. At Rebar, a funky, quirky downtown café, health food never tasted so good. Here you'll find inventive, delicious and guilt-free meals.

Victoria is also a city on the go, and the cafés that offer quick lunches and the best coffees to keep its denizens well-fuelled never lack patrons. Zambri's, located downtown in a tiny strip mall behind a London Drugs, holds the title as the best casual Italian restaurant. Order from Peter Zambri himself as he stands cooking at the stove in his small, open kitchen. He'll size you up and tell you what you should have. You can't go wrong with the illy espresso. There's Paradiso di Stelle on Bastion Square for gelato, soups and sandwiches. Bond Bond's, the city's top bakery, serves simple, fresh lunches.

A new trend is gourmet delicatessens that offer small meals. Great ambience can be found at the newly expanded Ottavio in Oak Bay and at La Collina on Cedar Hill Road. As well, both offer large selections of fine cheeses, pastries and other gourmet products. Of course, Barb's Fish 'n Ships at Fisherman's Wharf is the spot for reliable fish and chips, hauling in both Victorians and visitors to this funky dockside take-out.

SEAFOOD

Good seafood used to be harder to find than you would think for a coastal city, but this is changing thanks to a number of small seafood companies that have recently started supplying local restaurants. These days, most good restaurants offer well-prepared seafood. But four restaurants come to mind when the urge for fresh fish hits. The Blue Crab Bar & Grill in the Coast Harbourside Hotel is Pacific Northwest casual and has a great water view. Check out the blackboard for the specials of the day and don't skip the desserts here — they're delicious. The Marina Restaurant at the Oak Bay Marina is just the nautical setting to sample fine naturally smoked black cod braised in local Merridale cider. Newly opened is Lure in the Delta Ocean Pointe Resort and Spa. This sleek, contemporary room has the best seats for viewing the city's skyline across the waters of the Inner Harbour, including the Parliament Buildings. The menu is seafood-centric, and chef Michael Weaver delivers plenty of wow with plates such as prawn and seafood risotto with a fennel and onion marmalade served with an orange and ginger froth and Rockfish; house-smoked trout; and apple-cider poached halibut paired with pork belly. Twenty minutes outside the city, in Sidney, at another marina, Dock 503 keeps the focus finely tuned on the freshest seafood and farm-supplied produce. After dinner, take the time to explore Sidney's many used bookstores.

TOP: THE EMPRESS DINING ROOM
ABOVE: HIGH TEA AT THE EMPRESS

BREW PUBS

Ever since owner Paul Hadfield got an act of parliament to allow pubs to brew their own beer, Victoria has been a leader in craft brewing in Canada. Popular brews at his Spinnaker's Brew Pub include his light and lemony Hefeweizen wheat beer and a smoky Dunkleweizen. Their hot and sour soup, which is made from their own India Pale Ale malt vinegar, is worth a try. Other brew pubs worth a visit are Hugo's, Canoe, the Irish Times, the Penny Farthing and Swans.

A SPOT OF TEA

For many, Victoria and English High Tea are synonymous. The Fairmont Empress Hotel holds court as the queen of teas. It isn't cheap, but the chance to sit amid such splendour while sipping on properly steeped and poured tea

and munching on dainty sandwiches is worth the price of admission. Another fine spot for tea is Butchart Gardens outside town on picturesque Brentwood Bay. It is especially refreshing after a tramp around the spectacular gardens of Victoria's number-one attraction, the Butchart Gardens.

For more cost-effective yet equally satisfying teas, Blethering Place in Oak Bay, the James Bay Tearoom and Restaurant downtown, and historic Point Ellice House overlooking the gorge are all recommended.

ETHNIC EATERIES

A growing trend are the large number of small, owner-run Asian restaurants that are springing up all over town. Best of the new crop include the Daidoco Deli & Café, a small haiku of a room that excels at serving innovative small plates of cold and hot dishes cafeteria-style. Every bite seems to shimmer with freshness and clarity. Offerings include a cold salad of tiny bay scallops with organic asparagus, turnip, chickpeas and garlic oil.

Victoria's Chinatown, with its colourful history and other Asian influences, is shoulder-to-shoulder with grocery stores overflowing with the exotic and restaurants often serving the freshest fish in town. The always busy J & J Won Ton Noodle House, a simple noodle shop featuring tasty Chinese fare, is worth a visit. The Noodle Box began life as a street cart. Its spicy Asian takeaway dishes, famed for eight levels of heat, are now wok'd up at two locations, one near Chinatown and the other strategically placed on Douglas Street, a block from the Inner Harbour.

Excursions

WHISTLER

CONSTANCE BRISSENDEN

WHISTLER AND BLACKCOMB MOUNTAINS

SNOWBOARDER IN WHISTLER

Just when the world thought that Whistler, consistently voted North America's top ski and snowboard resort, couldn't get any bigger or better, it was awarded the 2010 Olympic and Paralympic Winter Games, sharing the honour with Vancouver. Working with the Olympic committee, the communities of Vancouver, Whistler and every place in between are working together to make the 2010 Olympic Games the best ever.

Forty years ago, Whistler was serviced by one ski lift. Travelling from Vancouver, 120 kilometres (75 miles) away, took seven hours on a rugged dirt road. By 1975, responding to tremendous growth, the Resort Municipality of Whistler, British Columbia's first and only resort designation, was created. This enlightened decision paid off.

Today, Whistler is an international mega-star as well as a four-season destination. More than two million people visit annually. The resort's infrastructure continues to expand, offering a complete range of services, including the Whistler Medical Centre, Whistler Public Library, Whistler Museum and Archives, grocery stores, schools, an excellent public transit system, and even a recycling depot. Spas are a major attraction, some of which are located in luxury hotels, while others are run independently. A First Nations Cultural Centre, reflecting local Interior Salish peoples, will soon be built near the Fairmont Chateau Whistler. Million-dollar chalets grace the mountainsides and lakeshores, but Whistler is still a small-town community with year-round residents now numbering 12,000.

For eight months of the year, there's action on the slopes: skiing and snowboarding on the side-by-side Whistler and Blackcomb mountains from late November to mid-June (to April 30 on Blackcomb), and from mid-June to mid-August on Blackcomb's Horstman Glacier. The resort's extensive lift system is capable of carrying nearly 60,000 skiers and riders per hour. With 15 high-speed lifts (out of a 33-lift system), Whistler and Blackcomb boast the most high-speed lifts at a single resort in North America. There's also cross-country skiing, snowmobiling, heli-skiing, heli-snowboarding, snowshoeing and sleigh rides. Ski and snowboarding lessons for adults and children are offered on both mountains.

In addition to accolades for its two mountains, Whistler Resort has been praised for best overall resort design, combining ski-in, ski-out convenience with distinctive nouveau European architecture. The original Whistler Village is now joined by Upper Village (also known as Blackcomb Benchlands) at the foot of Blackcomb Mountain and Village North off Lorimer Road. All three are within easy walking distance of one another. Creekside, the original Whistler site 4 kilometres (2.5 miles) south of Whistler Village, has experienced a recent building boom. The result is a more family-oriented alternative, with condominium-style lodging, child-friendly restaurants, and quick access to children and family zones on Whistler Mountain.

Shopping at Whistler is part of the fun, with six shopping areas selling everything from handmade

WHISTLER VILLAGE IN SUMMER

chocolates to locally made snowboards. Luxurious winter wear is a highlight. Nearly a dozen art galleries tempt visitors who may want to take home a First Nations carving, a nature-inspired oil painting, or finely designed piece of jewellery as a keepsake.

SNOWBOARDER

As befits an international resort, Whistler dining is exceptional. There are more than 90 restaurants, cafés and pubs. Visitors also enjoy a variety of live entertainment in clubs and lounges.

In 1914, Alex and Myrtle Philip opened the Rainbow Lodge and soon had visitors backpacking in to canoe and fish the five local lakes. In 1966, when the first ski lift opened on Whistler Mountain, summer took a back seat, but it's now returned as a major draw. In late spring and fall, expect to find a quieter Whistler. Prices are at their best, with special hotel and dining offers available, although a number of attractions such as the Whistler Gondola may be temporarily closed.

You get to Whistler by scheduled bus and air service as well as charter buses, taxis, limousines and charter air service. If you drive, take Highway 99 from Vancouver. Expect construction delays prior to the 2010 Olympic and Paralympic Winter Games. Free all-day parking is available in the day parking lots off Lorimer Road. Free short-term (maximum three hours) indoor parking is below the Royal Bank building (turn right off Village Gate Boulevard onto Whistler Way).

With the help of the Whistler Activity and Information Centre, it's easy to plan your holiday. For contact information, see Listings under Excursions/Whistler.

WHISTLER MOUNTAIN

Whistler and Blackcomb mountains are owned by Intrawest, which refers to them jointly as Whistler Blackcomb. An aggressive resort developer, Intrawest continues to invest in its dual property. The 2004/05 season saw $14.2 million in improvements, including Whistler Creekside's brand new look.

WINTER IN WHISTLER VILLAGE

Consider for a moment the thrill of Whistler Mountain's longest run, a satisfying 11 kilometres (6.8 miles). The mountain offers 1,480 hectares (3,657 acres) of skiable terrain, with 20 per cent designed for beginners, 55 per cent for intermediate skiers and 25 per cent for advanced to expert skiers. Between the easy runs and double black diamonds, there's something for every level of skier or snowboarder.

Choice is the name of the game. Take the gondola from Whistler Village or Whistler Creekside. A third Whistler Mountain access point was added in 1999 with the Fitzsimmons Quad, installed between the Blackcomb Excalibur Gondola and Whistler Gondola. It connects with the new Garbanzo Express that goes up, up, up with the greatest vertical rise of any chair on either mountain. On your way to the top, don't forget to count the more than 100 marked runs below.

Whistler Mountain also attracts enthusiastic snowboarders, with options for all. The Terrain Park is now 10.5 hectares (25 acres) of snowboarding freedom, ideal for newer riders. Expert boarders can get to the top by taking the Peak Chair or Harmony Express and working their way down to the intermediate and beginner runs. The Chipmunk Terrain Park debuted in 2002, an area more than 335 metres (1,100 feet) long with a vertical drop of 182 metres (600 feet). Snowboarders take hits on rollers, hip jumps and spines, with a mini snow-cross track within the park. The Whistler Pipe, 91 metres (300 feet) long with walls up to 4 metres (13 feet), is for experienced park riders.

To satisfy culinary cravings, check out Whistler Mountain's restaurants. The Chic Pea at the top of Garbanzo Express is a rustic 230-seat restaurant that serves pizzas, soups and humongous cinnamon buns. Familiar spots include the renovated 1,740-seat Roundhouse Lodge, with a full fast-food menu, and Pika's, which offers cafeteria-style food. Both eateries are at the top of the Whistler Express Gondola. Steep's, located in the Roundhouse Lodge, offers casual seated dining. The Raven's Nest, at the top of the Creekside Gondola, boasts spectacular views and outdoor seating as well as hearty soups, stews and salads. Located at the Whistler Creek Base (at the bottom of the Creekside Gondola), Dusty's Bar & Barbeque, home to the Canadian BBQ Championships, takes you from breakfast to après-ski fun with authentic BBQ offerings.

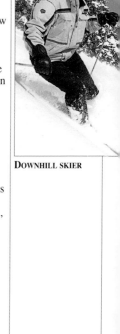

DOWNHILL SKIER

BLACKCOMB MOUNTAIN

Blackcomb's nickname is the Mile-High Mountain. Launched by Intrawest in 1980 as a brand-new facility, Blackcomb rivaled Whistler until the merger of both mountains in 1996. The merger has been spectacularly successful in terms of mountain improvements and Whistler's growth. Winter 2004/05 saw the addition of an outstanding new super pipe snowboarding facility on Blackcomb Mountain. Intrawest also added 161 hectares (400 acres) of terrain in a peak to creek expansion, and 283 hectares (700 acres) to the Flute Bowl. Total terrain on Blackcomb is now an awe-inspiring 3,683 hectares (9,100 acres).

KIDS AT WHISTLER RESORT

Blackcomb is serviced by three base areas: Excalibur Village Station, Upper

Village Blackcomb Base (known as the Daylodge) and Excalibur Base II Station. There are more than 100 marked runs. Fifteen per cent are designed for beginners, 55 per cent for intermediate skiers and 30 per cent for the advanced and expert group. A few seasons back, the mountain unveiled its superb Excalibur gondola system, featuring 97 eight-passenger sit-down cabins capable of carrying 2,600 skiers an hour. Combined with the Excelerator high-speed quad chair and the Glacier Express, skiers can climb from village to glaciers in 19 minutes.

Snowboarding has an impressive niche in Blackcomb's challenging 6.5-hectare (16-acre) snowboard Terrain Park, accessible by its own lift, the Catskinner Triple Chair. Like Whistler Mountain, Blackcomb has different parks aimed at different abilities. The Big Easy Terrain Garden is the place to start as an introduction to freestyle features. Work up to Highest Level, 525 metres (1,720 feet) long with a 148-metre (485-foot) vertical drop. Park features include big table tops, hips, spines, rails and jibs.

TOP: KAYAKING ON THE RIVER OF GOLDEN DREAMS MIDDLE: HORSEBACK RIDING IN WHISTLER

Dining on the mountain is a must. For a warm-up, there's freshly brewed coffee and lunch at the Mountain Grill, located in the Rendezvous at the top of Solar Coaster. Horstman Hut, at the top of 7th Heaven, serves a variety of hot food including soups, stews and jambalaya. Crystal Hut, with its rustic theme, offers wood-oven prepared steak and salmon, Belgian waffles and an evening fondue program. Glacier Creek, at the base of the Jersey Cream and Glacier Express quad chairs, is Blackcomb's largest dining facility. Upstairs is River Rock Grill, with 10 food market areas ranging from made-to-order deli sandwiches to Asian stir fry. Downstairs is the B.C. Eatery featuring fresh West Coast cuisine in a bistro-style atmosphere. For casual seated dining, head to Christine's in the Rendezvous with its view of Wedge Mountain and Armchair Glacier.

Blackcomb Benchlands is a mix of hotels, shops, restaurants and condominiums centered in and around Château Whistler Resort. The Château, built in the grand Canadian Pacific Railway style, features stone-clad fireplaces and domed ceilings painted with gold leaf. Just walking through is a vicarious pleasure. In 2004, the adjacent Four Seasons Hotel opened to rival the Château in luxury and glamour.

BLACK BEAR IN WHISTLER

SUMMER ACTIVITIES

You can still canoe down the River of Golden Dreams in Whistler, a favourite of Alex Philip in the early 1900s. The mountains, and the resort's five lakes (Alpha, Nita, Alta, Lost and Green), are still there. What has changed, however, is the way you experience them. Mountain biking on Whistler Mountain is hugely popular. As are summer skiing and snowboarding on

Blackcomb, helicopter and float plane flights, glider rides, paragliding, valley bus and four-wheel drive tours, in-line skating, horseback riding, hayrides, white-water rafting, jet boating, kayaking, fishing, and good old, unadorned hiking.

The memorable Ancient Cedars Trail is an easy, 4-kilometre (2.5 mile) hike to old-growth forest. A unique experience is a four-by-four jeep ride to active bear dens with bear researcher Michael Allen. Ride the lifts to sightsee on the glaciers on Blackcomb Mountain, but take a warm jacket. Golfing is also a favourite activity, with four local designer courses that boast mountain views.

CULTURAL ACTIVITIES

When you need a break from all that healthy physical stuff, take in some culture. Street entertainers, band concerts, art shows, jazz, blues and even symphony concerts will entertain you and your family. Throughout the year, annual festivals add energy to the scene. Among the best are Altitude, February's gay and lesbian ski and snowboard week; the TELUS World Ski & Snowboard Festival in mid-April; the Whistler Arts and Music Festival in July; and Cornucopia, a food and wine extravaganza in November.

ESPECIALLY FOR CHILDREN

Children get plenty of attention at Whistler and Blackcomb mountains. Ski and snowboard lessons, snowshoeing and snow cat adventures, dog sledding and sleigh rides are just a few of the winter activities. The year starts with First Night Whistler, a family-oriented, non-alcoholic New Year's Eve event.

Summer features the Adventure Zone Activity Centre at the base of Blackcomb with rock-climbing at the Great Wall Underground and other activities. Swim with the family at the Meadow Park Aquatic Centre or ice skate at the Meadow Park Arena. At the five local lakes, swimming, picnicking, fishing and canoeing are options. Château Whistler runs the Tennis Tigers camp daily in July and August. First-run movies are shown at the Rainbow Theatre and Village 8 Cinemas. In addition to nature walks, families can challenge sections of the easygoing 30-kilometre (18-mile) Valley Trail on rented bikes, skateboards or in-line skates. Children's mountain-bike camps are a big draw on Whistler Mountain. For more information on children's activities, contact the Whistler Activity and Information Centre.

GULF ISLANDS

ANNE SMART

MOUNT MAXWELL ECOLOGICAL RESERVE, SALTSPRING ISLAND	Located off the West Coast, nestled in the Strait of Georgia, is a group of islands each with its own unique character and charm. British naval Captain George Vancouver made his first sighting of these islands, home to several Coast Salish First Nations, in 1792. Mistakenly believing they were situated in a gulf, he named them the Gulf Islands. And the name stuck.

The Gulf Islands are well situated between British Columbia's mainland and Vancouver Island, and are easily accessible by B.C. Ferries, private vessels or floatplane. The islands are beloved for their Mediterranean climate and multitude of activities for visitors.

STOPOVERS

B.C. Ferries offers scenic ferry passage to the six main Gulf Islands. Five of the most southerly — Mayne, Saltspring, Pender, Galiano and Saturna — can be reached via a B.C. Ferries circle tour from Vancouver Island's Swartz Bay. To the north, Gabriola Island is a 20-minute ferry ride from Nanaimo. Accommodations are varied and include bed and breakfasts, hotels, cabins, resorts, |

provincial park campsites and private campgrounds.

In the busy summer months, it's best to plan ahead. Although slightly more expensive, consider making ferry reservations where available. It's also wise to book accommodations ahead of time.

Activities abound, most revolving around the outdoors. Hike, golf, kayak, sail, swim, cycle and shop. From May to October, many of the islands host Saturday morning outdoor markets selling the wares of residents. At these community events, discover eclectic goods such as glass beads, ceramic tiles, bird houses, specialty cheeses and local organic produce.

GABRIOLA ISLAND'S DRUMBERG PROVINCIAL PARK

SALTSPRING ISLAND

The largest of the southern Gulf Islands, Saltspring (also known as Salt Spring) is named for its salty north-end mineral springs. The island is 27 kilometres (17 miles) long and has 10,000 winter residents. The number triples in the summer months.

The commercial centre of the island is the village of Ganges, easily explored on foot. Visitors spend leisurely afternoons browsing the many galleries, craft stores and studios lining the main streets. Before leaving, stroll the Ganges sea walk to enjoy the views of the chain of small islands in the harbour and the yachts at anchor.

If you prefer a hike, head to Baynes Peak at Mount Maxwell Provincial Park. From the summit, the views of the entire Pacific Northwest are exquisite.

PENDER ISLAND

After a 40-minute ferry ride from Vancouver Island's Swartz Bay, you'll arrive at Otter Bay on Pender Island. Pender is actually two islands, appropriately named North and South, with a connecting one-lane bridge. The two islands combined are about 34 kilometres (21 miles) long.

On the south island, a hike up Mount Norman rewards the hearty with spectacular views of the southern region from the highest point on "the Penders." Beaumont Marine Park has both sandy beaches as well as provisions for boaters. On the north island, Roesland's 230 seaside hectares (568 acres) offers views of sunsets, harbour seals and eagles. Small Prior Centennial Provincial Park is a forested spot for campers. Near Magic Lake is the Golf Island Disc Park, a popular 27-hole wooded course for disc golf players from as far away as California. All ages can join in. Craft stores, artist galleries, restaurants and pubs are plentiful.

GALIANO ISLAND

With its shoreline ranging from high bluffs to sandy beaches, many consider Galiano the most scenic of the Gulf Islands. Nearly as long as Saltspring Island, Galiano is less than 9 kilometres (5 miles) at its widest, but boasts seven parks. Montague Harbour Provincial Marine Park features marine life and a lagoon that can be explored by an easy trail system. Birdwatchers delight in more than 120 species. At Sturdies Bay, on the south end, the Cabra Gallery Museum is dedicated to local artists and history, including the Spanish captain who gave the island its name.

MAYNE ISLAND

Some 150 years ago Mayne Island was the stopping point for miners enroute to B.C.'s goldfields. Its historical past attracts many visitors. Miners Bay, with its century-old buildings, is the commercial hub. Here, too, is the Springwater Lodge, one of the province's oldest hotels. There's the Plumper Pass Museum, and it's possible you might catch sight of a whale from Lighthouse Park on Georgina Point. A hike to the end of Campbell Bay offers expansive views of Mt. Baker in Washington State. On the east side of the island, discover one of the Gulf Islands finest beaches at Bennett Bay.

SATURNA ISLAND

One of the more remote of the Gulf Islands, Saturna offers an appreciated tranquility. Wildlife and more than 180 species of birds add a pleasant dimension. Cycling routes as well as paddles past galleries of natural sandstone sculptures are popular. With 320 permanent residents, Saturna is the least populated of the Gulf Islands, as most of the land is protected within a National Park Reserve. East Point Park has a swimming beach ideally situated to view orcas while Winter Cove features a tidal marsh popular among birdwatchers. On Canada's birthday, July 1, the entire island welcomes the world to the annual Saturna Lamb Barbecue.

GALIANO ISLAND

GABRIOLA ISLAND

Gabriola is an easy place to visit for a daytrip or overnight stay. The narrow island is 9 kilometres (5.5 miles) long. Although small, Gabriola offers a variety of places to stay, eat and shop, as well as several provincial parks with picnic facilities, hiking trails and beautiful views. The island community runs the Gabriola Museum, a compact spot with a historical collection that offers a glimpse of pioneer life. At Sands Provincial Park, the Malaspina Galleries is a series of outstanding natural limestone formations carved by the surf.

SUNSHINE COAST

KEVIN BARKER

The misty fiords immediately north of Greater Vancouver have endured many misconceptions since old George Gibsons first weighed anchor in Gibsons Harbour in 1886. But none is more enduring than the mistaken belief of just about everyone that the Sunshine Coast is an island.

Although a 40-minute ferry ride from Horseshoe Bay to Langdale is required to reach it, the Sunshine Coast is not an island but part of mainland British Columbia. It is, in fact, a highly recommended day-trip along a ribbon of highway that winds past seaside communities like Gibsons, Roberts Creek and Sechelt. When you finally reach the rocky shores of Jervis Inlet, you can embark on yet another ferry to Powell River and the northern terminus of Highway 101. Add another day for the extension.

Sunshine is indeed more plentiful on the Sunshine Coast. Unspoiled beaches like Bonniebrook and Davis Bay are in abundance, along with excellent hiking trails such as Cliff Gilker Park. Fishing, diving, canoeing, sailing and kayaking attract visitors to both the Lower and Upper Sunshine coasts. Not that culture doesn't get a nod: Gibsons' Elphinstone Pioneer Museum brings an old-time lifestyle of logging, fishing and farming to life while the Tems Awiya Museum at the east entrance to Sechelt is a showcase for the Shishalh First Nation's culture, art and artifacts.

Many visitors are sufficiently enamoured of the seaside town of Gibsons, located about 2 kilometres (1.2 miles) from the Langdale ferry dock, to talk about house prices with the several realtors who work along Marine Drive. Before you move on, check out Molly's Lane for antique stores and the Sunshine Coast Maritime History Museum. It's right behind Molly's Reach, an ancient maritime hotel that was the setting for a long-running television series, The Beachcombers.

SECHELT AND SURROUNDING AREA

A few kilometres past Gibsons is Cliff Gilker Park, with an excellent network of trails adjacent to the 18-hole Sunshine Coast Golf & Country Club. In Roberts Creek, turn left on Roberts Creek Road and drive to the the Gumboot Garden Café at the crossroad of Lower Road for a delectable lunch near the village square. For a lively evening, join in on the rather frequent hometown dances at the Roberts Creek Hall located near the corner of Roberts Creek Road and Highway 101.

Travelling northwest from "the Creek" one crosses a series of rivers before arriving in the mid-coast town of Sechelt, a narrow isthmus separating the Strait of Georgia from Sechelt Inlet. Downtown fronts a lovely sandy beach, with Snickett Park forming the west perimeter. Rockwood Lodge is a restored heritage house on Cowrie Street that hosts the annual Festival of the Written Arts in mid-August. The Sunshine Coast Arts Centre at the nearby corner of Trail and Medusa has local and off-coast visual arts. Local authors read from their works here. Note the unusual log construction of the building designed by pioneer builder Clarke Stebner.

A little further up the road, Halfmoon Bay's rustic General Store, built in 1938, suggests an earlier time when steamers made daily stops at the pier to drop off mail and pick up passengers. Situated on a picturesque bay, it is reached from Redrooffs Road, which detours off the highway and winds past Sargeant Bay and Coopers Green (great picnicking) before meeting the highway a stone's throw from the bay itself. Homesite Road, farther along, features an old growth forest and great hikes.

The coastline gets progressively rockier towards Secret Cove and finally Pender Harbour, where communities lie clustered in tiny coves linked by secondary roads and the meandering coastline. The popular Pender Harbour Jazz Festival, held in September, draws a laid-back crowd. Madeira Park, Garden Bay and Irvines Landing are centered around the waters of Pender Harbour itself. The Ruby Lake Resort enroute to Earls Cove is ideal for boating and fishing.

If weather permits, take the Egmont turnoff just before Earls Cove and hike to Skookumchuck Narrows, where tidal forces weave the placid waters into gigantic eddies and whirlpools. Check the tide table for the best viewing times.

ISLAND ALTERNATIVES

Foot passengers arriving at the Langdale ferry dock are welcome to board the tiny *Dogwood Princess* to visit Keats or Gambier islands across Howe Sound. Both offer day-trippers excellent trails, beaches and kayaking routes. Keats Island enjoys a commanding view of the Strait of Georgia. Gambier is home to a wonderful general store complete with home-baked goodies, a curlicued façade and a rugged mountain backdrop.

Boaters should try to arrive at dusk when the harbours and coves are at their most exquisite. Keats Island has excellent moorage at Plumpers Cove on the northwest side.

LISTINGS: CONTENTS

GETTING THERE

VANCOUVER

On the brink of the Pacific Ocean, at the foot of the Coast Mountains, Vancouver is well-served by air, land and sea routes.

BY AIR

Vancouver International Airport (YVR) is located south of Vancouver, approximately 15 minutes away in Richmond. A new international terminal was opened in 1996 as part of an expansion that included a new control tower and third runway. A major upgrade of the domestic terminal was completed in 2002. YVR serves 38 major carriers, and 19 regional and local airlines. General inquiries are taken at 604 207-7077. More information about YVR can be found at www.yvr.ca.

An Airport Improvement Fee (AIF) is levied from passengers departing from Vancouver: $5 when travelling within BC and the Yukon Territory, $10 when travelling to other North American destinations, and $15 when travelling to destinations outside North America. Children under two and passengers on same-day connecting flights are exempt.

From the airport, buses, shuttles, taxis and limousines are available curbside. TransLink, the city's public transit system (604 953-3333, www.translink.bc.ca), provides a connection from the airport into Vancouver and suburbs ($2.25 to $4.50 depending on distance and time of day). Take the #424 from the airport for the five-minute ride to Airport Station, then transfer to the limited-stop 98B-Line into downtown Vancouver 30 minutes away. Bus service to major downtown hotels is available via the Airporter ($12 one way, $18 return), 604 946-8866, 1-800-668-3141. Scheduled bus service is also available to Whistler, Victoria, Nanaimo, and Seattle, USA.

Courtesy shuttles are available to many local hotels. Taxis and limousines (Limojet Gold, 604 273-1331) picking up at the airport are regulated by the airport and are onsite 24 hours per day. Black Top and Checker Cabs (604 731-1111), MacLure's Cabs (604 683-6666), Vancouver Taxi (604 871-1111) and Yellow Cab Company (604 681-1111 or 1-800-898-8294) are the main taxicab companies. A typical trip downtown would cost $30 by taxi and $39 by limousine. Car rental companies operating from YVR include Avis, Alamo, Budget, Hertz, National and Thrifty, plus several local enterprises.

BY SEA

BC Ferries (250 386-3431 in Victoria and outside BC; other parts of BC call 1-888-223-3779) offers year-round passenger and vehicle service from Vancouver Island, the Gulf Islands and many other parts of BC. Vehicle reservations can be made for an additional fee. Peak season fares (subject to change) are $10.25 per adult, $5.75 per child 5-11 years and $35.75 per car. See www.bcferries.com for information on sailing and fares.

BY CAR

Three major highways connect Greater Vancouver to the rest of British Columbia, Canada and the United States. Highway 99 connects the north end of the city to Whistler before joining Highway 97, BC.'s main north-south highway. To the south, Highway 99 also connects Vancouver to Washington's Interstate 5 and Seattle. The TransCanada Highway (Highway 1) runs into Vancouver through the Lower Mainland and Fraser River Valley from the rest of Canada, where its feeders include Highway 97 and various connectors and highways from the US.

BY BUS

Pacific Central Station (1150 Station St.) is Vancouver's bus station. Visitors from many US and Canadian cities can get to Vancouver on Greyhound buses (604 482-8747 or 1-800-661-8747 in Canada, 1-800-231-2122 in the US). Seattle travellers can catch Quick Shuttle Bus Service (604 940-4428 or 1-800-665-2122).

BY RAIL

Pacific Central Station is also the city's train station. VIA Rail (1-888-842-7245, www.viarail.ca) offers Canadian transcontinental service three days a week. Travellers from Seattle may choose Amtrak (1-800-872-7245, www.amtrak.com), which operates one round-trip per day between Seattle and Vancouver.

VICTORIA

Three main options are available to the traveller:
- Fly to Victoria International Airport.
- Fly to Vancouver, then transfer to a plane or a bus plus a ferry.
- Fly to Seattle, then transfer to a plane or a ferry.

BY AIR FROM VANCOUVER

Thirty-five minute flights to Victoria from Vancouver are offered by the following:
- Harbour Air Seaplanes (250 384-2215 in Victoria, 604 274-1277 in Vancouver, 1-800-665-0212. Twin Otter seaplane service from downtown Vancouver and YVR to Victoria's Inner Harbour.
- Helijet International Incorporated (250 382-6222 in Victoria, 1-800-665-4354 in Vancouver). Helicopter service from downtown Vancouver or YVR to Victoria's Ogden Point, a five-minute drive from the Inner Harbour.
- West Coast Air (250 388-4521 in Victoria, 604 606-6888 in Vancouver, 1-800-347-2222). Float plane service from downtown Vancouver to Victoria's Inner Harbour.
- Air Canada (1-800-247-2262). Flights on small planes from airport to airport.

BY AIR FROM SEATTLE

- Horizon Air (1-800-547-9308). Flights to Victoria International Airport.
- Kenmore Air (425 486-1257 in Seattle, 1-800-543-9595 in the US and Canada). Fifty-five-minute seaplane flights from downtown Seattle (shuttles from Seattle-Tacoma Airport in summer) to Victoria's Inner Harbour.

The Victoria International Airport is located near Sidney, about 30 minutes from the downtown area. From the airport, the AKAL Victoria International Airporter (250 386-2525) runs to all hotels, motels and downtown on the half-hour, for $13 one way. Taxis are run by Victoria Taxi (250 383-7111), Empress Taxi (250 381-5577) and Blue Bird Cabs (250 384-1155). Fares are about $40.

BY SEA FROM VANCOUVER

BC Ferries (250 386-3431 in Victoria, 1-888-223-3779) crosses the Strait of Georgia between Vancouver and Victoria. Ferries make the journey from Tsawwassen (Vancouver) to Swartz Bay (Victoria) in approximately 95 minutes. The drive into Victoria is 32 kilometres (20 miles). Board as a walk-on passenger ($10.25 in peak season) or by car ($35.75 in peak season for car, passengers extra). Different rates apply to motorcycles, bicycles and oversized vehicles. Pacific Coach Lines runs buses directly from YVR and downtown Vancouver onto the ferry and into downtown Victoria. Call 1-800-661-1725, 604 662-8074 (Vancouver), or 250 385-4411 (Victoria) for rates and more information.

BY SEA FROM SEATTLE AND PORT ANGELES

- From Pier 69 in Seattle, Victoria Clippers' high-speed catamarans make the trip to Victoria in 2 to 2.5 hours. Rates and information can be found at 1-800-888-2535, 206 448-5000 (Seattle) and 250 382-8100 (Victoria).
- The MV Coho offers daily Port Angeles, Washington, ferries to Victoria on a no-reservations system. Call 250 361-9144 (Canada), 1-800-633-1589 or 360 452-8088 (US), www.victoriaexpress.com.

BY CAR

Driving to Victoria from any place off the Island involves taking a ferry. Allow extra time to make your selected sailing in peak season. From the Swartz Bay Ferry Terminal (and the Victoria International Airport) take Highway 17 south into the city.

BY BUS

Pacific Coach Lines runs buses directly from YVR and downtown Vancouver onto the ferry and into downtown Victoria. Call 1-800-661-1725, 604 662-8074 (Vancouver) or 250 385-4411(Victoria) for rates and more information.

TRAVEL ESSENTIALS

MONEY

Canadian cash consists of $1 (loonie) and $2 (toonie) coins, 1-cent, 5-cent, 10-cent and 25-cent coins and differently coloured $5, $10, $20, $50, $100 and $1000 bills. Main branches of Canadian chartered banks can exchange foreign currency, although small local branches may not exchange currency other than US dollars directly. Several foreign banks have offices in Vancouver, and will handle some foreign currencies directly. Banking hours in general are 9:30 a.m. to 4:30 p.m., Monday to Friday, with extended hours and weekends at some branches. Most banks have automatic teller machines posted in locations around the city, accessible 24 hours a day with bank cards on international banking networks such as Cirrus, Plus and Interac. Currency can also be exchanged at the many commercial money exchange outlets in each city.

Most businesses accept all major credit cards such as American Express, Diners Club, EnRoute, MasterCard and Visa. Smaller businesses, however, may accept only one or two of these cards. Traveller's cheques can be cashed in major hotels, some restaurants and large stores.

PASSPORTS

To enter Canada, citizens and permanent residents of the United States require a US birth certificate, US passport or green card. Proof of residence, such as a driver's licence, should also be carried. However, this is not accepted as proof of citizenship. All other international visitors must have a valid national passport and, in some cases, a visa. Check with the nearest Canadian Consulate or Embassy well in advance of travel.

CUSTOMS

Arriving

Travellers entering Canada must declare all goods. Reasonable amounts of personal effects and food are admitted free of duty. Special restrictions or quotas apply to certain specialty goods, especially to plant-agricultural- and animal-related materials. Each visitor over the age of 19 may bring into Canada, duty free, up to 40 ounces (1.1 litres) of liquor or wine, or 228 ounces (8 litres or 24 bottles) of beer. Visitors over the age of 19 may also bring up to 50 cigars, 200 cigarettes and 8 ounces (200 grams) of tobacco. Revolvers, pistols, and fully automatic firearms are not allowed into Canada. All other weapons (such as hunting rifles and shotguns) must be

declared. For more information contact: Canada Customs – Pacific Region Third Floor, 333 Dunsmuir Street, Vancouver, BC V6B 5R4 Canada, Fax: 604 666-3144 or 1-800-461-9999 Outside Canada: 1-204-983-3500 8 a.m. - 4:15 p.m., Monday - Friday

Departing

Before visiting BC, contact a US Customs office, where copies of the US customs information brochure "Know Before You Go" are available, to find out customs rules for entering or re-entering the United States. Visitors from other countries should check their own customs regulations before leaving home as well.

TAXES

The Federal Goods and Services Tax (GST) of 7% is applied to most goods and services whether the buyer is a resident of Canada or a visitor. Those from outside of Canada can obtain a GST rebate on most goods taken out of Canada within 60 days of purchase, and on accommodation of less than 30 days. Some restrictions apply. Detailed information is available in the Tax Refund for Visitors to Canada publication. Forms can be obtained within the city at major hotels and information centres and online at ww.rc.gc.ca/visitors. To order forms: 1-800-267-5177 (from US) or 1-613-952-3741 (outside Canada). For more information or assistance, call 902 432-5608 (outside Canada) or 1-800-668-4748 (within Canada). Visitors departing by air, rail, charter-bus or ferry must include boarding passes or a carrier ticket with the claim.

A non-refundable provincial sales tax (PST) of 7.5% applies to all retail purchases except liquor, which is taxed at 10%.

GETTING ACQUAINTED

TIME ZONE

Vancouver and Victoria are in the Pacific Standard Time Zone.

CLIMATE

These are the average high and low temperatures in Vancouver (source Environment Canada):

January	5.7°C to 0.1°C
	42°F to 32°F
February	8.0°C to 1.4°C
	46°F to 34°F
March	9.9°C to 2.6°C
	50°F to 37°F
April	12.7°C to 4.9°C
	55°F to 41°F
May	16.3°C to 7.9°C
	61°F to 46°F
June	19.3°C to 11.0°C
	67°F to 52°F
July	21.7°C to 12.7°C
	91°F to 55°F
August	21.7°C to 12.9°C
	71°F to 55°F
September	18.4°C to 10.1°C
	65°F to 50°F
October	13.5°C to 6.4°C
	56°F to 44°F
November	9.0°C to 3.0°C
	48°F to 37°F
December	6.1°C to 0.8°C
	43°F to 33°F

Average temperatures:

12.0°C (54°F) in spring
16.3°C (61°F) in summer
6.5°C (44°F) in fall
4.7°C (40°F) in winter

Average annual rainfall:

1,117.2 mm (44.0 inches)

Average annual snowfall:

54.9 cm (21.6 inches)

The average high and low temperatures in Victoria, near the water are (source Environment Canada, based on data from 1967 to 1990):

January	6.7°C to 1.6°C
	44°F to 35°F
February	8.4°C to 2.4°C
	47°F to 36°F
March	10.1°C to 3.0°C
	50°F to 37°F
April	11.9°C to 4.3°C
	53°F to 40°F
May	14.2°C to 6.7°C
	58°F to 44°F
June	16.4°C to 8.8°C
	62°F to 48°F
July	18.2°C to 9.9°C
	65°F to 50°F
August	18.6°C to 10.1°C
	65°F to 50°F
September	17.1°C to 8.8°C
	63°F to 48°F
October	13.1°C to 6.2°C
	56°F to 43°F

November	9.3°C to 3.8°C
	49°F to 39°F
December	6.9°C to 2.0°C
	44°F to 36°F

Average temperatures:

10.4°C (51°F) in spring
14.0°C (57°F) in summer
6.9°C (44°F) in fall
5.4°C (42°F) in winter

Average annual rainfall:

1,197.7 mm (47.2 inches)

Average annual snowfall:

29.3 cm (11.5 inches)

GUIDES AND INFORMATION SERVICES

BC has established a Visitor's Info Network with Visitor Info Centres in many communities to assist travellers throughout the province. Tourism BC's official website can be found at www.hellobc.com. Visitors can call 1-800-435-5622 in North America, 604 435-5622 in Vancouver and 250 387-1642 internationally, for reservations and help with accommodations and other travel plans.

VANCOUVER

• Vancouver Tourist Info Centre, Plaza Level, 200 Burrard St., Vancouver, BC V6C 3L6, 604 683-2000, Fax: 604 682-6839, www.tourismvancouver.com. Source for current information on the Greater Vancouver area, guides and maps. Visitors can make reservations for many accommodations, sightseeing, transportation and outdoor adventures.

VICTORIA

• Tourism Victoria Visitor Info Centre, 812 Wharf St., Victoria, BC V8W 1T3, 250 953-2033, 1-800-663-3883, Fax: 250 382-6539, www.tourismvictoria.com. Source for current information on seeing Victoria, with guides, maps and other travel services.
• Tourism Vancouver Island, Suite 203-335 Wesley St., Nanaimo, BC V9R 2T5, (250 754-3500, Fax: 250 754-3599, www.seetheislands.com). Source for travel information and reservations for Vancouver Island and Gulf Islands.

GETTING AROUND

PUBLIC TRANSIT

VANCOUVER

The TransLink public transit system is a network of buses, SeaBus ferries and light rapid transit (SkyTrain). Fares for buses, SkyTrain and SeaBus are the same: travel in one zone costs $2.25 for adults and $1.50 for concession (teenagers, children over five and seniors), travel in two zones costs $3.25/$2, and in three zones, $4.50/$3. Discount fares (single-zone amount for all zones) apply after 6:30 p.m. weekdays and all day weekends and holidays. Daypasses cost $8/$6. Faresaver books of 10 tickets ($18/one zone, $27/2 zone, $36/3 zone, $15/concession) are available at many convenience stores. Schedules can be found at the Vancouver Tourist Info Centre, public libraries, SkyTrain stations and City Hall.

Buses on most routes run until approximately 1 a.m., with some major routes running until 4 a.m. Drivers carry no change, so bring exact fare. A transfer is given as proof of payment and allows passengers to transfer between buses, SkyTrain and SeaBus until the time shown (90 minutes). Blue Buses serve West Vancouver and leave downtown at the corner of Granville and Georgia. The same fares and transfers apply. Call 604 985-7777 for more information on the Blue Buses.

SkyTrain is an automated rapid-transit line that runs on mostly elevated tracks from Vancouver's westernmost Waterfront Station through the municipalities of Burnaby and New Westminster to Surrey, as well from Sapperton Station to Commercial Station. These operate from downtown from 5 a.m. to 1:15 a.m., Monday through Saturday and on Sunday to 12:15 a.m. Tickets can be purchased or validated at machines in each station. SkyTrain carries bikes from 9:30 a.m. to 3:30 p.m. daily and after 6:30 p.m.

SeaBus carries passengers (and bikes) only. Leaving Waterfront Station every 15-30 minutes, the ferry crosses Burrard Inlet and arrives 12 minutes later at Lonsdale Quay in North Vancouver.

Most buses (except for trolleys) are wheelchair lift-equipped or have low floors for easy access. SkyTrains, SeaBuses and SeaBus terminals are wheelchair accessible. All SkyTrain stations except Granville Station have elevators.

For route and schedule information, call TransLink at 604 953-3333, or visit www.translink.bc.ca.

VICTORIA

The Victoria Regional Transit System operates over two zones. Adult fares are $1.75 for one zone; $2.50 for two zones, concession fares for seniors, children over five years of age and students are $1.10 for one zone, $1.75 for two zones. Exact change must be given on buses, and transfers are valid for one-way travel only. Sheets of 10 tickets may be purchased in advance from many stores. Daypasses are also available.

The majority of the Victoria Regional Transit System buses are wheelchair accessible with low-floor buses. For route and schedule information, call the 24-hour information line at 250 382-6161 or visit the website at www.bctransit.com.

CARS AND RENTALS

Most foreign drivers' licences are valid in British Columbia. Check with a BC Motor Vehicle Branch to find out specific requirements. Visiting motorists should bring registration documents and have insurance in place before driving. Insurance is available as an option in most car rental contracts, and Visitor to Canada Insurance can be purchased through the British Columbia Automobile Association (BCAA). United States motorists should have a Canadian Non-Resident Interprovince Motor Vehicle Liability Insurance Card, available only in the US. For more information or to obtain a copy of BC's "rules of the road," contact Driver Services Centre, 254-800 Hornby St., Vancouver, BC, 1-800-950-1498 (within North America), www.icbc.com.

Speed limits within Vancouver and Victoria are 50 km/h (30 mph) unless otherwise posted. The use of seat belts, child restraints and motorcycle helmets is mandatory. Vancouverites and Victoria residents believe in the pedestrian's right of way.

Distances, speed limits and fuel measurements are indicated in metric units. To convert kilometres to miles, multiply by 0.6; to convert miles to kilometres, multiply by 1.6. One litre equals about 1/3 of an American gallon or 1/5 of an Imperial gallon.

VANCOUVER

- Alamo Rent A Car, 1132 West Georgia St., 604 684-1401, 1-800-462-5266 or 1-800-327-9633, Vancouver International Airport, 604 231-1400, 1-800-462-5266 or 1-800-327-9633, www.alamo.com.
- Avis, 757 Hornby St., 604 606-2869, 1-800-272-5871, Vancouver International Airport, 604 606-2847, 1-800-272-5871, www.avis.com.
- Budget Rent A Car, 501 West Georgia St., 604 668-7000, 1-800-268-8900, Vancouver International Airport, 604 713-3102, 1-800-268-8900, www.bc.budget.com.
- Hertz, 1128 Seymour St., 604 606-4711, 1-800-263-0600, Vancouver International Airport, 604 606-3782, 1-800-263-0600, www.hertz.com.
- Lo-Cost Rent-A-Car Ltd., 1105 Granville St., 604 689-9664, 1-888-377-2277, www.locost.com.
- National Car Rental — Downtown, 1130 West Georgia St., 604 609-7150, 1-800-227-7368, Vancouver International Airport, 604 207-3730, 1-800-227-7368, www.nationalcar.com.
- Rent-A-Wreck, 1349 Hornby St., 604 688-0001, 1-888-665-3777, www.rentawreckvancouver.com.
- Thrifty Car Rentals, Century Plaza Hotel, 1015 Burrard St., 604 606-1666, 1-800-847-4389, Empire Landmark Hotel, 1400 Robson St., 604 681-4869, 1-800-847-4389, Vancouver International Airport, 604 606-1655, 1-800-847-4389, www.thrifty.com.

VICTORIA

- Avis, 1001 Douglas St., 250 386-8468, Victoria International Airport, 250 656-6033, www.avis.com.
- Budget Rent A Car, 757 Douglas St., 250 953-5300, 1-800-268-8900, Victoria International Airport, 250 953-5300, 1-800-268-8900, www.budget.com.
- Enterprise Rent-A-Car, Victoria International Airport, 250 656-4808, 1-800-325-8007.
- Hertz, 2634 Douglas St., 250 360-2822, Victoria International Airport, 250 656-2312, www.hertz.com.
- National, 767 Douglas St., 250 386-1213 or 2, Victoria International Airport, or 250 656-2541. www.nationalvictoria.com.
- Thrifty Car Rentals, 625 Frances Ave., 250 383-3659, 1-800-847-4389, www.thrifty.com.

Check the Telus Yellow Pages for more listings under Automobile renting.

TOURS

VANCOUVER

- AAA Horse and Carriage (Stanley Park horse-drawn tours). One-hour narrated, horse-drawn tours. Stanley Park, 604 681-5115, www.stanleyparktours.com.
- Accent Cruises. Yachts for charter cruises and special occasions. 100-1676 Duranleau St., 604 688-6625, www.accentcruises.ca.
- Gastown Business Improvement Society. Summer walking tours of Gastown. 207 Abbott St., 604 683-5650, www.gastown.org.
- Gray Line of Vancouver. A wide variety of sightseeing packages. 255 East 1st Ave., 604 879-3363, 1-800-667-0882, www.grayline.ca.
- Harbour Cruises. Sunset dinner cruises, harbour tours, luncheon cruises, day trips. North foot of Denman St., 604 688-7246, 1-800-663-1500, www.boatcruises.com.
- Landsea Tours. Guided tours of Vancouver, Victoria, Whistler and the North Shore. 875 Terminal Ave., 604 255-7272, www.vancouvertours.com.
- Pride of Vancouver Charters. Charters for luncheons, tours, carol ship dinners, fireworks viewing. Plaza of Nations, 604 687-5533, www.vancouvercharters.com.
- Rockwood Adventures. Walking tours of Chinatown and North Shore. 839-Unit C, West 1st St., North Vancouver, 604 980-7749, www.rockwoodadventures.com.
- Vancouver Trolley Company. A loop of 16 attractions in Vancouver with on/off privileges. 875 Terminal Ave., 604 801-5515, www.vancouvertrolley.com.
- Vancouver Yacht Charters. Yacht touring and cruises. 750 Pacific Blvd., 604 682-2070, www.boatcharters.net.

- Walkabout Historic Vancouver. Downtown, Gastown and Granville Island walks. 342-6038 Imperial St., 604 439-0448 or 604 720-0006, www.walkabouthistoricvancouver.com.
- West Coast City and Nature Sightseeing. Tours of Vancouver, Grouse Mountain, Whistler and Victoria in mini-coaches. 3945 Myrtle St., Burnaby, 604 451-1600, www.vancouversightseeing.com.

VICTORIA

- Fantasea Charters. Luxurious covered yacht for whale-watching or sightseeing. 1243 Miramar Dr., 250 658-6052, www.boatchartersvictoria.com.
- Gray Line of Victoria. Popular tours include Butchart Gardens and Whale Watching and Nature Tour. 700 Douglas St., 250 388-6539, 1-800-663-8390, www.grayline.ca/Victoria.
- Kabuki Kabs. Pedicabs with friendly and knowledgeable drivers. Generally downtown tours, but some operators have specialized tours. 613 Herald St., 250 385-4243, www.kabukikabs.com.
- Tallyho Tours. Horse-drawn carriage tours of up to 20 people as well as small private carriages. 7450 Veyaness Rd., Saanich, 250-383-5067, www.tallyhotours.com.
- Black Beauty Carriages. Private horse-drawn tours for six. Corner of Belleville and Menzies, 250 361-1220.
- Victoria Harbour Ferries. Full tours of the Gorge and Inner Harbour, evening cruises or short hops. Board at any one of 10 stops on the Inner Harbour, 250 708-0201, www.victoriaharbourferry.com.
- Victoria Bobby Walking Adventures.. One and a quarter hours of talk and touring of old-town Victoria. 414-874 Fleming St., 250 995-0233, www.walkvictoria.com.
- Victoria's Secret Gardens. A guided look into private gardens in Oak Bay. 3150 Midland Rd., 250 595-5333.

ACCOMMODATION

In both Vancouver and Victoria, a multitude of lodgings has evolved, both to accommodate the varied tastes of world travellers and to showcase the allure of the West Coast. The major and minor hotels and motels, most located in the downtown areas, put the traveller in each city's heart, while a host of charming bed and breakfasts beckon from quieter residential streets.

What follows is a cross-section of the hotels, bed and breakfasts, and budget establishments to be found in each city. Maps are provided at the beginning of this book. Prices indicated are approximate, based on the costs quoted at the time of publishing, for two people staying in a double room (excluding taxes) during peak season: $ = $50-$90, $$ = $90-$180, $$$ = above $180. Except for campgrounds and houseboats, rates quoted are subject to an 8% provincial hotel and motel room tax. Where approved, an additional 2% tourism tax is levied by the local municipal government. GST (7%) is also applied. Many establishments offer special Internet rates and online reservation services. HELLO BC (1-800-435-5622, www.hellobc.com) is a free service providing access to over 700 Tourism BC-approved lodgings and trip planning services.

VANCOUVER

HOTELS: VANCOUVER INTERNATIONAL AIRPORT

Most of Vancouver's hotels are within a short drive of the airport. The following, however, are considered the closest:

- Accent Inns, 10551 St. Edwards Dr., Richmond, BC V6X 3L8, 604 273-3311, Fax: 604 273-9522, www.accentinns.com. Well kept and comfortable. Exterior corridors, restaurant. Welcomes small pets. $$.
- Best Western Abercorn Inn, 9260 Bridgeport Rd., Richmond, BC V6X 1S1, 604 270-7576, 1-800-663-0085, Fax: 604 270-0001, www.abercorn-inn.com. Styled as a Scottish country inn, with antiques and fresh flowers. Spacious rooms, restaurant. $$.
- Best Western Richmond Hotel, 7551 Westminster Hwy., Richmond, BC V6X 1A3, 604 273-7878, 1-800-663-0299, Fax: 604 278-0188, www.richmond-hotel.ca. Two restaurants, four nightspots. Welcomes pets. $$.
- Comfort Inn, 3031 #3 Rd., Richmond, BC V6X 2B6, 604 278-5161, 1-800-663-0974, Fax: 604 207-2380,

www.comfortinnvancouver.com.
Location allows easy access to
casino, Fraser River trails and malls.
Welcomes pets. $$.

- Delta Vancouver Airport Hotel,
3500 Cessna Dr., Richmond, BC
V7B 1C7, 604 278-1241, 1-800-
268-1133, Fax: 604 276-1975,
www.deltavancouverairport.com.
Older hotel on nine landscaped acres
overlooking the Fraser River.
Heated pool. Welcomes small pets
($15.00). $$

- Executive Airport Plaza Hotel, 7311
Westminster Hwy., Richmond, BC
V6X 1A3, 604 278-5555, 1-800-663-
2878, Fax: 604 278-0255,
www.executivehotels.net. Large
rooms and suites. Heated pool, whirl-
pool. Two restaurants, lounge.$$.

- Fairmont Vancouver Airport, 3111
Grant McConachie Way, Richmond,
BC V7B 1X9, 604 207-5200,
www.fairmont.com. Newly opened,
world-class hotel brings
sophistication to the concept of
airport accommodation.
Globe@YVR Restaurant, Jetside
Lounge, pool, fitness centre. Offers
in-room airline check-in service.
Welcomes pets. $$-$$$.

- Four Points by Sheraton Vancouver
Airport, 8368 Alexandra Rd.,
Richmond, BC V6X 4A6, 604 214-
0888, 1-888-281-8888, Fax: 604
214-0887, www.fourpoints.com.
Modern hotel in Richmond's
shopping and entertainment district.
Heated pool, restaurant, lounge. $$.

- Hilton Vancouver Airport, 5911
Minoru Blvd., Richmond, BC V6X
4C7, 604 273-6336, 1-800-445-
8667, Fax: 604 273-6337,
www.vancouverairport.hilton.com.
Restaurant, lounge, pool, fitness
centre, tennis courts. $$.

- Holiday Inn Vancouver Airport,
10720 Cambie Rd., Richmond, BC
V6X 1K8, 604 821-1818, Fax: 604
821-1819, www.hi-airport.bc.ca.
Kid-friendly rooms include
bunkbeds, video games. $$.

- Quality Inn Airport, 725 S.E. Marine
Dr., Vancouver, BC V5X 2T9,
604 321-6611, 1-800-663-6715,
Fax: 604 327-3570,
www.qualityinnvancouverairport.com.
Bowling alley, liquor store and
sports bar onsite. $$.

- Radisson President Hotel and Suites,
8181 Cambie Rd., Richmond, BC
V6X 3X9, 604 276-8181, 1-800-
333-3333, Fax: 604 279-8381,
www.radisson.com. Home to Western-
style and Chinese seafood restaurants.
Heated pool, whirlpool. $$$.

- Ramada Plaza and Park Plaza
Vancouver Airport Conference
Resort, 10251 St. Edwards Dr.,
Richmond, BC V6X 2M9, 604
278-9611, 1-866-482-8444, Fax:
604 276-1121, www.vacr.bc.ca.
Three towers of rooms. Pools,
tennis, kids' centre. Welcomes pets
(per day charge). $$.

- Travelodge, 3071 St. Edwards Dr.,
Richmond, BC V6X 3K4, 604 278-
5155, 1-888-515-6375, Fax: 604
278-5125,
www.travelodgevancouverairport.com.
Comfortable setting. Heated pool,
whirlpool, restaurant, lounge. $$.

- Vancouver Airport Marriott, 7571
Westminster Hwy., Richmond, BC
V6X 1A3, 604 276-2112, 1-877-
323-8888, Fax: 604 276-0112,
www.marriott.com. Caters to
corporate travellers, with spacious
desks in comfortable rooms. Heated
pool. Welcomes small pets. $$.

HOTELS: DOWNTOWN VANCOUVER

In downtown Vancouver, over 10,000
rooms, from budget hostels to luxury
hotels, can be found amid a myriad of
shops, restaurants and a bustling
business district:

- Best Western Chateau Granville
Hotel, 1100 Granville St., Vancouver,
BC V6Z 2B6, 604 669-7070, 1-800-
663-0575, Fax: 604 669-4928,
www.chateaugranville.com.
Downtown hotel bordering the
business and shopping districts.
Wheelchair access, babysitting,
restaurant and lounge. Complimentary
passes to nearby health club. $$$.

- Best Western Downtown Vancouver,
718 Drake St., Vancouver, BC V6Z
2W6, 604 669-9888, 1-888-669-
9888, Fax: 604 669-3440,
www.bestwesterndowntown.com.
Great views. Rooftop fitness centre,
sauna, Jacuzzi. Complimentary
downtown shuttle. $$$.

- Blue Horizon Hotel, 1225 Robson St.,
Vancouver, BC V6E 1C3, 604 688-
1411, 1-800-663-1333, Fax: 604
688-4461, www.bluehorizonhotel.com.
Distinctive comfort with oversized

corner rooms and private balconies in all rooms. Harbour and city views, heated pool. $$$.

- Bosman's Hotel, 1060 Howe St., Vancouver, BC V6Z 1P5, 604 682-3171, 1-888-267-6267, Fax: 604 684-4010, www.bosmanshotel.com. Newly upgraded older hotel. Dining room, lounge, outdoor pool. $$.
- Century Plaza Hotel & Spa, 1015 Burrard St., Vancouver, BC V6Z 1Y5, 604 687-0575, 1-800-663-1818, Fax: 604 687-0578, www.century-plaza.com. Oversized suites with panoramic , mountain and city views. Seafood restaurant, lounge, café and cappuccino bar. Day spa, steam room, pool. $$-$$$.
- Crowne Plaza Hotel Georgia, 801 West Georgia St., Vancouver, BC V6C 1P7, 604 682-5566, 1-800-663-1111, Fax: 604 642-5579, www.hotelgeorgia.bc.ca. Magnificently restored to reflect its 1920s roots. Full service, with dining room serving afternoon tea. Lounge, fitness centre. Multilingual staff. $$$.
- Days Inn Vancouver Downtown, 921 West Pender St., Vancouver, BC V6C 1M2, 604 681-4335, 1-877-681-4335, Fax: 604 681-7808, www.daysinnvancouver.com. 1914 English-style heritage building, renovated 1998. Views restricted by neighbouring buildings. Restaurant, lounge. $$.
- Empire Landmark Hotel – Downtown Vancouver, 1400 Robson St., Vancouver, BC V6G 1B9, 604 687-0511, 1-800-830-6144, Fax: 604 687-2801, www.asiastandard.com. Vancouver's tallest, featuring the Cloud Nine Revolving Restaurant and Lounge. Sauna and whirlpool, fitness room, business centre and convention space. $$$.
- Executive Hotel Downtown Vancouver, 1379 Howe St., Vancouver, BC V6Z 2R5, 604 688-7678, 1-800-570-3932, Fax: 604 688-7679, www.executivehotels.net. Contemporary deluxe rooms and fully-furnished condos. $$-$$$.
- Fairmont Hotel Vancouver, 900 West Georgia St., Vancouver, BC V6C 2W6, 604 684-3131, Fax: 604 662-1929, www.fairmont.com/hotelvancouver. Heritage landmark that is home to the renowned restaurant Griffin's.

Beautiful guestrooms and suites. Indoor pool, healthclub, spa, business centre. $$$.

- Fairmont Waterfront , 900 Canada Place Way, Vancouver, BC V6C 3L5, 604 691-1991, Fax: 604 691-1999, Email: thewaterfronthotel@ fairmont.com, www.fairmont.com. Waterfrontage, terraced gardens. Enclosed walkway links hotel to Vancouver Convention and Exhibition Centre and cruise ship terminal. Heated pool. Welcomes dogs. $$$.
- Four Seasons Hotel Vancouver, 791 West Georgia St., Vancouver, BC V6C 2T4, 604 689-9333, 1-800-268-6282, CAN/ 1-800-332-3442 US. , Fax: 604 684-4555, www.fourseasons.com/vancouver. Luxurious hotel with the exclusive Chartwell Restaurant atop the shops of Pacific Centre. $$$.
- Georgian Court Hotel, 773 Beatty St., Vancouver, BC V6B 2M4, 604 682-5555, 1-800-663-1155, Fax: 604 682-8830, Email: info@georgiancourt.com, Website: www.georgiancourt.com. Intimate, European-style hotel, well-known William Tell Dining Room. Deluxe guestrooms and suites. Welcomes small pets. $$$.
- Greenbrier Hotel, 1393 Robson St., Vancouver, BC V6E 1C6, 604 683-4558, 1-888-355-5888, Fax: 604 669-3109, www.greenbrierhotel.com. Smallish hotel. Full kitchens in suites. $$.
- Hampton Inn & Suites – Vancouver Downtown, 111 Robson St., Vancouver, BC V6B 2A8, 604 602-1008, 1-877-602-1008, Fax: 604 602-1007, www.hamptoninnvancouver.com. West-Coast themed hotel. Breakfast buffet, daily newspaper, local calls, rooftop exercise facilities. $$$.
- Holiday Inn Hotel & Suites Vancouver Downtown, 1110 Howe St., Vancouver, BC V6Z 1R2, 604 684-2151, 1-800-663-9151, Fax: 604 684-4736, www.hivancouverdowntown.com. Offers some suites with extra-long beds. Unsupervised Kids PlayCentre with video games, jungle gym. Welcomes small pets. $$$.
- Howard Johnson Hotel, 1176 Granville St., Vancouver, BC V6Z 1L8, 604 688-8701, 1-888-654-6336,

Fax: 604 688-8335, www.hojovancouver.com. Beautifully renovated boutique hotel. Swing bar.. Free fitness passes. $$.

- Hyatt Regency Vancouver, 655 Burrard St., Vancouver, BC V6C 2R7, 604 683-1234, 1-800-233-1234, Fax: 604 639-4829, www.vancouver.hyatt.com. Luxury tower connected to Royal Centre plaza. Restaurant, kosher kitchen. coffee bar and two lounges, health club, outdoor pool. Multilingual staff. $$$.

- Listel Vancouver, 1300 Robson St., Vancouver, BC V6E 1C5, 604 684-8461, 1-800-663-5491, Fax: 604 684-7092, www.listel-vancouver.com. Features two gallery floors showcasing original work by regional and international artists. Restaurant and bar with live jazz nightly. $$$.

- Lord Stanley Suites on the Park, 1889 Alberni St., Vancouver, BC V6G 3G7, 604 688-9299, 1-888-767-7829, Fax: 604 688-9297, Location at entrance to Stanley Park offers unobstructed views of the water, mountains, and the city. Insuite office, washer and dryer. $$$.

- Marriott Pinnacle Hotel, 1128 West Hastings St., Vancouver, BC V6E 4R5, 604 684-1128, Fax: 604 298-1128, 1-800-228-9290. www.vancouvermarriott pinnacle.com. Sauna, whirlpool, indoor pool. Pet-friendly. $$$.

- Metropolitan Hotel, 645 Howe St., Vancouver, BC V6C 2Y9, 604 687-1122, Fax: 604 643-7267, www.metropolitan.com. Sumptuous surroundings, full-service rooms. Hosts elegant Diva at the Met Restaurant. Sports court. Welcomes small pets. $$$

- Opus Hotel, 322 Davie St., Vancouver BC V6B 5Z6, 604 642-6787, 1-866-642-6787, Fax: 604 642-6780, www.opushotel.com. Modern, stylish hotel with French brasserie Elixir and eclectic Opus Bar. $$$.

- Pacific Palisades Hotel, 1277 Robson St., Vancouver, BC V6E 1C4, 604 688-0461, Fax: 604 688-4374, www.pacificpalisadeshotel.com. All-suite hotel. Kitchens in some suites, health club with pool, steam room. . Complimentary shoe shine and daily newspaper. Welcomes small pets. $$$.

- Pan Pacific Hotel Vancouver, 300-999 Canada Place, Vancouver, BC V6C 3B5, 604 662-8111, 1-800-663-1515, Fax: 604 685-8690, www.panpacific.com. One of the city's best luxury hotels. Part of a complex shared by the cruise ship terminal, convention centre and the celebrated Five Sails Restaurant. Health club, harbour and mountain views, full service. Welcomes small pets. $$$.

- Quality Hotel Downtown, 1335 Howe St., Vancouver, BC V6Z 1R7, 604 682-0229, 1-800-663-8474, Fax: 604 662-7566, www.qualityhotel.ca. Sante Fe atmosphere. Heated outdoor pool, complimentary access to nearby fitness centre. Offers excellent "passport" featuring 50% savings at 35 Vancouver attractions, restaurants and entertainment. $$-$$$.

- Ramada Downtown Vancouver, 435 West Pender St.,Vancouver, BC V6B 1V2; 604 488-1088, 1 888 389-5888, Fax: 604 488-1090, www.ramadadowntownvancouver.com. European boutique-style non-smoking rooms. $$$.

- Ramada Inn & Suites Downtown Vancouver, 1221 Granville St., Vancouver, BC V6Z 1M6, 604 685-1111, 1-888-835-0078, Fax: 604 685-0707, www.ramadavancouver.com. Situated in the Granville Entertainment district, with Granville Island just an Aquabus ferry away. Restaurant, lounge, airport shuttle. $$-$$$.

- Renaissance Vancouver Hotel Harbourside, 1133 West Hastings St., Vancouver, BC V6E 3T3, 604 689-9211, 1-800-468-3571, Fax: 604 689-4358, www.renaissancevancouver.com. Guestrooms and suites with harbour and city views. Restaurant, heated pool, conference space, pet-friendly. $$$.

- Robsonstrasse Hotel, 1394 Robson St., Vancouver, BC V6E 1C5, 604 687-1674, 1-888-667-8877, Fax: 604 685-7808, www.robsonstrassehotel.com. Studio and deluxe suites with kitchenette. Personalized voice mail, ADSL hookup, free covered parking. $$$.

- Rosedale on Robson, 838 Hamilton St., Vancouver, BC V6B 6A2, 604

689-8033, 1-800-661-8870, Fax: 604 689-4426, www.rosedaleonrobson.com. Vancouver's newest all-suite hotel offers one- or two-bedroom suites. Recreation facilities, restaurant, lounge. $$$.

- Sheraton Vancouver Wall Centre Hotel, 1088 Burrard St., Vancouver, BC V6Z 2R9, 604 331-1000, 1-800-624-5140 Fax: 604 893-7200, www.sheratonvancouver.com. Luxurious guestrooms and suites, first-class service. $$$.
- St. Regis Hotel, 602 Dunsmuir St., Vancouver, BC V6B 1Y6, 604 681-1135, 1-800-770-7929, Fax: 604 683-1126, www.stregishotel.com. A boutique-style hotel. Steakhouse, bar and grill, breakfast lounge. $$.
- Sutton Place Hotel, 845 Burrard St., Vancouver, BC V6Z 2K6, 604 682-5511, 1-800-961-7555, Fax: 604 642-2928. www.suttonplace.com. Attentive staff, understated elegance. Home to award-winning Fleuri Restaurant. $$$.
- Sylvia Hotel, 1154 Gilford St., Vancouver, BC V6G 2P6, 604 681-9321, Fax: 604 682-3551, www.sylviahotel.com. A charming, ivy-covered heritage building immortalized by the children's book *Mister Got To Go*. Welcomes pets. $$.
- Wedgewood Hotel, 845 Hornby St., Vancouver, BC V6Z 1V1, 604 689-7777, 1-800-663-0666, Fax: 604 608-5348, www.wedgewoodhotel.com. Intimate and stylish European boutique hotel. Attentive staff, award-winning Bacchus restaurant. Afternoon tea, weekends only; lounge. $$$.
- Westin Bayshore Resort & Marina Vancouver, 1601 Bayshore Dr., Vancouver, BC V6G 2V4, 604 682-3377, 1-800-228-3000, Fax: 604 687-3102, www.westin.com/bayshore. Luxury in a waterfront setting. Two restaurants, two lounges, whirlpool, masseur, pools, some environmentally friendly rooms. Welcomes small dogs. $$$.
- YMCA Hotel, 955 Burrard St., Vancouver, BC V6Z 1Y2, 604 681-0221, Fax: 604 681-1630, www.vanymca.org. Clean, affordable co-ed accommodations. Daily maid service, shared bathrooms, café, complete fitness facility with pools. $.
- YWCA Hotel, 733 Beatty St., Vancouver, BC V6B 2M4, 604 895-5830, 1-800-663-1424, Fax: 604 681-2550, www.ywcahotel.com. Built in 1995 for women and men. Air-conditioning, private, shared or hall bathrooms, shared kitchen, laundry room. Complimentary access to YWCA Health and Wellness Centre with pool, steam room whirlpool, gym, fitness and aquatics drop-in classes. $-$$.

BED AND BREAKFASTS

Bedding down in one of Vancouver's bed and breakfasts gives travellers a glimpse of the enviable, everyday lifestyle of the West Coast.

The following reservations services can be of great help:
- Canada-West Accommodations (604 990-6730 or 1-800-561-3223).
- Old English B&B Registry www.bandbinn.com. (604 986-5069)

Vancouver B&Bs include:
- Anthem House/O Canada House, 1114 Barclay St., Vancouver, BC V6E 1H1, 604 688-0555, 1-877-688-1114, Fax: 604 488-0556, www.ocanadahouse.com. Five rooms in a beautifully restored 1897 home, where the national anthem O Canada was written in 1909. Fans, designated smoking area, breakfast. $$-$$$.
- Camilla House Bed & Breakfast, 2538 West 13th Ave., Vancouver, BC V6K 2T1, 604 737-2687. Four rooms in a private home with oriental touches in public areas. Breakfast plan. $$.
- Penny Farthing Inn, 2855 West 6th Ave., Vancouver, BC V6K 1X2, 604 739-9002, Fax: 604 739-9004, www.pennyfarthinginn.com. Two rooms, two suites in a renovated 1912 house. Guest living room, guest fridge, guest business room with computer, scanner, printer, email connection, fax, photocopier. Full breakfast. The three resident cats aren't permitted in guest rooms or suites. $$.
- West End Guest House, 1362 Haro St., Vancouver, BC V6E 1G2, 604 681-2889, Fax: 604 688-8812, www.westendguesthouse.com. Eight period rooms in a pink Victorian-era home. Resident ghost, designated smoking areas, breakfast plan. $$-$$$.

- Windsor House, 325 West 11th Ave., Vancouver, BC V5Y 1T3, 604 872-3060, Fax: 604 873-1147. Ten rooms, simple décor. Designated smoking areas, breakfast plan. $-$$.

HOSTELS AND EDUCATIONAL RESIDENCES

Hostels offer spartan but economical alternatives for accommodation. In the summer, a few educational institutes open their residences to travellers as well.

- C & N Backpackers Hostel, 927 Main St. and 1038 Main St., Vancouver, BC V6A 2V8 and V6A 2W1, 604 682-2441 and 604 681-9118, 1-888-434-6060, Fax: 604 682-2441 and 604 681-9118, www.cnnbackpackers.com. A 1926 heritage building with renovated interior near public transit. Staff speak many languages. Fully equipped kitchen, several showers per floor, laundry facility. Internet, guest phones, fax. $.
- Cambie International Hostel, 300 Cambie St., Vancouver, BC V6B 2N3, 604 684-6466, Fax: 604 687-5618, www.cambiehostels.com. Gastown hostel features a pub, general store and bakery/café. Full laundry, bike storage, email and Internet. Shuttle bus to bus station and airport. $.
- Cambie International Hostel (Seymour), 515 Seymour St., Vancouver, BC V6B 2H6, 604 684-7757, Fax: 604 687-5618, www.cambiehostels.com. Downtown location. Full laundry, bike storage, email and Internet. Shuttle bus to bus station and airport. $.
- Hostelling International — Vancouver Central, 1025 Granville St., Vancouver, BC V6Z 1L4, 604 685-5335, 1-888-203-8333, Fax: 604 685-5351, www.hihostels.ca. Renovated hostel offering private and dormitory rooms. Popular pub The Royal onsite. $.
- Hostelling International — Vancouver Downtown, 1114 Burnaby St., Vancouver, BC V6E 1P1, 604 684-4565, 1-888-203-4302, Fax: 604 684-4540, www.hihostels.ca. Shared and private rooms with fully equipped kitchen. Internet, TV room, game room and organized activities. Library/reading room, laundry room, bike rental/storage, limited parking. $.
- Hostelling International — Vancouver Jericho Beach, 1515 Discovery St., Vancouver, BC V6R 4K5, 604 224-3208, 1-888-203-4303, Fax: 604 224-4852, www.hihostels.ca. Shared and private rooms with fully equipped kitchen. Internet, laundry, licensed cafeteria. $.
- UBC Conference Centre, 5961 Student Union Blvd., Vancouver, BC V6T 2C9, 604 822-1000, Fax: 604 822-1001, www.ubcconferences.com. Arranges accommodations at four on-campus residences. $-$$.

VICTORIA

HOTELS: VICTORIA INTERNATIONAL AIRPORT

Because the Victoria International Airport is located on the Saanich Peninsula away from the city, Victoria itself has no "airport hotels." However, the towns bordering the airport extend a number of lodgings to serve travellers too tired to make the 30-minute drive to the core of Victoria:

- Best Western Emerald Isle Motor Inn, 2306 Beacon Ave., Sidney, BC V8L 1X2, 250 656-4441, 1-800-315-3377, Fax: 250 655-1351, www.bwemeraldisle.com. Huge guest rooms. Sauna, whirlpool, restaurant. $$.
- Sidney Waterfront Inn and Suites, 9775 First Street, Sidney, BC V8L 2X1 250 656-1131, 1-888-656-1131, Fax: 250 656-9396, www.sidneywaterfront.com. The hotel's location on the Sidney Harbour means access to whale-watching, fishing and other water-related activities. Some rooms with harbour views, kitchens. $$.
- Super 8 Motel Victoria/Saanichton, 2477 Mt. Newton X Road, Saanichton, BC V8M 2B7, 250 652-6888, 1-800-800-8000, Fax: 250 652-6800, www.super8.com. Modern comfort, economically styled. Welcomes pets. $$.
- Travelodge Victoria Airport Sidney, 2280 Beacon Ave., Sidney, BC V8L 1X1, 250 656-1176, 1-866-656-1176, Fax: 250 656-7344, www.airport travelodge.com. Older but remodelled digs. Courtyard, heated outdoor pool. Welcomes small pets. $$.

HOTELS: DOWNTOWN VICTORIA AND INNER HARBOUR

Victoria's downtown and Inner Harbour hotels perfectly situate the traveller in the thick of the city's attractions:

- Admiral Inn, 257 Belleville St., Victoria, BC V8V 1X1, 250 388-6267, 1-888-823-6472, Fax: 250 388-6267, www.admiral.bc.ca. Well-equipped rooms and suites in a harbourside hotel-class accommodation. Complimentary local calls, parking, continental breakfast and coffee. English and French-speaking staff. Welcomes pets. $$-$$$.
- Bedford Regency Hotel, 1140 Government St., Victoria, BC V8W 1Y2, 250 384-6835, 1-800-665-6500, Fax: 250 386-8930, www.bedfordregency.com. Architectural details lend old-world charm to this small but elegant 1800s hotel. Wood-burning fireplaces in some suites. Off-site parking only. Restaurant serving breakfast only. $$-$$$.
- Best Western Carlton Plaza, 642 Johnson St., Victoria, BC V8W 1M6, 250 388-5513, 1-800-663-7241, Fax: 250 388-5343, www.bestwesterncarltonplazahotel.com. Refurbishing has made for bright and spacious rooms. Air conditioning, restaurant. $$-$$$.
- Best Western Inner Harbour, 412 Quebec St., Victoria, BC V8V 1W5, 250 384-5122, 1-800-383-2378,1-888-383-2378 Fax: 250 384-5113, www.victoriabestwestern.com. Spacious, renovated rooms, all with private balconies. Jacuzzi, sauna, heated outdoor pool. $$-$$$.
- Chateau Victoria Hotel, 740 Burdett Avenue, Victoria, BC V8W 1B2, 250 382-4221, 1-800-663-5891, Fax: 250 380-1950, www.chateauvictoria.com. Full-service boutique hotel hosting Victoria's only rooftop restaurant. English, Chinese, German, Portuguese, Spanish and Swiss spoken. Lounge, heated pool. $$-$$$.
- Coast Victoria Harbourside Hotel and Marina, 146 Kingston St., Victoria, BC V8V 1V4, 250 360-1211, 1-800-663-1144, Fax: 250 360-1418, www.coasthotels.com. Waterfrontage with indoor/outdoor pools, health club. Award-winning Blue Crab Bar and Grill, lounge. $$$.
- Crystal Court Motel, 701 Belleville St., Victoria, BC V8W 1A2, 250 384-0551, Fax: 250 384-5125, martin.scott@crystalcourt.ca. Well-kept, older budget motel with mix of room size and style. Exterior corridors. $.
- Days Inn on the Harbour, 427 Belleville St., Victoria, BC V8V 1X3, 250 386-3451, 1-800-665-3024, Fax: 250 386-6999, www.daysinnvictoria.com. Restaurant, lounge, heated pool, whirlpool. $$-$$$.
- Delta Victoria Ocean Pointe Resort Hotel and Spa, 45 Songhees Road, Victoria, BC V9A 6T3, 250 360-2999, 1-800-667-4677, Fax: 250 360-1041, www.deltahotels.com/hotels/hotels. php?hotelId=51. Casually elegant with heated pool, sauna, whirlpool, racquetball and tennis courts, European spa Home to The Victorian Restaurant. Welcomes small pets. $$-$$$.
- Executive House Hotel, 777 Douglas St., Victoria, BC V8W 2B5, 250 388-5111, 1-800-663-7001, Fax: 250 385-1323, www.executivehouse.com. Older high-rise hotel with spacious rooms and suites. Sauna, steam room, whirlpool, restaurants. Welcomes small pets. $$.
- The Fairmont Empress Hotel, 721 Government St., Victoria, BC V8W 1W5, 250 384-8111, 1-866-540-4452, Fax: 250 389-2747, www.fairmont.com/empress. Elegance and service in a restored heritage setting as regal as the name implies. Restaurant and lounge, fitness facilities. World-famous afternoon tea. $$-$$$.
- Harbour Towers Hotel, 345 Quebec St., Victoria, BC V8V 1W4, 250 385-2405, 1-800-663-5896, Fax: 250 385-4453, www.harbourtowers.com. Spacious rooms. Indoor pool and fitness centre. Restaurant and lounge. $$$.
- Hotel Grand Pacific, 463 Belleville St., Victoria, BC V8V 1X3, 250 386-0450, 1-800-663-7550, Fax: 250 380-4475, www.hotelgrandpacific.com. Rooms all have private balconies, air conditioning. Pool, whirlpool, sauna, workout facilities, squash and

racquetball courts. Chinese, English, French, German, Spanish, Punjabi spoken. $$$.

- Laurel Point Inn, 680 Montreal St., Victoria, BC V8V 1Z8, 250 386-8721, 1-800-663-7667, Fax: 250 386-9547, www.laurelpoint.com. Resort-style downtown hotel with indoor pool, sauna, Jacuzzi. Free local calls. Two restaurants, lounge, business centre. English, French and Japanese spoken. $$$.
- The Magnolia Hotel and Spa, 623 Courtney St., Victoria, BC V8W 1B8, 250 381-0999, 1-877-624-6654, Fax: 250 381-0988, www.magnoliahotel.com. Opulent boutique hotel with floor-to-ceiling windows and lavish bathrooms. Restaurant, brewpub. $$$.
- Quality Inn Downtown, 850 Blanshard St., Victoria, BC V8W 2H2, 250 385-6787, 1-800-661-4115, Fax: 250 385-5800, www.victoriaqualityinn.com. Convenient, large rooms, small indoor pool, steam and fitness rooms. English-style pub, restaurant. $$.
- Queen Victoria Hotel & Suites, 655 Douglas St., Victoria, BC V8V 2P9, 250 386-1312, 1-800-663-7007, Fax: 250 381-4312, www.qvhotel.com. Pool, sauna, restaurant. $$-$$$.
- Ramada Huntingdon Manor, 330 Quebec St., Victoria, BC V8V 1W3, 250 381-3456, 1-800-663-7557, Fax: 250 382-7666, www.bellevillepark.com. Full-service hotel with English-style interiors. Sauna, whirlpool, aromatherapy. Restaurant, bar and grill, ice-cream parlour. Home to Artisans Lane. $$-$$$.
- Strathcona Hotel, 919 Douglas St., Victoria, BC V8W 2C2, 250 383-7137, 1-800-663-7476, Fax: 250 383-6893, www.strathconahotel.com. A 1913 building recently refurbished with charisma. Victorian-era pub, nightclub. Rooftop lounge and volleyball court. $-$$.
- Swans Suite Hotel, 506 Pandora St., Victoria, BC V8W 1N6, 250 361-3310, 1-800-668-7926, Fax: 250 361-3491, www.swanshotel.com. Restored heritage building with art collection in Olde Towne. Onsite brew pub, restaurant, club, beer and wine store. $$.

- Travellers Inn Downtown, 1850 Douglas St., Victoria, BC V8T 4K6, 250 381-1000, 1-888-254-6476, Fax: 250 381-1001, www.travellersinn.com. Spacious rooms. Top floor rooms with small patio deck. No pets. $.
- Victoria Plaza Hotel, 603 Pandora Ave., Victoria, BC V8W 1N8, 250 386-3631, 1-800-906-4433, Fax: 250 386-9452. Modern and clean rooms with fine service. $.
- Victoria Regent Hotel, 1234 Wharf St., Victoria, BC V8W 3H9, 250 386-2211, 1-800-663-7472, Fax: 250 386-2622, www.victoriaregent.com. Condominium-style accommodations with sundecks, kitchens and dining areas. $$-$$$.

BED AND BREAKFASTS

More than any other, the bed-and-breakfast experience evokes the graciousness and hospitality of a bygone era.

The following reservations service can help you find a B&B:
- AA-Accommodations West Reservation Agency (250 479-1986).

The following are but a few of the many bed and breakfasts that dot the Victoria area:
- A B&B at Swallow Hill Farm, 4910 William Head Rd., Victoria, BC V9C 3Y8, 250 474-4042, Fax: 250 474-4042, www.swallowhillfarm.com. Two suites with private baths on an apple farm on the southwest coast. Ocean and mountain views. Wildlife viewing. Farm breakfast served. No pets (resident dog), no smoking. $$.
- Abigail's Hotel, 906 McClure St., Victoria, BC V8V 3E7, 250 388-5363, 1-800-561-6565, Fax: 250 388-7787, www.abigailshotel.com. Twenty-two rooms on four floors in a Tudor-style country bed and breakfast inn. Antique furniture, no elevator. Breakfast served, hors d'oeuvres in library. German spoken. $$$.
- Beaconsfield Inn, 998 Humboldt St., Victoria, BC V8V 2Z8, 250 384-4044, 1-888-884-4044, Fax: 250 384-4052, www.beaconsfieldinn.com. Six rooms, three suites in a 1905 manse. Edwardian atmosphere, beamed ceilings and leaded glass windows. Gourmet breakfast, afternoon tea and sherry served. No pets, no smoking, no elevator (four stories). $$$.

- Binners' Bed and Breakfast, 58 Linden Ave., Victoria, BC V8V 4C8, 250 383-5442, 1-888-409-5800 Fax: 250 383-5885, www.aBeautifulIslandAway.com. Two serene modern suites and one bedroom, all with private baths, fireplaces, in-room telephones. Internet access. Full breakfast. Close to scenic Dallas Rd and Beacon Hill Park. $$.
- Gatsby Mansion Bed & Breakfast & Restaurant, 309 Belleville St., Victoria, BC V8V 1X2, 250 388-9191, 1-800-563-9656, Fax: 250 920-5651, www.bellevillepark.com. A collection of 18 suites in Belleville Park in a restored Queen Anne mansion (1877) and smaller house, with ocean views. Main house has antiques and large verandah. Licensed lounge, restaurant, gift shop. Full breakfast. No smoking, no pets. $$-$$$.
- Haterleigh Heritage Inn, 243 Kingston St., Victoria, BC V8V 1V5, 250 384-9995, Fax: 250 384-1935, www.haterleigh.com. Six rooms in a 1901 Victorian heritage mansion. Restored, with mix of modern and antique furnishings. Private Jacuzzis, gourmet breakfast. No smoking, no pets. $$$.
- Heathergate House B&B, 122 Simcoe St., Victoria, BC V8V 1K4, 250 383-0068, 1-888-683-0068, Fax: 250 383-4320, www.heathergatebb.com. Quiet, elegant, immaculate rooms with private baths as well as a 2-bedroom cottage in a delightful garden setting. Full English breakfast served. No smoking, no pets. $$
- Humboldt House Bed and Breakfast, 867 Humboldt St., Victoria, BC V8V 2Z6, 250 383-0152, 1-888-383-0327, Fax: 250 383-6402, www.humboldthouse.com. Five romantic rooms in authentic Victorian-era house. Large whirlpool, wood-burning fireplaces. Sherry served in sitting room. Gourmet champagne breakfast delivered to rooms. No smoking. $$$.
- Iris Garden Country Manor Bed and Breakfast, 5360 West Saanich Rd., Victoria, BC V9E 1J8, 250 744-2253, 1-877-744-2253, Fax: 250 744-5690, www.irisgardenvictoria.com. Four rooms with vaulted ceilings in an elegant country retreat. Three acres of irises, Douglas firs surround the 1960s character home. Guest living room. Full breakfast served. No smoking. $$.
- Oak Bay Guest House, 1052 Newport Ave., Victoria, BC V8S 5E3, 250 598-3812, 1-800-575-3812, Fax: 250 598-0369, www.oakbayguesthouse.com. Eleven rooms in a restored manor previously owned by an eccentric Oak Bay philosopher. Charming décor, lush landscape reflecting gentility of the Oak Bay suburb.No smoking. $$.
- Prior House B&B Inn, 620 St. Charles St., Victoria, BC V8S 3N7, 250 592-8847, 1-877-924-3300, Fax: 250 592-8223, www.priorhouse.com. Six rooms and suites in a restored 1912 manor house built originally for the lieutenant-governor. Lush landscaped grounds, gracious interior, wood-burning fireplace. No elevator, smoking outdoors. Breakfast and High Tea served. $$-$$$.
- Rosewood Victoria Inn, 595 Michigan St., Victoria, BC V8V 1S7, 250 384-6644, 1-800-335-3466, Fax: 250 384-6117, www.rosewoodvictoria.com. Seventeen rooms in a 1930s residence. Relaxed elegance, country antique items, charming library/ lounge with open-log fire. No elevator, no pets, designated smoking area. Breakfast served. $$-$$$.
- Ryan's Bed and Breakfast, 224 Superior St., Victoria, BC V8V 1T3, 250 389-0012, 1-877-389-0012, Fax: 250 389-2857, www.ryansbb.com. Eight rooms in 1892 restored home. Original fireplace, china cabinets, oil paintings in heavy gilded frames. Designated smoking area, small pets only. Breakfast served. $$-$$$.
- White Heather Cottage, 626 Simcoe St., Victoria, BC V8V 1M4, 250 383-0152, 1-888-383-0327, Fax: 250 383-6402, www.whiteheathercottage.com. Two guestrooms in beautiful 1925 English Cottage. Pine beds, ensuite baths with deep soaking or Jacuzzi tubs. Gourmet breakfast served with champagne and chocolate truffles. No pets. $$-$$$

HOSTELS AND EDUCATIONAL RESIDENCES

For the budget-conscious traveller not looking for pampering, hostels and schools are the accommodation of choice:

- Backpackers Hostel Turtle Refuge, 1608 Quadra St., Victoria, BC V8W 2L4, 250 386-4471, Fax: 250 386-4471. Dorm-style and private rooms. Four shared bathrooms, full kitchen facility, laundry room. Parking available. English and French spoken. $.
- Hostelling International Victoria, 516 Yates St., Victoria, BC V8W 1K8, 250 385-4511, 1-888-883-0099, Fax: 250 385-3232, www.hihostels.ca. Shared and private rooms. Equipment storage, self-service kitchen, laundry room. Hostel-based activities and tours. Games/TV room, Internet access. $.
- Ocean Island Backpacker's Inn, 791 Pandora Ave., Victoria, BC V8W 1N9, 250 385-1788, 1-888-888-4180, Fax: 250 385-1750, www.oceanisland.com. Spacious dorms with kitchen facilities. Licensed café, music room, Internet access. $.
- University of Victoria Student Residences, PO Box 1700, Stn CSC, Victoria, BC V8W 2Y2, 250 721-8395, Fax: 250 721-8390, housing.uvic.ca/Housing.htm. Available May to August. Single and double rooms with shared bath, coin-operated laundry, pay phones, lounge. Seven suites (Craigdarroch House) with private bath, desk, TV, phone, complimentary breakfast. Fully-furnished townhouses also available at higher rates. $.

DINING

Vancouver and Victoria restaurants take full advantage of their setting, poised on the edge of an ocean and surrounded by wilderness. Fresh flavours incorporating indigenous ingredients mark each restaurant, as do the creativity of each chef and the diverse origins of the people they serve. Smoking in Vancouver and Victoria restaurants is prohibited by law. Please smoke in designated areas only. Tips are not usually added to a restaurant bill. Tipping a server is standard practice at the rate of 15% to 20%. The following lists a select number of the multitude of restaurants in each city. Each listing includes the approximate price range for dinner for two, including a bottle of wine (where served), taxes and gratuity: $ = under $45, $$ = $45-$80, $$$ = $80-$120, $$$$ = $120-$180, $$$$$ = over $180. Keep in mind that many fine restaurants make a wide selection of wines available by the glass as well. Meals served are indicated as: B = breakfast, L = lunch, D = dinner, G = grazing, T-O = take-out, Late = open past midnight. The credit cards accepted by each establishment are also listed: AX = American Express, V = Visa, MC = Mastercard, DC = Diners Club.

VANCOUVER

ASIAN

Chinese

Most restaurants represent the Cantonese and Mandarin regions. Many other styles, however, are showing up at diverse locations. Dim sum is available at most establishments, with the exception of noodle houses.

- Floata Seafood Restaurant, 400-180 Keefer St., 604 602-0368. Sets a standard for good food and strong service in a huge venue. L/D/T-O, $$$, AX/V/MC/DC.
- Hon's Wun Tun House, 1339 Robson St., 604 685-0871. An institution for fast, cheap rice and noodles, potstickers, wun tun, and vegetarian dim sum. Multiple locations: 108-268 Keefer St., 604 688-0871; 268 Keefer St., 604 688-0871; 310-3025 Lougheed Hwy., Coquitlam, 604 468-0871; 408 6th St., New Westminster, 604 520-6661; 101-4600 #3 Rd., Richmond, 604 273-0871. L/D/T-O, $, AX/V/MC/DC.
- Imperial Chinese Seafood Restaurant, 355 Burrard St., 604 688-8191. Elevated Chinese Dining. L/D, $$$$, V/MC/DC.
- Kirin Mandarin Restaurant, 102-1166 Alberni St., 604 682-8833. Refined

dining from China's northern regions. L/D, \$\$\$\$, AX/V/DC.
- Pink Pearl Chinese Restaurant, 1132 East Hastings St., 604 253-4316. Come early for the dim sum, come late if you want to see a Chinese wedding banquet. L/D/T-O, \$\$\$, AX/V/MC/DC.
- Richmond Mandarin Chinese Restaurant, 2200-8181 Cambie Rd., 604 270-3003. A hotel restaurant in Richmond's Asia West just has to have authenticity, and it doesn't disappoint. L/D, \$\$\$, AX/V/MC.
- Shanghai Chinese Bistro, 1124 Alberni St., 604 683-8222. Chinese food, Shanghai-style and a dinner show in the form of noodle-pulling demonstration. L/D/Late, \$\$, AX/V/MC.
- Sun Sui Wah Restaurant, 3888 Main St., 604 872-8822. Every visiting food writer makes this stop for seafood and dim sum. Additional location in Richmond at 102-4940 #3 Rd., 604 273-8208. L/D, \$\$\$-\$\$\$\$, AX/V/MC.
- Szechuan Chongqing Seafood Restaurant, 1668 West Broadway Ave.,(upstairs) 604 734-1668. Showcases Chongqing regional cooking style. L/D, \$\$-\$\$\$, AX/V/MC.
- Won More Szechuan Cuisine, 201-1184 Denman St., 604 688-8856. Mainly spicy dishes in a crowded, upstairs space. D, \$\$, V/MC.

Japanese

- Ezogiku Noodle Café, 5-1329 Robson St., 604 685-8606. For ramen in all its forms (and more). An additional location is under the Rosedale Hotel at 270 Robson, 604 685-9466. L/D/T-O, \$, no credit cards.
- Gyoza King, 1508 Robson St., 604 669-8278. Gyozas galore: meat-based, vegetable-based, seafood-based. Noodle and rice dishes, too. D/Late, \$, V/MC.
- Musashi Japanese Restaurant, 780 Denman St., 604 687-0634. The West End's answer to sensibly-priced sushi. D, \$, AX/V/MC.
- Kamei Royale Japanese Restaurant, 1030 West Georgia St., 604 687-8588. An impressive second floor setting with experienced, creative sushi chefs. L/D, \$\$\$, AX/V/MC.
- Tojo's Restaurant, 202-777 West Broadway Ave., 604 872-8050. The ultimate in sushi springs from the hands of chef Hidekazu Tojo. Closed Sunday. D, \$\$\$\$, AX/V/MC.
- Yuji's Japanese Tapas, 2059 West 4th Ave., 604 734-4990. Appetizer dishes, sashimi, sushi. Open nightly and weekends, closed Monday. D, \$\$, AV/MC.

South Asian

- Maurya, 1643 West Broadway Ave., 604 742-0622. Modern fine dining. Indian. L/D/T-O, \$\$\$, AX/V/MC.
- Vij's Restaurant, 1480 West 11th Ave., 604 736-6664. Expect lineups (no reservations are taken) for Vij's BC-influenced Indian dishes. D, \$\$\$, AX/V/MC/DC.

Thai and Vietnamese

- Montri's Thai Restaurant, 3629 West Broadway Ave., 604 738-9888. Authentically hot, in every sense of the word. Closed Monday. D, \$\$\$, V/MC.
- Phnom Penh, 244 East Georgia St., 604 682-5777. A Vietnamese-Cambodian-Chinese mix of dishes in a family-run establishment. L/D, \$\$, AX/MC.

FRENCH AND ITALIAN

- Beach Side Café, 1362 Marine Dr., West Vancouver, 604 925-1945. Light, subtle food and stunning views. Brunch on weekends. L/D, \$\$\$\$, AX/V/MC.
- Bistro Pastis, 2153 West 4th Ave., 604 731-5020. Satisfying bistro classics. Closed Monday. L/D, \$\$\$, AX/V/MC.
- Café de Paris, 751 Denman St., 604 687-1418. Both the setting and fare bring to mind the classic Paris bistro. No lunch weekends. L/D, \$\$\$, AX/V/MC.
- Cioppino's Mediterranean Grill, 1133 Hamilton St., 604 688-7466. Light, fresh dishes melding Italian, French and Spanish flavours. L/D, \$\$\$-\$\$\$\$, AX/V/MC.
- Il Giardino di Umberto, 1382 Hornby St., 604 669-2422. A seaside villa recreated, serving excellent pasta and game. Closed Sunday, no lunch Saturday. L/D, \$\$\$\$, AX/V/MC/DC.
- La Régalade, 103-2232 Marine Dr., West Vancouver, 604 921-2228. Country French at bistro prices. L/D, \$\$, V/MC.

- Le Crocodile, 909 Burrard St., 604 669-4298. Offers the full, real Alsace experience. Closed Sundays, no lunch Saturday. L/D, $$$$, AX/V/MC./DC.
- Saveur, 850 Thurlow St., 604 688-1633. Fine French dining with locally sourced organic and fresh dishes at a prix fixe of $39.00 . Closed Sunday, no lunch Saturday. L/D, AX/V/MC/.
- Quattro on Fourth, 2611 West 4th Ave., 604 734-4411. Additional location at Gusto di Quattro, North Vancouver, L/D 604 924-4444. Mosaic and mahogany and marvellous food. D, $$$-$$$$, AX/V/MC/DC.
- Smoking Dog Grill, 1889 West 1st Ave., 604 732-8811. Simple French fare in the perfect people-watching place. L/D, $$-$$$, AX/V/MC.
- Villa Del Lupo, 869 Hamilton St., 604 688-7436. Generous and contemporary cooking in a charming old house. D, $$$$, AX/V/MC/DC.

PACIFIC NORTHWEST

- Liliget Feast House, 1724 Davie St., 604 681-7044. A rarity: original First Nations cuisine in a fabulous longhouse setting. D, $$$, AX/V/MC/DC.
- Rodney's Oyster House, 405-1228 Hamilton St., 604 609-0080. Oysters are the main attraction here, but other seafoods are popular too. L/D, $$$, AX/V/MC/DC.
- Blue Water Café and Raw Bar, 1095 Hamilton St., 604 688-8078. Local seafood plus a master sushi chef at the Raw Bar. Fabulous deserts and an excellent champagne list. L/D, $$$, AX/V/MC.
- Provence Marinaside, 1177 Marinaside Crescent, 604 681-1414. Meals from pasta to fresh seafood, plus afternoon tea by reservation and picnic baskets on order. L/D, brunch on weekends, $$$, AX/MC/V.
- glowbal grill & satay bar, 1070 Mainland St., 604 602-0825. The open kitchen conjures up award-winning regional dishes with a flourish. L/D, $$$, AX/V/MC.
- The Beach House, 150 25th St., West Vancouver, 604 922-1414. Strong on seafood. By Dundarave Pier, it's a great spot for Sunday brunch. L/D, $$$$, AX/V/MC/DC.

- The Cannery Seafood Restaurant, 2205 Commissioner St., 604 254-9606. Promises good seafood, and delivers. No lunch weekends. L/D, $$$$, AX/V/MC/DC.
- The Fish House in Stanley Park, 8901 Stanley Park Dr., 604 681-7275. Bold and creative seafood. Sunday brunch. L/D, $$$-$$$$, AX/V/MC/DC.
- The Pear Tree, 4120 Hastings St., Burnaby, 604 299-2772. Inventive food, reasonable prices. Closed weekends.. D, $$$, AX/V/MC/DC.
- Raincity Grill, 1193 Denman St., 604 685-7337. Ever-changing menu based on what's fresh. Weekend brunch. L/D, $$$$, AX/V/MC/DC.
- Seasons Hilltop Bistro, Queen Elizabeth Park, Cambie St. and West 33rd Ave., 604 874-8008. Good, conservative food in an intoxicating garden setting. Weekend brunch à la carte. L/D, $$$-$$$$, AX/V/MC.

FINE DINING AND HOTEL DINING

- Salmon House on the Hill, 2229 Folkstone Way, West Vancouver, 604 926-3212. High in the North Shore hills, this classic spot is romantic and traditional. Wild salmon is the specialty. L/D, $$$$, AX/V/MC.
- Bacchus Restaurant, Wedgewood Hotel, 845 Hornby St., 604 689-7777. Small, exclusive room with unfailingly good food. Afternoon tea served. Weekends only. B/L/D/Late (lounge), $$$$, AX/V/MC/DC.
- Bishop's Restaurant, 2183 West 4th Ave., 604 738-2025. Flawlessly prepared food, understated elegance and superb service. No lunch on weekends. L/D, $$$$, AX/V/MC/DC.
- C, 2-1600 Howe St., 604 681-1164. Intriguing dishes and a million-dollar marina view. D, lunch in summer months, $$$$-$$$$$, AX/V/MC/DC.
- Chartwell, Four Seasons Hotel, 791 West Georgia St., 604 689-9333. The classic dining choice. D, $$$$-$$$$$, AX/V/MC/DC.
- Diva at the Met, Metropolitan Hotel, 645 Howe St., 604 602-7788. Airy space with multi-tiered seating and stylish food preparation. Weekend brunch. B/L/D, $$$$, AX/V/MC/DC.
- Feenie's, 2563 West Broadway Ave., 604 739-7115. Casual Canadian

bistro cooking with flair includes burgers and spaghettini with prawns and scallops. B/L/D/, $$$, AX/V/MC/DC.

- Five Sails Restaurant, Pan Pacific Hotel, 300-999 Canada Place, 604 662-8111. Imaginative orchestration of flavours and breathtaking views. D, $$$$, AX/V/MC/DC.
- Fleuri Restaurant, Sutton Place Hotel, 845 Burrard St., 604 642-2900. A hidden treasure. Afternoon tea; jazz brunch every Sunday. Chocoholic Bar. B/L/D, $$$$, AX/V/MC/DC.
- Lumière, 2551 West Broadway Ave., 604 739-8185. Classic French preparation with contemporary flair. Now two rooms: Dining Room and The Tasting Bar. Superb tasting menus. Closed Mondays. D, $$$$- $$$$$, AX/V/MC/DC.
- West, 2881 Granville St., 604 738- 8938. Regional, seasonal fare. L/D. $$$$, AX/V/MC/.

SPECIALTY

Heritage

- Hart House on Deer Lake, 6664 Deer Lake Ave., Burnaby, 604 298-4278. The Tudor-style setting embraces both traditional and more daring fare. L/D, $$$-$$$$, AX/V/MC/.
- Sequoia Grill at the Teahouse at Ferguson Point, Stanley Park, 604 669-3281. Former officers' mess perfectly situated in the midst of one of the world's best and biggest urban parks. Weekend brunch. L/D, $$$$, AX/V/MC.

Vegetarian

- Habibi's, 7-1128 West Broadway Ave., 604 732-7487. Bargain-priced, vegetarian Lebanese fare makes for both a healthy body and a happy wallet. No lunch weekends, closed Sundays. L/D, $, no credit cards.
- Planet Veg, 1941 Cornwall Ave., 604 734-1001. A warning: lineups form fast for the Indian, Mexican and Mediterranean vegetarian fast foods. L/D/T-O, $, V/MC.

Tapas

- Bin 941 Tapas Parlour, 941 Davie St., 604 683-1246. Generously filled tasting bowls. D/Late, $$-$$$, V/MC.
- Bin 942 Tapas Parlour, 1521 West Broadway Ave., 604 734-9421.

Much like Bin 941, but bigger. D/Late, $$-$$$, V/MC.

CASUAL DINING AND BAKERIES

- Dockside Brewing Company, 1253 Johnston St., 604 685-7070. Pub, casual restaurant, microbrewery and smashing patio, all in one. B/L/D, $$, AX/DC/V/MC.
- Earl's Restaurants, 1601 West Broadway Ave., 604 736-5663. Fresh and healthy food that's fast. Good place to take children. Various additional locations: 901 West Broadway Ave., 604 734-5995 and 1185 Robson St., 604 669-0020. L/D, $$, AX/V/MC.
- Harambe Café, 2149 Commercial Dr., 604 216-1060.
- Havana Restaurant, 1212 Commercial Dr., 604 253-9119.
- Juicy Lucy's Good Eats, 1420 Commercial Dr., 604 254-6101. Juice bar and café. $.
- Les Amis Du Fromage, 1752 West 2nd Ave., 604 732-4218. Wide selection of cheese take-out at Vancouver's best cheese shop. T-O, $, AX/V/MC.
- Memphis Blues Barbeque House, 1465 West Broadway Ave., 604 738- 6806. Additional location at 1342 Commercial Dr., 604 215-2599. Southern baah-be-cue with all the Memphis favourites. L/D/T-O, $, AE/MC/V.
- Milestone's, several locations, original location at 1210 Denman St., 604 662-3431, www.milestonesrestaurants.com. L/D/G, $$, AX/V/MC.
- Patisserie Lebeau, 1728 West 2nd Ave., 604 731-3528. Fine Belgian waffles and jewel-like pastries and French breads, freshly baked. Eat-in or take-out. Closed Sunday and Monday, V/MC.
- Solly's Bagelry, 189 East 28th Ave., 604 872-1821. Order from the bagelry and deli, or sit with a coffee and something sweet (the best cinnamon bun in town, perhaps). Additional location at 2873 West Broadway Ave., 604 738-2121. B/L/G/T-O, $, V.
- Steamworks Brewing Company, 375 Water St., 604 689-2739. Some say the best beer in town is found in Steamworks' onsite brewery. B/L/D/Late, $$, AX/V/MC.

- Subeez, 891 Homer St., 604 687-6107. Popular industrial-style bistro. Brunch,L/D, $$-$$$, V/MC.
- Tomato Fresh Food Café, 3305 Cambie St., 604 874-6020. Distinctively healthy and colourful comfort food, with the same food available for takeout around the corner at Tomato to Go, 530 West 17th Ave., 604 873-4697. B/L/D/T-O, $$, AX/V/MC.
- Urban Fare, 177 Davie St., 604 975-7550. Café and gourmet supermarket B/L/D/T-O, $, AX/V/MC.
- Waazubee Café, 1622 Commercial Dr., 604 253-5299. Casual and upbeat spot on The Drive. L/D, $$, V/MC.
- White Spot Triple O, 1881 Cornwall Ave., 604 738-3888. The express version of Nat Bailey's famous White Spot. Fries, milkshakes and Vancouver's favourite burgers with legendary Triple O sauce are served fast. Other Vancouver locations: 805 Thurlow St., 604 609-7000, 1455 Quebec St. (Science World), 604 647-0003. B/L/D/T-O, $, V/MC.
- The Irish Heather, 217 Carrall St., 604 688-9779. As Irish as they come, from bangers 'n' mash to blueberry bread pudding. Over 100 single malts and Irish whiskeys are served. L/D, $$$, AX/V/MC.
- Go Fish!, 1505 W 1 Ave., 604 730-5040. Mostly takeaway but with a few tables under a canopy roof by the waterside. Halibut, salmon and cod are cooked fresh from the dock. L/D, $, V/MC.

VICTORIA

FINE DINING

- Aerie Resort, 600 Ebadora Lane, Malahat, 250 743-7115. French class and quality well worth the price. L/D, $$$$-$$$$$, AX/V/MC/DC.
- Arbutus Grille, Brentwood Bay Lodge & Spa, 849 Verdier Avenue, Victoria. Fine dining featuring west coast regional food Haida Feast Platter, a spectacular offering presented on hand carved yellow and red cedar ceremonial dishes. 250.544.2079 FAX : 250.544.2069 reservations : 1-888-544-2079. Email: reservations@brentwoodbaylodge.com B/L/D. $$$. A/X,V, M/C.
- Café Brio, 944 Fort St., 250 383-0009. Contemporary Pacific Northwest creations in a lively, art-filled room. No lunch weekends. L/D, $$$-$$$$, AX/V/MC.
- Fire and Water Fish and Chophouse, Victoria Marriott Inner Harbour, 728 Humboldt St., 250 480-3800, 1-877-333-8338. Regional cuisine in a serene atmosphere, with all-seasons patio. $$$. B/L/D, A/X, M/C, DC.
- Rosemeade Dining Room, Old English Resort, 429 Lampson St., Esquimalt, 250 412-7673, rosemeade@englishinnresort.com. Roast duck from the nearby Cowichan Valley, seasonally inspired salads and seafood. Kitchen tours and chef's table. B/L/D, $$$-$$$$, AX/V/MC.
- Deep Cove Chalet, 11190 Chalet Road, Deep Cove, Sidney, 250 656-3541. Exceptional French cuisine, specializing in local seafood. L/D, $$$$, AX/V/MC.
- Sooke Harbour House, 1528 Whiffen Spit Rd., Sooke, 250 642-3421. Innovative, even eccentric, one of Canada's gastronomic treasures. D, $$$$$, V/MC/DC.
- Victoria Harbour House, 607 Oswego St., 250 386-1244. Old-style elegance, Continental dining. D, $$$, AX/V/MC.
- The Temple, 525 Fort St., 250 383-2313. Contemporary regional cuisine in cosmopolitan ambience. L/D, $$$, MC/V/AX.

BISTROS AND CAFÉS

- Barb's Fish & Chips, 310 St. Lawrence St., 250 384-6515. Look inside the blue-painted shack for authentic halibut fish and chips. Closed November to March. L/D/G/T-O, $, no credit cards.
- Bond Bond's, 1010 Blanshard St., 250 388-5377. The city's top bakery makes lunch items, too. Closed Sunday. G/T-O, $, no credit cards.
- Brasserie L'Ecole, 1715 Government St., 250 475-6260. Classic French bistro dishes using Vancouver Island ingredients. D, $$$, MC/V.
- La Collina Bakery, 3115 Cedar Hill Rd., 250 595-2624. Italian bakery featuring pastries, breads and small dinner menu in the evening. L/D, $$$, MC/V.
- Ottavio Gastronomia, 2272 Oak Bay Ave., 250 592-4080. Italian bakery specializing in cheese, pastries, organic gelato and sandwiches. L/D, $$, V.

- Paprika Bistro, 2524 Estevan Ave., 250 592-7424. Vivid, yet light dishes with a Hungarian history. Closed Sunday. D, $$$, AX/V/MC.
- Paradiso di Stelle, 10 Bastion Sq., 250 920-7266. The place to go for a gelato fix. Open 7 days. V/MC.
- Rebar Modern Foods, 50 Bastion Sq., 250 361-9223. Inventive, delicious, healthy food. Kid-friendly. B/L/D, $$, AX/V/MC/DC.
- Zambri's, 110-911 Yates St., 250 360-1171. Best Italian café in town. L/D, $$, AX/V/MC.

SEAFOOD

- Blue Crab Bar and Grill, Coast Victoria Harbourside Hotel, 146 Kingston St., 250 480-1999. Look for Pacific Northwest casual and look out for dessert. B/L/D, $$$, AX/V/MC/DC.
- Dock 503 Waterfront Café, 2320 Harbour Rd., Sidney, 250 656-0828. Zeroes in on the freshest seafood in Sidney. Breakfast, weekend brunch in summer. B/L/D/G, $$$, AX/V/MC/DC.
- Lure, Delta Victoria Ocean Pointe Resort and Spa, 45 Songhees Rd., 250 360-2999. Sleek and contemporary, with impeccable service. B/I /D, $$$$, AX/V/MC/DC.
- Marina Restaurant, 1327 Beach Dr., 250 598-8555. The natural setting for a nautical meal. Sunday Brunch. L/D, $$$-$$$$, AX/V/MC/DC.

BREWPUBS

- Canoe Brewpub, Marina and Restaurant, 450 Swift St., 250 361-1940. Historic waterfront brewpub with modern food. L/D, $$-$$$, MC/V/AX/DC.
- Hugo's Grill and Brewhouse, Magnolia Hotel, 625 Courtney St., 250 920-4846. Hotel brewpub worth a visit. L/D/Late, $$-$$$.
- Irish Times Pub. 1200 Government Street. 250-383-7775. Lots of wood timbers and fireplaces in this historic former bank dating from 1900. Live celtic music nightly. L/D/T-O/Late. $-$$. MC/V/AX.
- Penny Farthing Olde English Pub, 2228 Oak Bay Ave., 250 370-9008. Lively pub that appeals to all ages. L/D, $$-$$$, MC/V/AX.
- Spinnakers Brewpub, 308 Catherine St., 250 384-2739.

Traditional brewery, sausage kitchen, smokehouse and bakery. B/L/D, $$, AX/V/MC.
- Swans Brewpub, Swans Suite Hotel, 506 Pandora St., 250 361-3310. In-house brews and reasonably priced food makes this a popular hangout. B/L/D/Late, $$, AX/V/MC.

TEA

While in Victoria, one must have tea. Keep in mind that many places make a distinction between "Afternoon" or "Light" Tea — small sandwiches, scones, clotted cream, jam, berries and coffee or tea — and High Tea, a more substantial tea with trifles and more of the above.

- Blethering Place Tea Room and Restaurant, 2250 Oak Bay Ave., 250 598-1413. A cozy place in Oak Bay Village. Light Tea, Full Tea, $$, AX/V/MC.
- Butchart Gardens, 800 Benvenuto Ave., Central Saanich, 250 652-8222. Tea in the garden, a fine idea. Afternoon Tea, $$, AX/V/MC.
- Empress Room, the Fairmont Empress Hotel, 721 Government St., 250 384-8111. Afternoon tea served as it should be. Reserve ahead. Dress code in Tea Lobby. High Tea, $$$$, AX/V/MC/DC.
- James Bay Tearoom and Restaurant, 322 Menzies St., 250 382-8282. A favourite for friendliness and prices. Afternoon Tea, High Tea Sunday, $, AX/V/MC.
- Point Ellice House, 2616 Pleasant St., 250 380-6506. Tea served out on the lawn, complete with white wicker, against a heritage house setting overlooking the Gorge. Light Tea, High Tea, $$ per person. AX/V/MC.

ETHNIC

- Daidoco, 633 Courtenay St., 250 388-7383. Open only Mon-Fri, 10a.m. – 6 p.m. Japanese homestyle small plates. Go early as they sell out fast. L, D, T-O, $, V/MC.
- J & J Won Ton Noodle House, 1012 Fort St., 250 383-0680. Savory noodles, soups, mein, fun, simply served. L/D, $, V/MC.
- The Noodle Box, 818 Douglas st., 250 384-1314. Asian-styled wok-cooked takeaway with eight levels of heat. A local favourite. Also at 626 Fisgard. L/D, $, V/MC.

TOP ATTRACTIONS

VANCOUVER

The list that follows gives the sights that define Vancouver to the rest of the world. Travellers who spend even a weekend here, however, will agree there's much more to see and do.

- Vancouver Museum. Fronted by Vancouver's pet stainless steel crab, this odd structure encloses Vancouver's past. Also hosts visiting and temporary exhibits. 1100 Chestnut St., 604 736-4431, www.vanmuseum.bc.ca.

- H. R. MacMillan Space Centre. Space comes to Earth with the Space Centre's hands-on galleries, interactive computer displays, multimedia and laser shows and live demonstrations, while the H.R. MacMillan Planetarium snares the stars on a 20-metre dome. 1100 Chestnut St., 604 738-7827, www.hrmacmillanspacecentre.com.

- Vancouver Maritime Museum. A historic ship, Heritage Harbour, the Children's Maritime Discovery Centre and permanent as well as temporary exhibits pay tribute to Vancouver's seagoing heritage. 1905 Ogden Ave., 604 257-8300, www.vmm.bc.ca.

- Vancouver Aquarium Marine Science Centre. Brings the denizens of different sea habitats into close focus through displays of 60,000 aquatic creatures. Also features special events, behind-the-scenes tours, sleepovers and animal encounters. Stanley Park, 845 Avison Way, 604 659-3474, www.vanaqua.org.

- Canada Place/CN IMAX Theatre. Five white sails hover over the Canada Place convention centre with its wraparound outdoor walkway and stunning views of Vancouver harbour. Included is the CN IMAX Theatre, where the steeply pitched amphitheatre seating, a five-story screen and six-channel IMAX Digital wraparound sound make film-viewing an intense experience. 999 Canada Place Way, 604 682-4629, www.imax.com/vancouver.

- Science World/Alcan OMNIMAX Theatre. Science and entertainment merge in creative, hands-on exhibits inside the mirrored geodesic dome.

The Alcan OMNIMAX Theatre runs documentaries to tremendous effect. 1455 Quebec St., 604 443-7440, www.scienceworld.bc.ca.

- Grouse Mountain/The Peak of Vancouver. Hike up Grouse or take the Skyride aerial tram for panoramic views, fine and casual dining and winter and summer sports at the top. 6400 Nancy Greene Way, North Vancouver, 604 984-0661, www.grousemountain.com.

- Capilano Suspension Bridge and Park. A structure of sturdy steel cables sways high above the forested Capilano River canyon. 3735 Capilano Rd., North Vancouver, 604 985-7474, www.capbridge.com.

- Vancouver Art Gallery. The neo-classical building is a permanent home to a collection of works by Emily Carr, among others, and hosts touring exhibitions, demonstrations and lunch-hour concerts. 750 Hornby St., 604 662-4700, www.vanartgallery.bc.ca.

- UBC Museum of Anthropology. Research and teaching museum-cum-gallery, with artifacts from around the world and one of the world's finest collections of Northwest Coast First Nations art. Free outdoor sculpture garden with totem poles and Haida houses. 6393 N.W. Marine Dr. (University of British Columbia campus), 604 822-5087, www.moa.ubc.ca.

- Stanley Park. One thousand acres of urban wilderness. While its rim has been adapted for recreation, its centre is untamed. 604 257-8400, www.parks.vancouver.bc.ca.

- Dr. Sun Yat-Sen Classical Chinese Garden. A serene garden set in the heart of Chinatown reflects perfect equilibrium in all elements, from design through use. 578 Carrall St., 604 662-3207, www.vancouverchinesegarden.com.

- Storyeum. A journey through BC history performed by talented actors on remarkable underground sets. 142 Water Street, 604 687-8142; 1 800 687 8142, www.storyeum.com.

VICTORIA

- Parliament Buildings. The seat of the Provincial Legislature. Free tours and a live "performance" when the house is in session.

501 Belleville St., 250 387-3046, www.legis.gov.bc.ca.

- Inner Harbour and Fisherman's Wharf. Outdoors where buskers and artisans offer their talents against a view of the harbour. On one side is Fisherman's Wharf, where commercial fishing boats dock. In front of The Fairmont Empress Hotel and Parliament Buildings.
- The Fairmont Empress Hotel. Grand, chateau-style heritage hotel. Famed afternoon tea. 721 Government St., 250 384-8111, www.fairmont.com/empress.
- Chinatown. Two crammed blocks' worth of browsing, shopping and eating almost hides narrow Fan Tan Alley, current home to artist studios and boutiques, former haven for opium dens. Fisgard and Government streets.
- Emily Carr House. Artist and writer Emily Carr's family home, restored and updated with computerized information centre and Canadian artists' gallery. 207 Government St., 250 383-5843, www.heritage. gov.bc.ca/emily/emily.htm.
- Helmcken House. Oldest house in BC still on its original site. Douglas and Belleville Streets, 250 361-0021, www.heritage.gov.bc.ca/helm/ helm.htm.
- Point Ellice House. Meticulously restored house and garden with unusual collection of Victoriana. 2616 Pleasant St., 250 380-6506, www.heritage.gov.bc.ca/point/ point.htm.
- Craigdarroch Castle. Monumental Dunsmuir family stone mansion. No wheelchair access. 1050 Joan Crescent, 250 592-5323, www.craigdarrochcastle.com.
- The Art Gallery of Greater Victoria. 1889 mansion attracting internationally renowned exhibits and housing contemporary BC and other Canadian art, North American, European, Japanese and Chinese works. Moss Street Paint-In festival every August. 1040 Moss St., 250 384-1531 or 250-4101, www.aggv.bc.ca.
- Royal British Columbia Museum. Three permanent galleries — Natural History Gallery, Open Ocean Gallery and the First Peoples and Modern History Gallery — plus multiple exhibits and the National Geographic

IMAX Theatre. 675 Belleville St., 250 356-7226, 1-888-447-7977, www.royalbcmuseum.bc.ca.
- Maritime Museum of British Columbia. Original 1889 provincial courthouse houses artifacts documenting the province's oceangoing history. Treasure hunt for kids. 28 Bastion Sq., 250 385-4222, www.mmbc.bc.ca.

GALLERIES AND MUSEUMS

VANCOUVER

Vancouver's galleries number more than 100 and cover a wide range of expressions: historic art, contemporary, avant garde and traditional. The art is made by First Nations people, Canadians, Asians and Europeans. Check the Thursday editions of *The Georgia Straight* and *Queue Magazine* in the *Vancouver Sun* for details of current shows. *Preview: The Gallery Guide* listings and maps are also useful. An online version can be found at www.preview-art.com.

Galleries

- Access Gallery. New art installations. 206 Carrall St., 604 689-2907.
- Art Emporium. Canadian art. 2928 Granville St., 604 738-3510.
- Artspeak. Phototext and interactive video. 233 Carrall St., 604 688-0051.
- Atelier Gallery. Contemporary art. 2421 Granville St., 604 732-3021.
- Bau-Xi Gallery. Contemporary art. 3045 Granville St., 604 733-7011.
- Bjornson Kajiwara Gallery. Exhibits recent art grads and emerging artists in various genres. 1725 West 3rd Ave., 604 738-3500.
- Buschlen Mowatt Gallery. International art. 1445 West Georgia St., 604 682-1234.
- Catriona Jeffries Gallery. Emphasis is on contemporary art. 3149 Granville St., 604 736-1554.
- Le Centre Culturel Francophone de Vancouver. Shows by French-speaking artists. 1551 West 7th Ave., 604 736-9806.
- Centre A. Shows of Asian art. 849 Homer St., 604 683-8326.
- Charles H. Scott Gallery. Located in the Emily Carr Institute of Art and Design. 1399 Johnston St., Granville Island, 604 844-3809.

- Circle Craft Gallery. Works by BC craft artists. 1-1666 Johnston St., Granville Island, 604 669-8021.
- Crafthouse. BC craft artists. 1386 Cartwright St., Granville Island, 604 687-7270.
- Contemporary Art Gallery. Vanguard works. 555 Nelson St., 604 681-2700.
- Crafthouse Gallery. BC crafts. 1386 Cartwright St., Granville Island, 604 687-6511.
- Diane Farris Gallery. Contemporary art. 1590 West 7th Ave., 604 737-2629.
- Douglas Udell. Western contemporary. 1558 West 6th Ave., 604 736-8900.
- Douglas Reynolds Gallery. Northwest Coast art. 2335 Granville St., 604 731-9292.
- Dundarave Print Workshop. Limited edition prints. 1640 Johnston St., Granville Island, 604 689-1650.
- Equinox Gallery. Contemporary Canadian works. 2321 Granville St., 604 736-2405.
- Gallery of BC Ceramics. Talented local potters. 1359 Cartwright St., Granville Island, 604 669-5645.
- grunt Gallery. First Nations and avant garde art. 116-350 East 2nd Ave., 604 875-9516.
- Harrison Galleries. Traditional Canadian. 2932 Granville St., 604 732-5217.
- Havana Gallery. Emerging artists. 1212 Commercial Dr., 604 253-9119.
- Heffel Gallery. Group of Seven and 19th-century artists. 2247 Granville St., 604 732-6505.
- Inuit Gallery. Museum-quality Inuit art. 206 Cambie St., 604 688-7323.
- Jacana. Oriental furniture and contemporary art. 2435 Granville St., 604 879-9306.
- Kurbatoff Gallery. International art. 2427 Granville St., 604 736-5444.
- Leona Lattimer Gallery. Northwest Coast artists. 1590 West 2nd Ave., 604 732-4556.
- Malaspina Printmakers Gallery. Limited edition prints. 1555 Duranleau St., Granville Island, 604 688-1827.
- Marion Scott Gallery. Inuit art. 308 Water St., 604 685-1934.
- Monte Clark Gallery. Contemporary photography. 2339 Granville St., 604 730-5000.
- Morris and Helen Belkin Gallery at the University of British Columbia. Exhibitions of international and Canadian art. 1825 Main Mall, 604 681-6730.
- New-Small and Sterling Studio Glass. Hot glass blowing and glass works. 1440 Old Bridge St., Granville Island, 604 681-6730.
- The Or Gallery. Conceptual art. 103-480 Smithe St., 604 683-7395.
- Simon Patrich Gallery. Some Latin-American art. 2329 Granville St., 604 733-2662.
- Spirit Wrestler Gallery. First Nations works. 8 Water St., 604 669-8813.
- Spirits of the North. First Nations works. 2327 Granville St., 604 733-8516.
- Uno Langmann. Antiques. 2117 Granville St., 604 736-8825.
- Vancouver Art Gallery. Traditional and contemporary Canadian and European art. 750 Hornby St., 604 662-4719.
- The Waterfall. Four galleries under one roof. 1540 West 2nd Ave., no telephone.

Museums
- BC Sports Hall of Fame and Museum. Chronicles BC's professional and amateur sports and recreation history through displays, hands-on exhibits and multimedia. Gate A, BC Place Stadium, 777 Pacific Blvd. S. 604 687-5520, www.bcsportshalloffame.com.
- Burnaby Village Museum. A turn-of-the-century town with authentically costumed "residents" and restored 1912 carousel called the "Carry-Us-All." 6501 Deer Lake Ave., Burnaby, 604 293-6501.
- Chinese Cultural Centre Museum and Archives. Temporary exhibits Chinese artists, archive of Chinese history in BC. 555 Columbia St., 604 658-8880.
- Granville Island Museums. Three international collections: Sport Fishing Museum, Model Trains Museum, Model Ships Museum. 1502 Duranleau St., Granville Island, 604 683-1939, www.sportfishingmuseum.bc.ca.
- Hastings Mill Store Museum. A charmingly cluttered museum inside Vancouver's oldest building shelters items such as muskets, Native baskets, period clothes, clocks and a coach. 1575 Alma St., 604 734-1212.
- UBC Museum of Anthropology.

Research and teaching museum-cum-gallery, with artifacts from around the world and Northwest Coast First Nations art. Outdoor sculpture garden with totem poles and Haida houses. 6393 N.W. Marine Dr. (University of BC campus), 604 822-5087, www.moa.ubc.ca.

- Vancouver Maritime Museum. A historic ship, Heritage Harbour, the Children's Maritime Discovery Centre and permanent as well as temporary exhibits pay tribute to Vancouver's seagoing heritage. 1905 Ogden Ave., 604 257-8300, www.vmm.bc.ca.
- Vancouver Museum. Vancouver's past plus visiting and temporary exhibits. 1100 Chestnut St., 604 736-4431, www.vanmuseum.bc.ca.
- Vancouver Police Centennial Museum. Crime and crime-fighting paraphernalia, including old photos, gambling displays, artifacts and accounts of ancient unsolved murders. 240 East Cordova St., 604 665-3346.

VICTORIA

Museums

- Maritime Museum of British Columbia. The original 1889 provincial courthouse houses artifacts documenting British Columbia's oceangoing history. Treasure hunt for kids. 28 Bastion Sq., 250 385-4222, www.mmbc.bc.ca.
- Royal British Columbia Museum. Three permanent galleries (Natural History Gallery, Open Ocean Gallery and the First Peoples and Modern History Gallery) plus multiple exhibits and the National Geographic IMAX Theatre. 675 Belleville St., 250 356-7226, 1-888-447-7977, www.royalbcmuseum.bc.ca.
- Royal London Wax Museum. Wax figures of famous and infamous characters in history, show business and literature. 470 Belleville St., 250 388-4461, www.waxworld.com.

VANCOUVER ENTERTAINMENT

In addition to a well-known film and television production industry, entertainment in Vancouver can be found live at clubs, theatres and arts centres around town. Alliance for Arts and Culture (www.allianceforarts.com) is a valuable resource, and *The Georgia Straight* publishes weekly events listings as well. Ticketmaster operates an Arts Line at 604 280-3311. Note that those under 19 years of age are not allowed in nightclubs serving alcohol.

CLUBS

- Au Bar, 647 Seymour St., 604 647-2227. Popular, chic dance club.
- Body Perve Social Club, last Saturday of each month. Lotus Sound Lounge, 455 Abbott St., 604 685-7777. Fetish.
- The Gérard Lounge (Sutton Place Hotel), 845 Burrard St., 604 682-5511. Attracts celebrities and a moneyed crowd.
- Honey Lounge, 455 Abbott St., 604 685-7777. Elegant mixed club that is lesbian friendly.
- Lick, 455 Abbott St., 604 685-7777. Women only.
- Numbers Cabaret, 1042 Davie St., 604 685-4077. Four split-levels and a pair of bars are crammed with a regular gay clientele.
- Odyssey, 1251 Howe St., 604 689-5256. Caters to a loyal gay crowd, features alternative dance music.
- Pumpjack Pub, 1167 Davie St., 604 685-3417. Gay club.
- Richard's On Richards, 1036 Richards St., 604 687-6794. Posh club with local bands, international recording acts and DJ dance music.
- Skybar, 670 Smithe St., 604 697-9199. Three levels with open rooftop.

THEATRE

- Arts Club Mainstage and Revue Theatre, 1585 Johnston St., Granville Island, 604 687-1644. Western Canada's largest regional theatre and a local institution.
- Firehall Arts Centre, 280 East Cordova St., 604 689-0926. Converted fire station specializing in alternative theatre, performance art and dance.
- Hoarse Raven Theatre, 1160 Rossland St., 604 258-4079, www.hoarseraven.com
- Metro Theatre Centre, 1370 S.W. Marine Dr., 604 266-7191. Attracts a loyal, mature audience looking for British comedy.
- Norman Rothstein Theatre, 950

West 41st Ave., 604 257-5111. State-of-the-art theatre in the Jewish Community Centre.
- Presentation House Arts Centre, 333 Chesterfield Ave., North Vancouver, 604 990-3473. Terrific community theatre.
- Queen Elizabeth Theatre. 600 Block Hamilton St., 604 665-3050. Glitzy, glamorous Broadway-style productions.
- St. Andrew Wesley's Church (Tony & Tina's Wedding), 1012 Nelson St., 604 280-3311 (Ticketmaster). Dinner theatre that begins in a real church and ends with the reception a short distance away.
- Stanley Theatre, 2750 Granville St., 604 687-1644. The Arts Club's third stage in a former vaudeville venue and movie theatre.
- Urban Well Kits Beach, 1516 Yew St., 604 737-7770. Adult improv comedy.
- Vancouver Playhouse. 600 Block Hamilton St., 604 873-3311. One of the best regional theatres in Canada.
- Waterfront Theatre, 1410 Cartwright St., Granville Island, 604 685-6217. Big stage in a small theatre where many Canadian works debut.

MUSIC AND DANCE
- Chan Centre for the Performing Arts, 6265 Crescent Rd., University of BC, 604 822-9197. Best acoustics in town.
- The Commodore Ballroom, 868 Granville St., 604 739-7469. Hosts an eclectic range of artists.
- Judith Marcuse Dance Projects, 604 606-6425. Ambitious, long-time local company performs at various locations.
- Kokoro Dance, 604 662-7441. Small, innovative company performs at various locations.
- Orpheum Theatre, 884 Granville St., 604 665-3050. Old-time, elegant home of the Vancouver Symphony Orchestra.
- Vancouver East Cultural Centre (The Cultch), 1895 Venables St., 604 251-1363. BC's most diverse performance space.
- Vogue Theatre, 918 Granville St., 604 331-7909. Hosts top musical acts and film screenings during the Vancouver International Film Festival.
- Seb's Market Café, 592 East Broadway, 604 298-4403. Cozy restaurant with jazz trio.
- The Cellar Jazz Club, 3611 West Broadway, 604 738-1959. Mellow jazz in a neighbourhood setting.
- The Yale, 1300 Granville St., 604 681-9253. One of the world's best blues bars.

PARKS AND GARDENS

Mild in climate and outdoors-oriented, Vancouver and Victoria are rife with gardens. The following lists a few that shouldn't be missed:

VICTORIA
- Beacon Hill Park, bounded by Dallas Rd. and Douglas, Southgate and Heywood streets, 250 361-0600. Victoria's oldest and largest park with wading pool, swans, ducks, English-style rose garden and exotic trees.
- Butchart Gardens, 800 Benvenuto Ave., Central Saanich, Vancouver Island, 250 652-4422, www.butchartgardens.com. Twenty-two hectares of lush gardens on the historic site of a former rock quarry.

VANCOUVER
- Century Gardens at Deer Lake Park, 6344 Deer Lake Ave., Burnaby, www.city.burnaby.bc.ca. Rhododendrons are Burnaby's official flower, and flourish on the grounds of the Burnaby Art Gallery.
- Dr. Sun Yat-Sen Garden, 578 Carrall St., 604 662-3207, www.vancouverchinesegarden.com. Authentic, full-scale classical Chinese garden offering tours and a popular summertime evening concert series.
- Park & Tilford Gardens, 440 - 333 Brooksbank Ave., North Vancouver, 604 984-8200. A garden oasis on the edge of a shopping centre.
- Queen Elizabeth Park and Bloedel Floral Conservatory, West 33rd Ave. and Cambie St., 604 257-8570, www.parks.vancouver.bc.ca. Quarry garden atop Little Mountain offers showy natural surroundings and a view of the city. The Conservatory, Canada's largest triodetic dome, encloses tropical birds and plants as well as desert and exotic plants.
- Riverview Lands Davidson Arboretum, 500 Lougheed Hwy., Coquitlam, 604 290-9910. Free spring to fall tours are offered by the

Riverview Horticultural Society of the more than 1,800 trees on the Riverview Hospital grounds.
- Stanley Park's gardens. Stanley Park, 604 257-8400 or 604 257-8544 for nature walks, www.parks.vancouver.bc.ca. Gardens flourishing in heavily forested Stanley Park include the Rose Garden and the Ted and Mary Grieg Rhododendron Garden.
- UBC Botanical Garden, 6804 S.W. Marine Dr., 604 822-9666, www.ubcbotanicalgarden.org. A living teaching and research library spread over 30 hectares (74 acres). UBC also includes Alpine, Asian, Japanese Nitobe Memorial and BC native gardens with unusual and new locally developed plants. Parking is free.
- VanDusen Botanical Garden, 5251 Oak St., 604 878-9274, www.vandusengarden.org. Themed gardens on 22 hectares of former golf course include Asian, Children's, Fragrance, Meditation, and Canadian Heritage gardens, a maze and fern dell.

ACTIVITIES AND SPECTATOR SPORTS

Vancouver is host to professional and amateur sports, as well as a wide range of year-round outdoor activities.

SPORTS

- Alcan Dragon Boat Festival. Colourful dragon boats compete as part of the Alcan Dragon Boat Festival. False Creek, 604 688-2382, www.adbf.com.
- BC Lions Football. Canadian Football League franchise. BC Place Stadium, 765 Pacific Blvd., 604 661-7373 or 604 589-7627, www.bclions.com.
- BC Sports Hall of Fame and Museum. Gate A, BC Place Stadium, 604 687-5520, www.bcsportshalloffame.com.
- Fraser Downs Racecourse. Harness racing from October to April. 17755 60th Ave., Surrey, 604 576-9141, www.fraserdowns.com.
- Hastings Racecourse. Thoroughbred racing live or via satellite. Located in Hastings Park, off Renfrew, Gate 6. 604 254-1631,

www.hastingsracecourse.com.
- Vancouver Canadians. Minor league affiliate of Oakland Athletics. Nat Bailey Stadium, 4601 Ontario St., 604 872-5232, www.canadiansbaseball.com.
- Vancouver Canucks. National Hockey League franchise. General Motors Place, 800 Griffiths Way, 604 899-4610, www.canucks.com.
- Vancouver Giants. Western Hockey League team. Pacific Coliseum, 100 North Renfrew St., 604 444-2687, www.vancouvergiants.com.
- Vancouver Whitecaps/Whitecaps Women. Professional men's and women's soccer, Swanguard Stadium, Central Park, Burnaby, 604 669-9283, www.whitecapsfc.com.
- Western Lacrosse Association. 604 421-9755, www.theboxrocks.com. Six BC teams (five local) compete in this fast-paced, all-Canadian game at several venues in the Lower Mainland.

OUTDOOR ACTIVITIES

Cycling, hiking, swimming and lying on the beach can be done at will, almost anywhere. Beaches and parks in the city are the responsibility of the Vancouver Board of Parks and Recreation (604 257-8400). The following list provides useful information for a number of other recreational activities.

Cycling

- Cycling British Columbia, 1367 West Broadway, 604 737-3034, www.cycling.bc.ca. Information on BMX, road and track and mountain biking competitions.

Skiing and Snowboarding

- Cypress Mountain. Great place for toboggans and inner tubes, with groomed trails for skiing. West Vancouver. Weather and trail information: 604 926-6007. Programs: 604 926-5612. www.cypressmountain.com.
- Grouse Mountain. Sleigh rides and outdoor ice-skating as well as downhill and cross-country skiing and snowboarding. 6400 Nancy Greene Way, North Vancouver. Snow reports: 604 986-6262. Programs: 604 984-0661. www.grousemountain.com.
- Mount Seymour. Backcountry and

downhill skiing, toboggans and inner tubes. 1700 Mount Seymour Rd., North Vancouver. Weather and conditions: 604 718-7771. Programs and special events: 604 986-2261. www.mountseymour.com.

Birdwatching

• Reifel Bird Sanctuary, 5191 Robertson Road on Westham Island, Ladner, 604 946-6980, www.reifelbirdsanctuary.com. Wetlands environment is especially attractive to shorebirds and migrating birds.

Canoeing, Kayaking, Windsurfing

• Canoeing, whitewater kayaking and sea kayaking information is available from the Outdoor Recreation Council of British Columbia, 604 737-3058, www.orcbc.ca.

Golfing

• Fraserview Golf Course, 7800 Vivian Dr., 604 257-6923 (Pro Shop) or 604 280-1818 (Tee Time), www.vancouver.bc.ca. A busy South Vancouver course.
• Furry Creek Golf and Country Club, 150 Country Club Rd., Furry Creek, 604 896-2224, www.golfbc.com. For water views and a course carved from a mountainside.
• Langara Golf Course, 6706 Alberta St., 604 713-1816 (Pro Shop) or 604 280-1818 (Tee Time). Popular city golf course. www.parks.vancouver.bc.ca.
• Mayfair Lakes Golf & Country Club, 5460 #7 Rd., Richmond, 604 276-0585, www.golfbc.com. Challenges the golfer with many water hazards.
• Stanley Park Pitch & Putt, 2099 Beach Ave., 604 681-8847 (seasonal). City-operated course in park setting. www.parks.vancouver.bc.ca.
• Queen Elizabeth Park Pitch & Putt, 33rd Ave. and Cambie St., 604 874-8336. Scenic park setting. www.parks.vancouver.bc.ca.
• University Golf Club, 5185 University Blvd., 604 224-1818. Beautiful, well-maintained course on the UBC grounds. www.universitygolf.com.

Swimming

• Kitsilano Pool, 2305 Cornwall Ave., 604 731-0011. Gigantic outdoor

saltwater pool o www.parks.vanc May to Aug.
• Vancouver Aquatic Beach Ave., 604 66 www.parks.vancouv
• Vancouver beaches, www.parks.vancouver.bc.ca.

KIDS' STUFF

INDOORS

• Alcan OMNIMAX Theatre, Science World. Runs documentaries to tremendous effect. 1455 Quebec St., 604 443-7440, www.scienceworld.bc.ca.
• CN IMAX Theatre, Canada Place. Film-viewing becomes an intense experience with big sound and bigger screens. Check with staff to determine if the film is too intense for young children. 999 Canada Place Way, 604 682-4629, www.imax.com/vancouver.
• H. R. MacMillan Space Centre and Planetarium. Hands-on galleries, interactive computer displays, multimedia and laser shows and live demonstrations bring space and the stars down to Earth. 1100 Chestnut St., 604 738-7827, www.hrmacmillanspacecentre.com.
• Science World. Science and entertainment merge in creative, hands-on exhibits inside the mirrored geodesic dome. 1455 Quebec St., 604 443-7440, www.scienceworld.bc.ca.
• Vancouver Aquarium Marine Science Centre. Brings the denizens of different dark sea habitats into close focus through aquatic displays, live shark dives, feedings and dolphin shows. Also features the new Pacific Canada Pavilion, behind-the-scenes tours, sleepovers and special animal encounters. Stanley Park, 845 Avison Way, 604 659-3474, www.vanaqua.org.

OUTDOORS

• Capilano Suspension Bridge. Hang high above the forested Capilano River canyon on a swaying structure of sturdy steel cables, visit the totem poles and exhibits. 3735 Capilano Rd., North Vancouver, 604 985-7474, www.capbridge.com.
• Reifel Bird Sanctuary. Feed the birds or view a wetlands ecosystem.

..obertson Rd., Ladner, . 946-6980, www.reifelbirdsanctuary.com.
- Greater Vancouver Zoo. Home to 93 animal species. 5048 264th St., Aldergrove, 604 856-6825, www.greatervancouverzoo.com.
- Lynn Canyon Park. Begin a hike in Lynn Headwaters Regional Park with a visit to the Ecology Centre and brave the swinging footbridge high above the rapids of Lynn Creek. Lynn Canyon entrance on Park Rd., 604 981-3103.
- Maplewood Farm. Small petting farm with seasonal special events and weekend pony rides. 405 Seymour River Pl., North Vancouver, 604 929-5610, www.maplewoodfarm.bc.ca.
- Pacific Spirit Regional Park. Experience BC's coastal cedar and fir forests firsthand with an easy hike through the many trails. West 16th Ave. and Blanca (Visitor Centre), 604 224-5739.
- Playland. Outdoor amusement park rides, midway games and cotton candy from April to Labour Day. Pacific National Exhibition Park, 604 253-2311, www.pne.bc.ca.
- Stanley Park. Kids' attractions include the Children's Farm Yard and Miniature Railway, and the totem poles at Lower Brockton Oval. 2099 Beach Ave., 604 257-8400.
- VanDusen Botanical Garden. Themed gardens on 55 acres include Children's Garden and Heritage and Elizabethan Hedge Maze. Many popular special events. 5251 Oak St., 604 878-9274, www.vandusengarden.org.

WATERPLAY

- Canada Games Pool and Fitness Centre. Olympic-size pool and teaching/toddler pool. 65 East 6th Ave., New Westminster, 604 526-4281.
- Eileen Dailly Leisure Pool and Fitness Centre. Burnaby's best indoor pool and community centre. 240 Willingdon Ave., Burnaby, 604 298-7946.
- Granville Island Water Park. Wet adventure playground with water cannons, spouts, waterslide and wading areas. Near Sutcliffe Park, Granville Island, 604 666-5784.
- Kitsilano Pool. Gigantic outdoor saltwater pool. 2305 Cornwall Ave., 604 731-0011. (May to August)
- Newton Wave Pool. Metre-high waves for bodysurfing and waterslides. 13730 72nd Ave., Surrey, 604 501-5540, 604 594-7873.
- Second Beach Pool. Features three small waterslides. Stanley Park, 604 783-8535 (mid-May to mid-October).
- Splashdown Park. Twisting waterslides, hot tubs and smaller-sized equipment for little kids. 4799 Nu Lelum Way, Tsawwassen, 604 943-2251.
- Stanley Park Water Park. Wet adventure playground with equipment suitable for children with physical disabilities. Near Lumberman's Arch, Stanley Park, 604 257-8400.
- Vancouver Aquatic Centre. Olympic-size indoor and outdoor pools and toddler pool. 1050 Beach Ave., 604 665-3424.
- Vancouver beaches. Second and Third Beach, English Bay, Sunset Beach, Kits Beach, Jericho Beach, Locarno Beach and Spanish Banks. Beach information: 604 665-3418, mid-May to mid-September.

CHILDREN'S CULTURE

- Arts Umbrella. Classes in dance, acting, animation and filmmaking for those on longer stays. 1286 Cartwright St., Granville Island, 604 681-5268, www.artsumbrella.com.
- Buschlen Mowatt Gallery. Hosts annual visual art show by budding artists in spring. 1445 West Georgia St., 604 682-1234.
- Vancouver East Cultural Centre Kids' Series. Saturday afternoon musical or dramatic performances monthly. Also a Youth Program discounting admission for youth to $2. 1895 Venables St., 604 251-1363, www.vecc.bc.ca.
- Vancouver International Children's Festival. Week-long event featuring quality performances, roving entertainers, face painters and a multicultural community stage. Vanier Park, 1100 Chestnut St., 604 708-5655, www.childrensfestival.ca.
- Vancouver Public Library. Children's floor has CD-ROM stations, videos, books and displays of children's art. 350 West Georgia St., 604 331-3600.

- Vancouver International Comedy Festival. Free and funny street entertainment and some ticketed family-oriented events. Granville Island, 604 683-0883, www.comedyfest.com.
- Vancouver International Writers (and Readers) Festival. Mid-October writers' festival has three days of children's events. Granville Island, 604 681-6330, www.writersfest.bc.ca.
- Vancouver Kidsbooks. Readings, book launches and book signings complement the huge variety of children's books. 3083 West Broadway Ave., 604 738-5335, www.kidsbooks.ca.

HISTORY AND LIVING CULTURE

- BC Sports Hall of Fame and Museum. BC's past professional and amateur sports and recreation history. Displays, a Participation Gallery and multimedia. Gate A, BC Place Stadium, 765 Pacific Blvd. South, 604 687-5520, www.bcsportshalloffame.com.
- Burnaby Village Museum and Carousel. Recreation of a 1920s village with hands-on activities, restored carousel and special events. 6501 Deer Lake Ave., Burnaby, 604 293-6501.
- Cedar Cottage/Trout Lake Pow Wow. Mother's Day event featuring intertribal dancing, drumming, hoop dancing, pageant and displays presents the cultural traditions of Canada's First Nations people. Trout Lake Community Centre, 3350 Victoria Dr., 604 874-4231.
- Fort Langley National Historic Park. Sample life as it was in the last century in this reconstructed Hudson's Bay Company post. 23433 Mavis, Fort Langley, 604 513-4777.

VANCOUVER ANNUAL EVENTS

JANUARY

- Polar Bear Swim. A New Year's Day plunge into the Pacific Ocean on English Bay. Vancouver Aquatic Centre, 604 665-3418.
- Brackendale Winter Eagle Festival and Count. Just after the New Year begins, an eagle count is taken, and related events are hosted all month. Squamish-Brackendale area, 604 898-3333.
- Chinese New Year's Festival. Chinatown greets the first day of the lunar year (in January or February) with festivals and events, 604 273-1655.

FEBRUARY

- Vancouver International Boat Show. Consumer show featuring the latest in boating. BC Place Stadium, Coal Harbour Marina, 604 678-8820.
- BC Home and Garden Show. The largest consumer home show in Western Canada. BC Place Stadium, 604 433-5121.

MARCH

- Festival du bois. Maillardville celebrates voyageur traditions and French-Canadian music, dance and food. Maillardville, Coquitlam.
- Vancouver Playhouse International Wine Festival. Week-long fund-raising celebration of good wine and food. Vancouver Convention and Exhibition Centre, 604 872-6622, www.playhousewinefest.com.

MAY

- Vancouver International Marathon. Canada's largest marathon. Starts at the Plaza of Nations, 604 872-2928, www.vanmarathon.bc.ca.
- Vancouver International Children's Festival. A week of quality performances, roving entertainers, face painters and a multicultural community stage, all for kids. Vanier Park, 604 708-5655, www.youngarts.ca.

JUNE

- Alcan Dragon Boat Festival. Dragon boats race in the largest dragon boat festival in North America. False Creek, 604 688-2382, www.adbf.com.
- Vancouver International Jazz Festival. Something for every jazz lover in the 400 or so performances held downtown, 604 872-5200, www.jazzvancouver.com.
- Bard on the Beach. Shakespeare is staged in a backless tent to take advantage of the magical natural backdrop. Shows from June to September. Vanier Beach, 604 739-0559 or 737-0625, www.bardonthebeach.org.

JULY

- Vancouver International Comedy Festival. Performances from a diverse mix of comic artists. Granville Island, 604 683-0883, www.comedyfest.com.
- Celebration of Light fireworks. Pyrotechnicians from different countries set fireworks to music in a four-day competition from late July to early August. English Bay, www.celebration-of-light.com.
- Festival Vancouver. Two-week-long festival featuring an array of classical, jazz and world music. Various venues throughout the city, 604 688-1152, www.festivalvancouver.bc.ca.
- Vancouver International Folk Music Festival. Hugely popular annual celebration of folk music. Jericho Beach, 604 602-9798, www.thefestival.bc.ca.

AUGUST

- Abbotsford International Airshow. Aerial displays and aerobatics. Abbotsford Airport, 604 852-8511.
- Pacific National Exhibition. Demolition derby, petting farm, Superdogs show, exhibits, midway games and amusement park rides. Win a house, win a car, eat candy floss and corndogs. Pacific National Exhibition Park, 604 253-2311, www.pne.bc.ca.
- Powell Street Festival. A celebration of Japanese-Canadian history and traditional Japanese food, music and entertainment. Oppenheimer Park, Powell St., 604 682-4335.
- Squamish Nations Pow Wow, Aboriginal Cultural Festival. Traditional dancing and drumming and cuisine. Capilano Reserve, Squamish Territory, North Vancouver, 604 986-2120, www.squamish.net.

SEPTEMBER

- Chilliwack Bluegrass Festival. Camp out for the bluegrass performances, 604 792-2069.
- Vancouver Fringe Festival. Alternative theatre performances by emerging and established companies, 604 257-0350, www.vancouverfringe.com.
- Vancouver International Film Festival. Over 250 innovative and accessible films from around the world. Various venues, 604 685-0260, www.viff.org.

OCTOBER

- Vancouver International Writers (and Readers) Festival. One week of readings, talks and other events featuring local and international writers. Granville Island, 604 681-6330, www.writersfest.bc.ca.

DECEMBER

- Carol Ships Parade of Lights. Carollers sail on ships decked out with lights. Vancouver Harbour, 604 682-2007.

EXCURSIONS

WHISTLER

- Whistler Activity and Information Centre. 4010 Whistler Way, Whistler, BC V0N 1B4, 604 938-2769, 1-877-991-9988, www.mywhistler.com.
- Whistler's Central Reservations Service. Official central reservations for Whistler Resort. 604 664-5625 in Vancouver;1-800-944-7853 in Canada and the US; 604 664-5625 direct; Fax: 604 938-5758, www.mywhistler.com.
- Resort Reservations Whistler. Intrawest's accommodations and activities centre also books customized vacation packages. 604 932-3434, 1-866-218-9690, www.whistlerblackcomb.com.
- Vancouver/Whistler 2010 Olympic and Paralympic Winter Games. www.winter2010.com.

THE GULF ISLANDS

- Tourism Vancouver Island, Old City Square, 203-335 Wesley St., Nanaimo, BC V9R 2T5, 250 754-3500, Fax: 250 754-3599, www.islands.bc.ca

THE SUNSHINE COAST

- Big Pacific, Lower Coast Visitor Info, 604 885-0662, Upper Coast Visitor Info, 604 485-4701, www.bigpacific.com. Provides information on the Sunshine Coast and helps visitors find accommodations, dining and entertainment.

SHOPPING

VANCOUVER

NEIGHBOURHOODS

Georgia and Granville

- The Bay, Georgia & Granville streets, 604 681-6211.
- Bentall Centre, Burrard and Dunsmuir streets, 604 661-5656.
- Cadillac Fairview Pacific Centre, 700 West Georgia St., 604 688-7236.
- Royal Centre, 1055 West Georgia St., 604 689-1711.
- Vancouver Art Gallery Shop, 750 Hornby St., 604 662-4706.

Robson Street

- Banana Republic, 1098 Robson St., 604 331-8285.
- The Gap, 9-1121 Robson St., 604 683-0906.
- Mexx, 1119 Robson St., 604 801-6399.
- Roots, 1001 Robson St., 604 683-4305.

Gastown

- Deluxe Junk, 310 West Cordova St., 604 685-4871.
- Hill's Native Art, 165 Water St., 604 685-4249.
- Inuit Gallery, 206 Cambie St., 604 688-7323.
- Salmegundi West, 321 West Cordova St., 604 681-4648.
- The Edinburgh Tartan Gift Shop, The Landing, 375 Water St., 604 646-3915.

Granville Island

- Edie's Hats, 11-1666 Johnston St., 604 683-4280.
- El Greco Jewellery, 1660 Johnston St., 604 681-0942.
- Granville Island Public Market, 1689 Johnston St., 604 666-6477.
- Kids Only Market (Kids Market) 1496 Cartwright St., 604 689-8447.

ANTIQUES AND COLLECTIBLES

- Ages Ago Used Furniture and Antiques, 4373 Main St., 604 876-3055.
- Baker's Dozen, 3520 Main St., 604 879-3348.
- Farmhouse Collections, 2915 Granville St., 604 738-0167 and 1098 S.W. Marine Dr. SW, 604 261-3681.

- Folkart Interiors, 3651 West 10th Ave., 604 731-7576.
- Small Comforts Antiques, 1525 West 6th Ave., 604 222-4992.
- Hampshire Antiques, 3007 Granville St., 604 733-1326.
- Second Time Around, 4428 Main St., 604 879-2313.
- William Robert Antiques, 1529 West 14th Ave., 604 731-0808.

BOOK STORES

- Banyen Books and Sound, 3608 West 4th Ave., 604 732-7912.
- Chapters, 788 Robson St., 604 682-4066. Additional locations: 4700 Kingsway, Burnaby, 604 431-0463 and 2505 Granville St., 604 731-7822 and 8171 Ackroyd Rd., Richmond, 604 303-7392.
- Duthie Books, 2239 West 4th Ave., 604 732-5344.
- Granville Book Company, 850 Granville St., 604 687-2213.
- Kidsbooks, 3083 West Broadway Ave., 604 738-5335. Additional location: 3040 Edgemont Blvd., North Vancouver, 604 986-6190.
- Little Sister's Book Store, 1238 Davie St., 604 669-1753, 1-800-567-1662.

CANADIAN CLOTHING DESIGNERS

- A-Wear Clothing, 757 West Hastings St., 604 685-9327.
- Dorothy Grant, 1656 West 75th Ave., 604 681-0201.
- JC Studio, 46 West 6th Ave., 604 688-5222.
- Margareta Design, 2448 West 41st Ave., 604 264-4625.
- Tilley Endurables, 2401 Granville St., 604 732-4287.
- Zonda Nellis Design, 2203 Granville St., 604 736-5668.

CHILDREN'S STORES

- Bobbit's for Kids, 2935 West 4th Ave., 604 738-0333.
- Isola Bella Design, 5692 Yew St., 604 266-8808.
- Kaboodles Toy Store, 4449 West 10th Ave., (604) 224-5311 and 1496 Cartwright St., Granville Island, 604 684-0066.
- Kidsbooks, 3083 West Broadway Ave., 604 738-5335. Additional location: 3040 Edgemont Blvd., North Vancouver, 604 986-6190.
- Kids Only Market (Kids Market), 1496 Cartwright St., Granville Island, 604 689-8447.

- Please Mum, 2041 West 41st Ave., 604 264-0366 and 2951 West Broadway Ave., 604 732-4574. Also in many malls.
- The Toybox, 3002 West Broadway Ave., 604 738-4322.
- Toys R Us, 1154 West Broadway Ave., 604 733-8697.

CHINA AND CRYSTAL
- Atkinson's, 1501 West 6th Ave., 604 736-3378.
- Chintz and Company, 950 Homer St., 604 689-0022.
- W.H. Puddifoot & Co., 2375 West 41st Ave., 604 261-8141.

DESIGNER BOUTIQUES
- Bacci Design, 2788 Granville St., 604 733-4933.
- Boboli, 2776 Granville St., 604 257-2300.
- Chanel, 900 West Hastings St., 604 682-0522.
- Dyanna's, 355 Howe St., 604 685-4225.
- Edward Chapman's Ladies Shops, 2596 Granville St., 604 732-3394. Also at 750 West Pender St., 604 688-6711 and Oakridge Centre, 604 261-8161.
- Enda B Fashions, 4346 West 10th Ave., 604 228-1214 and 2625 Granville St., 604 733-2000.
- Gianni Versace Boutique, 757 West Hastings St., 604 683-1131.
- Leone Fashions, 757 West Hastings St., 604 683-1133.
- Plaza Escada, 757 West Hastings St., 604 688-8558.

FIRST NATIONS ART AND JEWELLERY
- Hill's Native Art, 165 Water St., 604 685-4249.
- Inuit Gallery, 206 Cambie St., 604 688-7323.
- Lattimer Gallery, 1590 West 2nd Ave., 604 732-4556.
- Marion Scott Gallery, 308 Water St., 604 685-1934.
- Museum of Anthropology, 6393 N.W. Marine Dr. (University of BC campus), 604 822-5087.

GIFT SHOPS
- Bookmark — Vancouver Public Library Gift Shop, 350 West Georgia St., 604 331-4040.
- Chachkas, 1075 Robson St., 604 688-6417.
- Circle Craft Co-op, 1-1666 Johnston St., Granville Island, 604 669-8021.

- Moulé, 1944 West 4th Ave., 604 732-4066.
- The Museum Company, 53D-701 West Georgia St., 604 688-1502.
- Obsessions Gift Shop, 289 Davie St., 604 683 0188; 1124 Denman St., 604 605-8890; 101 - 595 Howe St., 604 684-0748.
- Vancouver Art Gallery Shop, 750 Hornby St., 604 662-4706.

HOME FURNISHINGS
- Country Furniture, 3097 Granville St., 604 738-6411.
- Industrial Revolution, 2306 Granville St., 604 734-4395.
- Jordan's, 1470 West Broadway Ave., 604 733-1174.
- Koolhaus, 2199 West 4th Ave., 604 875-9004.
- Sofa So Good, 2219 Cambie St., 604 879-4878.
- Upholstery Arts, 2430 Burrard St., 604 731-9020.

JEWELLERY
- Birks Jewellers, 698 West Hastings St., 604 669-3333 and 118-650 West 41st Ave., 604 266-2301.
- Karl Stittgen Goldsmiths, 2203 Granville St., 604 737-0029.
- Martha Sturdy Originals, 3039 Granville St., 604 737-0037.
- Tiffany & Co. at Holt Renfrew, 633 Granville St., 604 681-3121.

LEATHER
- Castle Milano, 248-757 West Hastings St., 604 647-0202.
- Danier Leather, 1018 Robson St., 604 689-7330. Also in Pacific Centre, 604 683-6846 and Oakridge, 604 266-0775. Factory outlet, 3003 Grandview Hwy., 604 432-6137.
- Mack's Leathers, 1043 Granville St., 604 688-6225.
- French Laundry By Neto, 252 East 2nd Ave., 604 875-8474.

MALLS
- Aberdeen Centre, 4400 Hazelbridge Way, Richmond, 604 273-1234.
- Arbutus Village Square, 4255 Arbutus St., 604 732-4255.
- Bentall Centre, Burrard and Dunsmuir streets, 604 661-5656.
- Brookfield Royal Centre, 1055 West Georgia St., 604 689-1711.
- Cadillac Fairview Pacific Centre, 700 West Georgia St., 604 688-7236.
- Central City Shopping Centre, 102 Ave. and King George Hwy., Surrey,

604 588-6431.
- City Square, 555 West 12th Ave., 604 876-5165.
- Guildford Town Centre, 2695 Guildford Town Centre, Surrey, 604 585-1565.
- Lougheed Mall Shopping Centre, 9855 Austin, 604 421-2882.
- Metropolis at Metrotown, 4700 Kingsway, Burnaby, 604 438-4715.
- Oakridge Centre, 650 West 41st Ave., 604 261-2511.
- Park Royal Shopping Centre, 2002 Park Royal South, West Vancouver, 604 925-9576.
- Richmond Centre, 6551 #3 Rd., Richmond, 604 713-7467.
- Vancouver Centre, 650 West Georgia St., 604 688-5658.
- Yaohan Centre, 3700 #3 Rd., Richmond, 604 231-0601.

MUSIC
- A & B Sound, 556 Seymour St., 604 687-5837. Also at 3433 East Hastings St., 604 298-0464, 3434 Cornett Road, 604 430-2999, and 732 S.W. Marine Dr., 604 321-5112.
- Highlife Records & Music, 1317 Commercial Dr., 604 251-6964.
- HMV Canada, 1160 Robson St., and Metropolis at Metrotown, 604 430-1699.
- Zulu Records, 1972 West 4th Ave., 604 738-3232.

MEN'S CLOTHING
- Boboli, 2776 Granville St., 604 257-2300.
- Boys' Co., 1044 Robson St., 604 684-5656. Also at Oakridge Centre, 604 266-0388, 910 Richards St., 604 687-2221, Metrotown Centre, 604 431-1866 and Richmond Centre, 604 303-0374.
- Chevalier Creations, 620 Seymour St., 604 687-8428 or 604 687-4643.
- Eddie Bauer, Oakridge Centre, 604 261-2621, Pacific Centre, 604 683-4711, Park Royal Centre, 604 925-0858.
- Enda B Fashion, 4346 West 10th Ave., 604 228-1214 and 2625 Granville St., 604 733-2000.
- Harry Rosen Men's Wear, 700 West Georgia St., 604 683-6861 and Oakridge Centre, 604 266-1172.
- Holt Renfrew, 633 Granville St., 604 681-3121.
- Leone Fashions, 757 West Hastings St., 604 683-1133.

- Mark James, 2941 West Broadway Ave., 604 734-2381.
- Roots, 1001 Robson St., 604 683-4305; Metropolis at Metrotown, 604 435-5554; Guildford Town Centre, 604 583-0689; Grandview Factory Outlet, 3695 Grandview Hwy., 604 433-4337; Oakridge Centre, 604 266-6229; Richmond Centre, 604 244-9113; Park Royal Shopping Centre, 604 925-2166.
- S. Lampman, 2126 West 41st Ave., 604 261-2750.
- Tilley Endurables Adventure Clothing, 2401 Granville St., 604 732-4287.
- Vasanji Boutique, 1012 Mainland St., 604 669-0882.

SHOE STORES
- Dayton Boots, 872 Granville St., 604 682-2668 and 2250 East Hastings St., 604 253-6671.
- Ingledew's Shoes 535 Granville St., 604 687-8606.
- John Fluevog Boots and Shoes, 837 Granville St., 604 688-2828.
- Salvatore Ferragamo, 918 Robson St., 604 669-4495 or 604 669-2218.
- Stephane de Raucourt Shoes, 1067 Robson St., 604 681-8814 and Oakridge Centre, 604 261-7419.

VICTORIA

FAIRMONT EMPRESS HOTEL AND VICTORIA CONVENTION CENTRE
- Art of Man Gallery, 721 Government St., 250 383-3800.
- The Body Shop, 1150 Douglas St., 250 383-0881
- Collections by Madison Avenue, 736 Douglas St., 250 380-0697.
- La Cache, 1150 Douglas St., 250 384-6343.
- Stephen Lowe Art Gallery, 752 Douglas St., 250 384-3912.

GOVERNMENT STREET
- British Importers, the Bay Centre, 250 386-1496.
- Christmas House, 1209 Wharf St., 250 388-9627.
- Copithorne and Row, 901 Government St., 250 384-1722.
- The Bay Centre Mall, 1150 Douglas St., 250 952-5680.
- Harbour Trading Company, 811 Wharf St., 250 381-1022.
- Irish Linen Stores, 1019 Government St., 250 383-6812.

- Original Christmas Village, 1323 Government St., 250 380-7522.
- Purdy's Chocolates, the Bay Centre, 250 361-3024.
- Rogers' Chocolates, 913 Government St., 250 384-7021, 1-800-663-2220.
- Sydney Reynolds, 801 Government St., 250 383-3931.
- The Spirit of Christmas, 1022 Government St., 250 385-2501.
- W&J Wilson Clothiers, 1221 Government St., 250 383-7177.

YATES STREET AREA

- Cowichan Trading Company, 1328 Government St., 250 383-0321.
- English Sweet Shop, 738 Yates St., 250 382-3325.
- Grandpa's Antique Photo, 1252 Wharf St., 250 920-3800.
- Hill's Native Crafts, 1008 Government St., 250 385-3911.
- Starfish Glassworks, 630 Yates St., 250 388-7827.
- The British Candy Shoppe, 635 Yates St., 250 382-2634.

MARKET SQUARE

- Fat Phege's Fudge Factory, 560 Johnson St., 250 383-3435.
- Foxglove Toys, 162-560 Johnson St., 250 383-8852.
- Marigold Galleria, 101-560 Johnson St., 250 386-5339.
- Out of Hand, 560 Johnson St., 250 384-5221.

CHINATOWN

- Chinatown Trading Company, 551 Fisgard St., 250 381-5503.
- Fan Tan Gallery, 541 Fisgard St., 250 382-4424.
- Quonley's, 1628 Government St., 250 383-0623.

ANTIQUE ROW

- Charles Baird, 1044A Fort St., 250 384-8809.
- Faith Grant, 1156 Fort St., 250 383-0121.
- Old Vogue Shop, 1034 Fort St., 250 380-7551.
- Recollections Antiques and Collectibles Mall, 817A Fort St., 250 385-1902.
- The Glass Menagerie, 1036 Fort St., 250 475-2228.

WHISTLER

ACCOMMODATIONS LISTINGS

For two people staying in a double room (excluding taxes) during peak season: $ = $50-$90, $$ = $90-$180, $$$ = $180-$250, $$$$ = above $250. Rates quoted are subject to a 7% federal tax and a 10% hotel tax.

WHISTLER VILLAGE

- Coast Whistler Hotel, 4005 Whistler Way, Whistler, BC V0N 1B4, 604 932-2522, 1-800-663-5644, Fax: 604-932-6711, www.coastwhistlerhotel.com. Value and location are very good. Free buffet-style breakfast. Covered pool, hot tub, sauna, exercise room. $$.
- Crystal Lodge, 4154 Village Green, Whistler, BC V0N 1B4, 604 932-2221, 1-800-667-3363, Fax: 604 932-2635, www.crystal-lodge.com. Casual, friendly, renovated. Short walk to Whistler Mountain gondolas, good price. Tuck shop, two family restaurants on site (Tex Corleone's and The Old Spaghetti Factory) plus lounge. Up to three bedrooms available. Pool. $$-$$$.
- Delta Whistler Resort, 4050 Whistler Way, Whistler, BC V0N 1B4, 604 932-1982, 1-800-515-4050, Fax: 604 932-7332, www.deltawhistler.com. Luxury hotel with big rooms, big beds, great mountain views. Some rooms with double Jacuzzis, dry saunas. Health Club, pool, hot tub, spa. Lounge, restaurant. Pet-friendly. $$$-$$$$.
- Timberline Lodge, 4122 Village Green, Whistler, BC V0N 1B4, 604 932-5211, 1-866-580-6649, Fax: 604 932-2306, www.whistler-timberline.com or www.whistlerlodgingco.com. Smaller hotel, European-style, some rooms with lofts/dens. Full kitchens. Hot tub, saunas. $$$.
- The Westin Resort & Spa, 4090 Whistler Way, Whistler, BC V0N 1B4, 604 905-5000, 1-888-634-5577, Fax: 604 905-5640, www.westinwhistler.com. Condo-style, luxury all-suite hotel, spa, health club, pools, Whistler Kids Club program, lounge, restaurant. Deluxe beds, down duvets. Full kitchen, dining room, living room in all suites. $$$-$$$$.

VILLAGE NORTH

- The Alpenglow, 4369 Main St., Whistler, BC V0N 1B4, 604 905-7078, 1-866-580-6642, Fax: 604 905-7053, www.whistler-alpenglow.com. Newer, lodge-style with smaller-size studio, one- and two-bedroom suites. Good value, central location. Fireplaces, full kitchens, air conditioning, fitness facilities with lap pool, hot tub, steam room, sauna. $$$.
- Whistler's Marketplace Lodge, 4360 Lorimer Rd., Whistler, BC V0N 1B4, 604 938-6699, 1-800-663-7711, Fax: 604 932-6622, www.resort-questwhistler.com. Low-frills lodging, good price, full kitchen, living and dining area with gas fireplace. No pool. Free parking. $$.

UPPER VILLAGE

- The Fairmont Chateau Whistler, 4599 Chateau Blvd., Whistler, BC V0N 1B4, 604 938-8000, 1-800-441-1414, Fax: 604 938-2291, www.fairmont.com. Rated one of the top ski resort hotels. Canadian Chateau-style luxury with double queen- and king-size beds and goose-down duvets. Restaurant, lounge, shopping on-site. Ski-in/ski-out Blackcomb Mountain. Pool, spa, sauna, fitness facilities. $$$$.
- Four Seasons Resort Whistler, 4591 Blackcomb Way, Whistler BC V0N 1B4, 604 935-3400, Fax: 604 935-3455, www.fourseasons.com/whistler. Newcomer to Whistler, with 242 spacious "modern rustic" rooms (95 suites) at the base of Blackcomb Mountain. Spa with luxury treatments, full fitness club. Pool, steam room, 24-hour concierge, restaurants. $$$$
- Residence Inn by Marriott, 4899 Painted Cliff Rd., Whistler, BC V0N 1B4, 604 905-3400, 1-866-580-6648, Fax: 604 905-3432, www.whistler-marriott.com. Ski-in/ski-out location on Blackcomb Mountain. Large rooms, fireplaces, full kitchens, pool, hot tubs. Free shuttle bus to and from Whistler Village. Free breakfast buffet, excellent fitness facilities. Pet-friendly. $$$$.
- Summit Lodge, 4359 Main St., Whistler, BC V0N 1B4, 604 932-2778, 1-888-913-8811, Fax: 604 932-2716, www.summitlodge.com. Intimate boutique hotel with exceptional service. All suites have full kitchen and gas fireplaces. Free shuttle to Whistler Village and gondolas. Pool, hot tub. $$$.

CREEKSIDE

- Lake Placid Lodge, 2050 Lake Placid Rd., Whistler, BC V0N 1B2, 604 932-6699, 1-800-663-7711, Fax: 604 932-6622, www.resortquestwhistler.com. Good value. Ski in/ski out access to Creekside Gondola. Large pool and patio area. One- to three-bedroom suites, gas fireplaces, fully equipped kitchens. Free underground parking. $$-$$$.
- Legends Whistler Creek, 2036 London Lane, Whistler BC V0N 1B2, 1-800-332-3152, Fax: 604 983-9699, www.lodgingovations.com. Ski-in/ski-out access to Creekside Gondola. Opened by Intrawest in 2002, luxury one- to three-bed-room condo-style suites with full kitchens. Family and adult fitness facilities, indoor kids' play area, movie room, two pools, two Jacuzzis. $$$-$$$$.

OTHER LOCATIONS

- Edgewater Lodge and Dining Room, 8841 Hwy. 99. Mailing address: Edgewater Lodge, Box 369, Whistler, BC V0N 1BO; 604 932-0688, 1-888-870-9065, Fax: 604-932-0686, www.edgewater-lodge.com. Small motel-like lodge in forest setting overlooking Green Lake. Deluxe breakfast, tea and coffee all day, gourmet restaurant. One bedroom units with bathtub and extra pullout twin bed. Shower-only in six units. Free parking. $$-$$$.
- Hostelling International Whistler, 5678 Alta Lake Rd., Whistler, BC V0N 1B5, 604 932-5492, Fax: 604 932-4687, www.hihostels.ca. Located in a former fishing lodge on Alta Lake. Wood-burning stove, common kitchen, dining room, sauna. Dorm rooms, private room sleeps up to four (children must stay with family in private room). Reservations recommended. $.
- Riverside RV Resort and Campground and Cabins, 8018 Mons Rd., Whistler, BC V0N 1B8, 604 905-5533, 1-877-905-5533, Fax: 604 905-5539, www.whistlercamping.com. Tent camping and RV with amenities in lodge including grocery store and

Internet café. Fourteen log cabins with lofts, showers only in units. Free parking. $$.
- The Shoestring Lodge, 7124 Nancy Greene Dr., Whistler, BC V0N 1B0, 604 932-3338, 1-877-551-4954, Fax: 604 932-8347, www.shoestringlodge.com. North of Whistler Village. Dorms sleep four to six people with bunk beds and TV, private double and queen rooms available. Free parking, free bus shuttle in winter. $.

BED & BREAKFASTS
For information on more than 25 B&B members, contact Whistler Chamber of Commerce, PO Box 181, Whistler, BC V0N 1B0, 604 932-5528, Fax: 604 932-3755, www.whistlerchamber.com.
- Alpine Lodge Pension, 8135 Alpine Way, Whistler, BC V0N 1B8, 604 932-5966, Fax: 604 932-1104, www.alpinelodge.com. Casual, European-style pension in a huge cedar lodge. Continental breakfast buffet,, down duvets, steam room, Japanese spoken. Communal kitchen open to guests. Free parking, free shuttle bus to mountains. $–$$$.
- Cedar Springs Bed & Breakfast Lodge, 8106 Cedar Springs Rd., Whistler, BC V0N 1B8, 604 938-8007, 1-800-727-7547, www.whistlerbb.com. Pretty cedar and pine lodge. Gourmet breakfast, dining room has wood-burning fireplace, tea and coffee always on. Sauna, hot tub. Showers only in rooms, except family room with soaker tub. Next to Meadow Park and the Valley Trail. Free shuttle in winter. $$.
- Durlacher Hof Pension Inn, 7055 Nesters Rd., Whistler, BC V0N 1B7, 604 932-1924, 1-877-932-1924, Fax: 604 938-1980, www.durlacherhof.com. Impressive guest rooms, extra-long twin or queen beds, goose-down duvets, private baths with Jacuzzi tubs or showers. Full breakfast, afternoon tea. No telephone or television in rooms. Free hot breakfast with Austrian sweet pancakes. Whirlpool, sauna. No children. $$$.

WHISTLER DINING
All major credit cards accepted.

FINE DINING ON THE MOUNTAINS
- Christine's, Blackcomb Mountain, 604 938-7437. Elegant, full-service dining, BC ingredients includes fish and shellfish, pasta specials. L, $$$, V/MC/AX/DC.
- Steeps Grill, Whistler Mountain, 604 905-2379. Alpine bistro at 1,158 meters (3,800 vertical ft.). Seasonal BC fare, includes grilled salmon and chowder. L, $$$, V/MC/AX/DC.

CASUAL DINING ON THE MOUNTAINS
Whistler Mountain

Ski in to these casual eateries and enjoy the view and people-watching.
- Chic Pea – top of Garbanzo Express. Pizza, soup and cinnamon buns. $.
- Roundhouse Lodge – top of Whistler Express Gondola. Fast food, great views. $.
- Raven's Nest – top of Creekside Gondola. Hearty soups, stews and salads. $.
- Dusty's BBQ & Grill – bottom of Creekside Gondola. Breakfast to BBQ, delicious all day long. $.

Blackcomb Mountain

- Mountain Grill – top of Solar Coaster. Coffee and lunch. $.
- Horstman Hut – top of 7th Heaven. Soups, stews and jambalaya. $.
- Crystal Hut – steak, salmon and Belgian waffles. Fondue in the evenings. $.
- Glacier Creek – base of Jersey Cream and Glacier Express. River Rock, upstairs, features 10 market areas, serving up fresh deli sandwiches to Asian stir fry. $. BC Eatery, downstairs, fresh West Coast cuisine, Bistro style. $.

Asian

- Amami Restaurant, 4274 Mountain Square, Westbrook Hotel, Whistler Village, 604 932-6431. Japanese and Chinese dishes in a casual setting. L/D, $$, V/MC/AX/DC.
- Mongolie Grill, 201-4295 Blackcomb Way, Upper Village, 604 938-9416. Notable Chinese stir-fry restaurant, including seafood and noodles,

18 gourmet sauces. No reservations accepted. L/D, $$, V/MC/AX.

- Tandoori Grill, 201-4368 Main St., Village North, 604 905-4900. Mild to hot authentic East Indian dishes. Reservations recommended. Take out and delivery available. L/D, $$$, V/AX/MC.
- Teppan Village Japanese Steak House, 4291 Mountain Square, Delta Whistler Resort, Whistler Village, 604 932-2223. Teppan-yaki-style restaurant features steak, also chicken and seafood. Reservations suggested in peak seasons. D, $$$, V/AX/MC/DC.
- Thai One On, 108-4557 Blackcomb Way, Upper Village, 604 932-4822. Hot and not-so-hot gourmet Thai dishes such as coconut prawns and satays. Reservations recommended. Free underground parking. D, $$, V/AX/DC/MC.
- Zen Japanese Restaurant, 2202 Gondola Way, First Tracks Lodge, Creekside, 604 932-3667. Sleek restaurant features traditional Japanese cuisine with West Coast influences. L/D, $$$, V/AX/MC/DC.

Cafés

- Chef Bernard's Ciao-Thyme Bistro, 1-4573 Chateau Blvd., Whistler Village, 604 932-7051. Tiny café with a great chef and fresh local produce. Soups, salads, cinnamon buns. B/L/D, $, AX/MC/V.
- Esquires Coffee House, 127-4338 Main St., Village North, 604 905-3386. Excellent coffee and teas with quiches, wraps and panini. B/L/D, $, AX/DC/MC/V.
- Southside Deli, 2102 Lake Placid Rd, Creekside, 604 932-3368. Famous for "Beltch" breakfast special of bacon, eggs, cheese and ham, burgers, sandwiches, soups, blackened snapper and BBQ charbroiled pork tenderloin. B/L/D, $$, AX/V.
- Splitz Grill, 4369 Main St., Alpenglow Hotel, Village North, 604 938-9300. Burgers galore including all-beef burger and spicy lentil vegetarian. L/D, $$, V.
- Uli's Flipside, 2021 Karen Cres., Creekside, 604 935-1107. Pasta, pizza, perogies, schnitzel, spicy Italian salsiccia sausage and chicken dishes. Casual atmosphere, children's menu. L/D, $$, V/MC.

Alpine

- Bavaria Restaurant, 4369 Main St., Village North, 604 932-7518. Traditional fondue, schnitzel and all dishes Austrian from a superb chef. Deserts include home-made apple strudel and Kaiserschmarrn, a caramelized crepe. D, $$$$, AX/MC/V.

Family/Casual

- Caramba! Restaurante, 12-4314 Main St., Village North, 604 938-1879. Pizzas, pastas in a cheery, lively setting. New York steak and calamari a la Plancha on the menu. L/D, $$$, AX/MC/V.
- Gaitors Bar & Grill, 7124 Nancy Green Drive, north of Whistler Village, 604 938-5777. Above the Shoestring Lodge, a fun spot for casual fare. Burgers, veggie enchiladas, curried prawns, soups, Mexican food. Sunday brunch buffet. L (weekdays), B/L/D Sat.-Sun, $$, AX/MC/V.
- Old Spaghetti Factory, 4154 Village Green, Crystal Lodge, Whistler Village, 604 938-1081. Adult and children's menu of soups, salads, pastas, sourdough bread, New York steak, vegetarian lasagna, ice cream. L/D, $$$, AX/MC/V.
- The Original Ristorante, 4270 Mountain Square, Whistler Village, 604 932-6408. Fast-paced service starting with breakfast. Pizzas and pastas. B/L/D, $$, V/AX/MC.
- Tex Corleone's, 4154 Village Green, Crystal Lodge, Whistler Village, 604 932-7427. Chicago-style deep-dish pizza, chicken, Alberta-beef ribs. Breakfast buffet or individual items start the day. Children's coloring activities. B/L/D, $$$, DC/MC/V.

Mediterranean

- Pasta Lupino Gourmet, 121-4368 Main St., Village North, 604 905-0400. Fresh pasta and sauces in a tiny, popular café. L/D, $$$, MC/V.
- Quattro at Whistler, 4319 Main St., Village North, 604 905-4844. Country Italian cooking and extensive wine list. D, $$$, AX/DC/MC/V.
- Trattoria di Umberto, 4417 Sundial Place, Whistler Village, 604 932-5858. Tuscan cooking features linguine, spaghetti, fettuccine and more. Seafood cioppino is chef Umberto

Menghi's specialty. L/D, $$$$, AX/DC/MC/V.

- Zeuski's Taverna, 40-4314 Main St., Village North, 604 932-6009. Lunch, dinner, and children's menus include Greek-style chicken burgers, falafels and wraps, roasted lamb, baklava. L/D, $$$, AX/DC/MC/V.

Seafood & Steak

- Brewhouse, 4355 Blackcomb Way, Village North, 604 905-2739. Wood-fired pizza and rotisserie-grilled prime ribs and chicken, sandwiches and tuna melts. L/D, $$, AX/MC/V.
- The Crab Shack, 4005 Whistler Way, Whistler Village, 604 932-4451. Casual dining. Features are hand-shucked oysters and steak. Live music at specified times. B/L/D, $$$, DC/MC/V.
- Creekside Grillroom, 2129 Lake Placid Rd., Creekside, 604 932-4424. Friendly ambience, features 10 variations of Alberta beef, as well as chicken and salmon. D, $$$, AX/MC/V.
- Rimrock Café, 2117 Whistler Rd., Creekside, 604 932-5565. Seabass, ahi tuna, grilled prawns as well as steak and lobster. Very popular, free parking. D, $$$$, AX/MC/V.

West Coast Cuisine

- Araxi Restaurant & Bar, 4222 Village Square, Whistler Village, 604 932-4540. Superb menu and 12,000-bottle wine list. West Coast with Italian and French influences. D, $$$$, AX/DC/MC/V.
- The Aubergine Grille, 4090 Whistler Way, Westin Resort & Spa, Whistler Village, 604 935-4344. Breakfast, lunch, dinner with a mountain view. West Coast seafood and salmon plus rustic pizza, certified Angus Beef, pastas. Dazzling deserts. B/L/D, $$$$, AX/MC/V.
- Edgewater Lodge Lakeside Dining Room, 8841 Hwy 99, north of Whistler Village, 604 932-0688. Secluded waterfront setting offering gourmet locally grown fare. Venison medallions, chicken, steaks. D, $$$$, AX/MC/V.
- Evergreens Restaurant, 4050 Whistler Way, Delta Whistler Resort, Whistler Village, 604 932-7346. Elegant and casual, occasional live piano. Taste of British Columbia Salmon specialty offers three in one.

Venison striploin a specialty. B/L/D, $$$$, AX/DC/MC/V.

- La Rua Restaurante, 4557 Blackcomb Way, Upper Village, 604 932-5011. Great food and great wines with six gourmet pasta selections. D, $$$, AX/DC/MC/V.
- The Wildflower, 4599 Chateau Blvd., Fairmont Chateau Whistler, Upper Village, 604 938-2033. Daily breakfast buffet, Sunday brunch, lunches. Dinner includes Fraser Valley duck, rib-eye steak, free-range chicken, venison. Over 2,500 bottles of wine. B/L/D, $$$-$$$$, AX/DC/MC/V.